SHOW & TELL

SHOW & TELL

ARCHITEKTUR SAMMELN | COLLECTING ARCHITECTURE

HERAUSGEGEBEN VON | EDITED BY
ANDRES LEPIK

MIT TEXTEN VON | WITH TEXTS BY
BARRY BERGDOLL, PETER CHRISTENSEN, JEAN-LOUIS COHEN, ANDRES LEPIK, KIERAN LONG UND | AND **IRENE MEISSNER**

SOWIE EINEM GESPRÄCH ZWISCHEN | AND A CONVERSATION BETWEEN
SIMONE BADER, MARGHERITA GUCCIONE UND | AND **PIPPO CIORRA**

A.M.

HATJE CANTZ

AUSSTELLUNGSANSICHT
SHOW & TELL,
ARCHITEKTURMUSEUM DER
TU MÜNCHEN, 2014

EXHIBITION VIEW
SHOW & TELL,
ARCHITEKTURMUSEUM DER
TU MÜNCHEN, 2014

AUSSTELLUNGSANSICHT
SHOW & TELL,
ARCHITEKTURMUSEUM
DER TU MÜNCHEN, 2014

EXHIBITION VIEW
SHOW & TELL,
ARCHITEKTURMUSEUM
DER TU MÜNCHEN, 2014

SHOW & TELL
ODER: WO STEHT DAS
ARCHITEKTURMUSEUM
AM ANFANG DES
21. JAHRHUNDERTS?

»Im Idealfall sollten Museen alle fünfzig Jahre geplündert und
ihre Sammlungen wieder in Umlauf gebracht werden.« [1]
BRUCE CHATWIN

Dass sich Architektur in gebauter Form nicht sammeln lässt wie Armbanduhren, Oldtimer oder Meissener Porzellan, kann sowohl als Vor- als auch als Nachteil gesehen werden. Der Vorteil ist, dass Architektur kein leicht bewegliches Spekulationsobjekt darstellt, das wie die Kunst auf dem Kunstmarkt zwischen Sammlern, spezialisierten Galerien und Museen in einer auf ökonomische Interessen abgestimmten Mechanik herumgereicht und dabei kontinuierlich im Wert gesteigert werden kann. Aus ihrer Eigenschaft als »Im-mobilie« resultiert für die Architektur jedoch andererseits auch der Nachteil, dass sie innerhalb eines Museums sehr viel schwerer als Kunst, Design oder Grafik zu präsentieren und zu vermitteln ist. Denn nur bei gebauten Ausstellungen im Außenraum, wie etwa der Weißenhofsiedlung in Stuttgart, kann ein Besucher die wirkliche und unmittelbare Erfahrung von Architektur machen – wobei er zumeist auf die Besichtigung von außen angewiesen ist und somit schließlich doch nur einen Teil dessen erfassen kann, wofür Architektur geplant ist.

Bei der Präsentation von Architektur im Innenraum ist der Kurator daher auf sekundäre und referenzielle Objekte angewiesen. Diese kann er sammeln, lagern und in verschiedenen thematischen Zusammenhängen präsentieren. Sekundäre Objekte verweisen auf den Entwurfs- oder Denkprozess geplanter Architektur, also beispielsweise Architekturzeichnungen, Renderings, Fotomontagen oder Modelle. Referenzielle Objekte sind Fotografien, Videos, nachgebaute Modelle und ähnliches, die gebaute Architektur ganz oder in Teilen abbilden, aber von dieser abhängig sind und ebenfalls keine reale Erfahrung von Architektur vermitteln.

ANDRES LEPIK

SHOW & TELL
OR: WHAT IS THE ROLE OF THE ARCHITECTURE MUSEUM AT THE BEGINNING OF THE 21ST CENTURY?

"Ideally, museums should be looted every fifty years,
and their collections returned to circulation."[1]

BRUCE CHATWIN

There is both an advantage and a disadvantage to the fact that architectural structures cannot be collected like watches, classic cars, or Meissen porcelain. The advantage is that architecture is not a readily transportable object of speculation. It cannot be passed back and forth between collectors, specialist galleries, and museums in an economically driven dynamic—like the art market—in order to enhance its value. However, the static nature of architecture poses a disadvantage and makes it much more difficult to present within a museum context than art, industrial design, or drawings. Only in a built, outdoor exhibition, such as the Weißenhofsiedlung in Stuttgart, can visitors truly and immediately experience architecture—although even in this case they must reconcile themselves to viewing architecture from the outside, and therefore they ultimately only gain a sense of this one aspect of the intentions underlying the design.

When showing architecture in an interior space, the curator must rely on secondary and referential objects, which can be collected, stored, and presented in various thematic contexts. Secondary objects include, for example, architectural drawings, renderings, photo montages, or models, and they serve as documentation of a design or conceptual process, which is associated with architectural projects in planning. Referential objects are photographs, videos, reconstructed models, and the like, which depict an existing building in its entirety or in part, but they are dependent on this source and do not convey any kind of real architectural experience.

Architectural collections were not originally established with the aim of presenting public exhibitions. In the beginning, such collections were used for professional training, that is, to give future architects the opportunity to learn

AUSSTELLUNG *SHOW & TELL*,
BAUKÄSTEN VOM 19. JAHRHUNDERT
BIS HEUTE

FROM THE EXHIBITION *SHOW & TELL*,
BUILDING BLOCKS FROM THE
NINETEENTH CENTURY TO TODAY

Architektursammlungen sind zunächst auch gar nicht mit dem Ziel öffent-
licher Ausstellungen entstanden. In der Anfangszeit wurden sie zur professionellen Ausbildung angelegt, um also zukünftige Architekten an konkreten
Vorbildern wie Gipsabgüssen von Reliefen, Skulpturen und Modellen oder
Vorlagenblättern lernen zu lassen. In der Zeit vor der einfachen Verfügbarkeit
gedruckter Bilder und der nur sehr eingeschränkten Möglichkeit des Reisens
für Studenten der Architektur waren solche Sammlungen besonders wichtig.
Dass diese didaktisch konzipierten Architektursammlungen in einigen Fällen
später in Museen gewandelt wurden, also Einrichtungen, die nicht nur für
Ausbildung und Forschung sammeln, sondern dauerhafte oder auch wech-
selnde öffentliche Ausstellungen organisieren, hängt eng mit der Geschichte
des Kunstmuseums zusammen. Die Gründung von Architekturmuseen als
eigenständige öffentliche Institutionen reicht etwa über 200 Jahre zurück
und liegt damit fast zeitgleich mit den Kunstmuseen.[2] Die Idee »nationaler«
Architekturmuseen, die einen volksbildenden Zweck erfüllen sollten, das heißt
die Baukultur eines Landes durch Ausstellungen und Sammlungen befördern,
war ein wichtiges Motiv für viele solche Gründungen. Mit der Zielrichtung

by studying specific examples, such as casts of reliefs, sculptures, architectural models, or design and pattern books. These kinds of collections were particularly important at a time before printed images were readily available and when students of architecture had very limited opportunities to travel. That some of these didactically oriented collections later became museums—institutions that not only collected for purposes of training and study but also organized changing or permanent public exhibitions—is linked to the history of the art museum. The founding of architecture museums as independent, official institutions has a two-hundred-year history, and these origins date to approximately the same time as those of art museums.[2] The concept of a "national" museum of architecture was a guiding idea that inspired the founding of many such museums, which were conceived to educate the public and foster the respective national building culture through their exhibitions and collections. Beginning in the mid-nineteenth century, museums of arts and crafts were founded in Europe with the aim of improving public taste and increasing the quality of crafted objects. In special cases, architecture museums were even dedicated to a single architect, as was the Sir John Soane's Museum in London, which opened shortly after his death in 1837, or the Schinkel Museum on the second story of the Bauakademie in Berlin, which was inaugurated in 1844.[3] Both institutions elevated individual architects to figures of exemplary national importance and can thus be ascribed to this pedagogical tradition. Nevertheless, in contrast to art museums, which proliferated at an almost exponential rate, particularly in the twentieth century, the number of architecture museums remains very modest even today, and these institutions are dispersed throughout a few, mostly European countries. Entire continents, including India and Africa, are not represented at all in the International Confederation of Architectural Museums.[4]

The difficulty of presenting architecture indoors has in some cases been met by bringing original architectural components into the museum, as a means of enabling the viewer to have some kind of direct access to these works. One of the most significant examples is the Musée des monuments français in Paris, which was founded in 1879. It is certainly representative of this type of architecture museum, in which large, original architectural elements and casts are placed on view with a museum to provide viewers with a one-to-one experience. Also, the original building of the Pergamonmuseum in Berlin was designed in 1901 to allow visitors to experience the famous Pergamon Altar in its original architectural constellation. This real-life experience of

der Verbesserung des Volksgeschmacks und der Hebung der handwerklichen Qualität wurden auch die Kunstgewerbemuseen seit der zweiten Hälfte des 19. Jahrhunderts in Europa eingerichtet. Im besonderen Fall wurden Architekturmuseen sogar einem einzelnen Architekten gewidmet, etwa das Sir John Soane's Museum in London, das schon 1837 unmittelbar nach seinem Tod öffnete, oder das Schinkel-Museum im 2. Obergeschoß der Bauakademie in Berlin, eröffnet im Jahr 1844.[3] Beide erhoben einen einzelnen Architekten zu einem nationalen Vor- und Leitbild und stehen damit ebenfalls in der erzieherischen Tradition. Im Unterschied zu den Kunstmuseen jedoch, die speziell im 20. Jahrhundert eine beinahe exponentielle Vermehrung erlebt haben, bleibt die Zahl der Architekturmuseen bis heute zahlenmäßig sehr überschaubar und ist auf wenige, meist europäische Länder verteilt. Ganze Kontinente wie Indien und Afrika sind daher in der Internationalen Föderation der Architektursammlungen ICAM überhaupt nicht vertreten.[4]

Der Schwierigkeit, Architektur im Innenraum zu präsentieren, ist gelegentlich damit begegnet worden, originale Architekturteile ins Museum zu bringen. Dies sollte zumindest in gewisser Form den unmittelbaren Zugang des Besuchers ermöglichen. Eines der wichtigsten Beispiele ist das Musée des monuments français, 1879 in Paris gegründet, das auch den ersten Fall eines Architekturmuseums darstellt, das große originale Architekturteile, aber auch Abgüsse im Innenraum eines Museums sichtbar macht und damit für die Besucher eine Eins-zu-eins-Erfahrung ermöglicht. Auch das Berliner Pergamonmuseum wurde 1901 in seiner ersten Form als Gebäude angelegt, in dem der berühmte Pergamonaltar in seiner ursprünglichen Aufstellung erlebt werden konnte. Dieses reale Raumerlebnis antiker Architektur wurde sofort zu einem durchschlagenden Publikumserfolg, der bis heute anhält. Im Schinkel-Wettbewerb von 1905 wurde dann die Planung eines eigenen Architekturmuseums für Berlin angeregt,[5] das am Ende zwar nicht gebaut wurde, aber dazu führte, dass mit dem 1930 errichteten Neubau des Pergamonmuseums als ein »Architekturmuseum der Antike« die Architektur den Weg ins Kunstmuseum fand.[6]

Wegen der erheblichen Schwierigkeit, ganze Bauten oder Teile ab- und wiederaufzubauen, blieben solche Ansätze auf wenige Beispiele beschränkt und konnten nur von sehr einflussreichen Institutionen verwirklicht werden (beispielsweise der spanische Renaissancehof im New Yorker Metropolitan Museum), teilweise – wie im Fall des Victoria and Albert Museums in London – dann auch durch Gipsabgüsse im originalen Maßstab. Diese

AUSSTELLUNG *SHOW & TELL*,
PRÄSENTATIONSMODELL
FÜR DIE ENTLASTUNGSSTADT
NEUPERLACH, MÜNCHEN, 1971

FROM THE EXHIBITION *SHOW & TELL*,
PRESENTATION MODEL FOR
THE DEVELOPMENT OF
NEUPERLACH, MUNICH, 1971

ancient architecture was a resounding success with the public, and still is today. In 1905 the Schinkel Competition initiated the planning of an architecture museum for Berlin,[5] which was ultimately never built. However, it did pave the way for the introduction of architecture into the art museum via the new building for the Pergamonmuseum, which was built in 1930 as an "architecture museum of antiquity."[6]

Given the substantial difficulties associated with reconstructing entire buildings or portions thereof, this kind of approach remained limited to a few instances and could only be put into practice by highly influential institutions (one example being the Spanish Renaissance patio from the Castle of Vélez Blanco at the Metropolitan Museum in New York), or to a certain extent through the use of plaster casts in original scale—as in the case of the Victoria and Albert Museum in London. This impressive but also quite cumbersome form of presenting architecture remained limited to displaying examples from different historical periods and thus had little contemporary relevance, at best serving to legitimize the prevailing historicism of the era through the presentation of originals from antiquity or other epochs. Museums specializing in architecture

eindrückliche, aber zugleich auch recht schwerfällige Form der Architekturpräsentation blieb darauf beschränkt, historische Objekte exemplarisch vorzuführen, und hatte damit nur wenig konkreten Bezug zur eigenen Gegenwart – allenfalls um den ohnehin vorherrschenden Historismus mit den originalen Vorlagen der Antike oder anderer Epochen zu legitimieren. Die ganz auf Architektur spezialisierten Museen blieben daher auch im weiteren Verlauf die Ausnahme und spielten weder in der öffentlichen Wahrnehmung noch in der akademischen Debatte eine aktive Rolle. Vielmehr wurden sie wie die Nachlässe von Architekten in den Akademien und anderen Einrichtungen, die Architektur sammelten, als Forschungsquelle betrachtet, die meist keine oder nur eine sehr begrenzte eigene Ausstellungstätigkeit entfalteten.

Der radikalste Schritt, um die öffentliche Wahrnehmung von Architektur aus der Position eines Museums heraus zu prägen und zugleich in eine neue Richtung zu lenken, ging im 20. Jahrhundert von einem modernen Kunstmuseum aus. Es war die Ausstellung *Modern Architecture. International Exhibition,* die das New Yorker Museum of Modern Art (MoMA) 1932 zeigte, kuratiert von Philip Johnson und Henry-Russell Hitchcock. Ihr durchschlagender Erfolg, obwohl sie im Grunde nur aus Fotoreproduktionen und einigen Modellen bestand, beruhte nicht zuletzt darauf, dass die Ausstellung auf Tournee durch viele amerikanische Städte geschickt wurde. Die Schau selbst und ihre begleitenden Publikationen wurden zum Vorreiter für ein Format von Architekturausstellungen, das bis heute Standards setzt:[7] Es ist die thesenhafte Ausstellung, die eine aktuelle Entwicklung in der Architektur herausgreift und als beispielhaft an die Öffentlichkeit bringt, um ihr zu weiterem Erfolg zu verhelfen. Der große Erfolg von *Modern Architecture* war Anlass für die Einrichtung einer eigenen Architekturabteilung am MoMA, die sich anfangs aber nur wenig um den Aufbau einer eigenen Sammlung bemühte (siehe Barry Bergdoll, S. 116). Dem Vorbild des MoMA sind andere moderne Kunstmuseen gefolgt und haben Architekturabteilungen eingerichtet, die auch Sammlungen angelegt haben (beispielsweise das San Francisco Museum of Modern Art oder das Art Institute of Chicago). Auch die Architekturabteilungen des Centre Pompidou (seit 1977) und des Musée d'Orsay (seit 1987) in Paris stehen in dieser Genealogie (zur Geschichte der französischen Sammlungen und Museen siehe Jean-Louis Cohen, S. 148). Das MAXXI in Rom dürfte zu den allerjüngsten Einrichtungen dieser Art gehören (siehe Gespräch zwischen Simone Bader, Margherita Guccione und Pippo Ciorra, S. 194).

AUSSTELLUNGSANSICHT *SHOW & TELL*,
ARCHITEKTURMUSEUM DER TU MÜNCHEN,
PINAKOTHEK DER MODERNE, 2014

EXHIBITION VIEW *SHOW & TELL*,
ARCHITEKTURMUSEUM DER TU MÜNCHEN,
PINAKOTHEK DER MODERNE, 2014

thus remained an exception to the rule and did not feature prominently in the public eye, nor did they play an active role in scholarly debates. Instead, like the papers left by architects to academies and other institutions that collected architectural materials, museums were viewed as a basis for study, which did not serve the purpose of exhibitions, or only to a limited extent.

The most radical steps made on the part of a museum towards shaping the public perception of architecture and forging a new direction altogether were initiated in the twentieth century by a museum of modern art: the exhibition *Modern Architecture. International Exhibition,* presented by the New York Museum of Modern Art (MoMA) in 1932 and curated by Philip Johnson and Henry-Russell Hitchcock. Although it basically only consisted of reproduced photographs and a few models, the show was a resounding success, not least because it toured many American cities. The exhibition itself and its accompanying publication served as a model for the type of architecture exhibition that continues to set the standard.[7] Putting forward a thesis, this kind of exhibition

AUSSTELLUNG *SHOW & TELL,*
EXEMPLARISCHE AUSWAHL
ZUR SAMMLUNGSGESCHICHTE

FROM THE EXHIBITION *SHOW & TELL,*
A SELECTION OF OBJECTS REPRESENTING
THE HISTORY OF THE COLLECTION

DER ÖKONOMISCHE WERT

Der durchschlagende Erfolg des Kunstmuseums im 20. Jahrhundert beruht zu weiten Teilen auf dem Erfolg des Kunstmarkts. Da im Kunstmuseum ökonomische und kulturelle Interessen ineinandergreifen, bildet es den zentralen Ort »der Infrastruktur, in der sich der Marktwert eines Kunstwerks konstituiert«.[8] Architekturzeichnungen oder Architekturmodelle waren dagegen seit jeher Teil eines Arbeitsprozesses und haben glücklicherweise nie jenen autonomen ökonomischen Wert zugeschrieben bekommen, als dass sich daraus ein funktionierender Markt etabliert hätte. Die wenigen bekannten Galerien, die seit den 1970er-Jahren versucht haben, mit Architekturzeichnungen oder auch -modellen einen ähnlichen Markt aufzubauen, haben sich meist nicht lange gehalten.[9] Private Sammler von Architekturzeichnungen gibt es dementsprechend weltweit nur wenige, meist sind es Architekten, die aus Leidenschaft oder Forschungsinteresse

singles out a current development in architecture, presenting examples of this trend as a means of furthering its success. The overwhelming response to *Modern Architecture* resulted in the establishment of an independent architecture department at MoMA, which initially did not make much attempt to form its own collection (see Barry Bergdoll, p. 117). Other modern art museums followed the example of MoMA by setting up architecture departments that also assembled collections (the San Francisco Museum of Modern Art and the Art Institute of Chicago, for example). Also the architecture departments of the Centre Pompidou (established in 1977) and the Musée d'Orsay (established in 1987) in Paris belong to this genealogy (on the history of French collections and museums, see Jean-Louis Cohen, p. 149). The MAXXI in Rome is one of the most recent institutions of this kind (see conversation between Simone Bader, Margherita Guccione, and Pippo Ciorra, p. 195).

ECONOMIC VALUE

The resounding success of the art museum in the twentieth century is largely based on the success of the art market. Since economic and cultural interests are aligned in the institution of the art museum, it forms a central node of "the infrastructure in which the market value of an artwork is constituted."[8] In contrast, architectural drawings and models have always been tied to a working process and have happily never been attributed with the kind of independent economic value that would foster a functioning market. The few notable galleries that have tried since the nineteen-seventies to establish a similar market for architectural drawings or models have not generally not been very robust.[9] On a global scale there are correspondingly few private collectors of architectural drawings; usually they are architects themselves, who collect historical drawings due to passionate interest or for research, or they purchase works directly from colleagues as a means of lending financial support.[10] Some architects refuse to accept that architecture museums do not operate in the same way as art museums. Convinced of the "artistic" value of their work (see Peter Christensen, p. 217), they wish to further capitalize on the archives that they have amassed over the course of their career, but that have usually already been a source of compensation in the form of professional fees. The most obvious and independent solution is for architects to establish their own archives, as have Richard Meier, Renzo Piano, and Oswald Mathias Ungers.

AUSSTELLUNG *SHOW & TELL*,
BLICK IN EINE DER FILMKABINEN
MIT ZEITZEUGENBERICHTEN,
FILM: CORINNE ROSE

FROM THE EXHIBITION *SHOW & TELL*,
VIEW OF A SCREENING
AREA FOR INTERVIEWS FILMED
BY CORINNE ROSE

historische Zeichnungen sammeln oder direkt von Kollegen kaufen, um diese finanziell zu unterstützen.[10] Dass Architekturmuseen eben nicht wie Kunstmuseen operieren wird von manchen Architekten nicht akzeptiert. Sie wollen aus ihren Archiven, die sie am Ende einer Karriere angehäuft haben und in der Regel durch die professionellen Honorare längst abgegolten sind, noch einmal zusätzliches Kapital schlagen, weil sie fest an den »künstlerischen« Wert ihrer Arbeit glauben (siehe Peter Christensen, S. 216). Die konsequenteste und unabhängigste Entscheidung ist es freilich, wenn Architekten wie Richard Meier, Renzo Piano oder Oswald Mathias Ungers gleich ihre eigenen Archive anlegen.

DAS ARCHITEKTURMUSEUM DER TECHNISCHEN UNIVERSITÄT MÜNCHEN

Auch die heutige Sammlung der Technischen Universität (TU) München ist 1868 zunächst als Lehrsammlung der Polytechnischen Schule gegründet worden, in die als Grundstock bedeutende Architekturbestände der Akademie übergeben wurden (zur Geschichte der Sammlung siehe Irene Meissner, S. 34). Friedrich von Thiersch regte schon 1908 an, in dem von ihm geplanten Neubau der Hochschule ein »ein gut beleuchtetes, geräumiges Architekturmuseum« einzurichten. Wie sehr er dabei bereits an die Präsentation für eine breitere Öffentlichkeit dachte, sei dahin gestellt, doch die Räume der Architektursammlung (wie sie dann doch weiterhin genannt wurden) im 2. Obergeschoß der Gabelsbergerstraße mit ihren herausragenden Objekten wie den berühmten Korkmodellen von Carl und Georg May, Gipsabgüssen, Stichen und Zeichnungen waren in jeder Hinsicht sehr repräsentativ. Sie blieben über lange Zeit aber hauptsächlich den Spezialisten bekannt – eine ähnliche Situation wie an der Technischen Universität Berlin und anderen architektonischen Spezialsammlungen, die keine öffentlichen Schauräume besaßen.[11] Die reichen Bestände, die Thiersch auch für den Unterricht nutzte, wurden unter seinem Nachfolger German Bestelmeyer schon wieder teilweise aufgelöst, weil er deren Wert nicht mehr anerkannte, und teils an andere Sammlungen abgegeben, teils sogar absichtlich zerstört. Nach den Wirren der Kriegs- und Nachkriegsjahre mit Auslagerungen, Schäden und weiteren Verlusten blieb die Sammlung über lange Zeit ohne

ANDRES LEPIK

THE ARCHITEKTURMUSEUM DER TECHNISCHEN UNIVERSITÄT MÜNCHEN

The current collection of the Technische Universität München was originally established in 1868 as the teaching collection of the Polytechnische Schule (Polytechnic College), to which important architectural holdings of the Königliche Bayerische Akademie (Academy of Fine Arts) were donated as a foundation (on the history of the collection, see Irene Meissner, p. 35). In 1908 Friedrich von Thiersch suggested installing a "well lit, spacious architecture museum" in the new building that he had designed for the college. To what extent he had envisioned this presentation as serving as wider public is unclear. In any case, the rooms of the architecture collection on the second floor of the building on Gabelsbergerstrasse constituted quite a prestigious display and included distinguished objects, such as the famous cork models produced by Carl and Georg May, plaster casts, engravings, and drawings. For a long time the collection remained known largely among specialists—a situation comparable to that of the Technische Universität Berlin and other specialized architectural collections lacking any public exhibition space.[11] These rich holdings, which Thiersch also used for teaching, were then partially disbanded by his successor, German Bestelmeyer, who no longer considered them of value. Some items were given to other collections; others were purposely destroyed. After the chaos of the war and postwar era, during which the collection had been in storage and had suffered damage and further losses, it did not have any public impact for a long time. At the initiative of individuals such as Friedrich Krauss, Otto Bauer, Heinz Thiersch, and Gottfried Gruben, the collection was transformed into an archive after World War II. Nevertheless, important bequests were acquired, such as the papers of Theodor Fischer, and the architectural collections of the city of Munich (Sammlung der Landeshauptstadt München) were transferred to the university in 1970. It was not until Winfried Nerdinger's thirty-seven-year tenure, that the holdings of some 150,000 plans and a few models were increased almost by a fourfold. Beginning with an in-depth, historical examination of important teachers from the architecture department of the TU, Nerdinger consistently broadened the scope of the institution's research and collection. He incessantly added to the collection, encouraged—through numerous publications—research on the history of architecture and the use of original sources, and also established the independent exhibition activities of the collection.

öffentliche Wirkung. Auf Initiative von Personen wie Friedrich Krauss, Otto Bauer, Heinz Thiersch und Gottfried Gruben wandelte sich die Sammlung nach dem Zweiten Weltkrieg in ein Archiv. Immerhin konnten bedeutende Nachlässe von Theodor Fischer und 1970 die Übernahme der Sammlung der Landeshauptstadt München verzeichnet werden. Aber erst während der 37-jährigen Amtszeit Winfried Nerdingers vervielfachte sich der Bestand von vormals rund 150 000 Plänen und wenigen Modellen fast um ein vierfaches. Ausgehend von der inhaltlichen Aufarbeitung der Geschichte der großen Lehrer an der Architekturfakultät der TU erweiterte Nerdinger das Spektrum von Forschung und Sammlung immer mehr. Er verfolgte einen konsequenten Ausbau der Sammlung, regte die architekturhistorische Forschung anhand von Originalen durch vielfältige Publikationen an und baute andererseits eine eigene Ausstellungstätigkeit auf.

Architekturausstellungen von überregionaler Bedeutung wurden in München bis dahin vor allem in der Neuen Sammlung gezeigt. Schon 1926, ein Jahr nach ihrer Ausgliederung aus dem Bayerischen Nationalmuseum, präsentierte sie *Neue amerikanische Baukunst*. Später dann, mit Ausstellungen wie *Anonyme Architektur* (1968 als Übernahme Bernard Rudofkys *Architecture Without Architects* von 1964 aus dem MoMA) und eigenen Produktionen wie *Profitopolis* von 1971 erzielte die Neue Sammlung auch starke Resonanz in der öffentlichen Architekturdiskussion. In den 1970er-Jahren konstituierte sich über die wachsende Kritik an der Internationalen Moderne und ihren Auswirkungen allgemein ein verstärktes Interesse an der Relevanz historischer Quellen. Die verbindenden Interessen der historisch orientierten Architektursammlungen und Museen wurden zum ersten Mal auf der gemeinsamen Konferenz der Architekturmuseen als ICAM im Jahre 1979 in Helsinki öffentlich diskutiert. Weil diese Tagung in die Planungsphase des Deutschen Architekturmuseums in Frankfurt am Main fiel, das Heinrich Klotz angeregt hatte, wurden die gemeinsamen Fragen in einem Sonderheft von *Kunstforum International* zum Thema »Architekturmuseen – Architekturvermittlung« veröffentlicht.[12] Es war genau die Zeit, in der sich im Zeichen der Postmoderne der Versuch etablierte, einen Markt für Architekturzeichnungen zu schaffen, und der Zusammenschluss der Architektursammlungen sollte mithin ein Zeichen setzen, »wichtige Belege aus der Architekturgeschichte nicht den Privatsammlern und den Spekulanten zu überlassen, sondern in öffentliches Eigentum, in Museen zu überführen«.[13]

<table>
<tr><td>

AUSSTELLUNG *SHOW & TELL,*
RICHARD J. DIETRICH,
MODELL ZUR METASTADT, 1970

</td><td>

FROM THE EXHIBITION *SHOW & TELL,*
RICHARD J. DIETRICH, MODEL FOR THE
METASTADT BUILDING SYSTEM, 1970

</td></tr>
</table>

Up until this point, architectural exhibitions of national and international importance had been presented in Munich largely by Die Neue Sammlung. In 1926, just one year after it was founded by a transfer of holdings from the Bayerisches Nationalmuseum, it presented *Neue amerikanische Baukunst.* Later, through exhibitions such as *Anonyme Architektur* (1968, a traveling version of Bernard Rudofky's *Architecture Without Architects* from 1964 at the MoMA) and in-house productions including *Profitopolis* from 1971, Die Neue Sammlung also generated substantial responses within public discussions on architecture. In the 1970s, before the backdrop of a growing critical stance toward International Style and its impact, historical sources became more relevant. The interests shared by historically oriented architectural collections and museums were discussed publicly for the first time at the initial conference of architectural museums (ICAM) in 1979 in Helsinki. Since the conference took place at the time when the Deutsches Architekturmuseum in Frankfurt am Main—initiated by its founding director Heinrich Klotz—was in planning, these common issues and questions were discussed in a special issue of *Kunstforum International* on the topic of "Architekturmuseen— Architekturvermittlung" (Architecture Museums—Architectural Education).[12]

Winfried Nerdinger hatte schon 1976 eine Kooperation mit dem Stadtmuseum in München begonnen, um mit einer Serie von Ausstellungen die Bestände der Technischen Universität einer breiteren Öffentlichkeit vorzustellen. Einzelne Ausstellungen wurden darüber hinaus auch in der Bayerischen Akademie der Schönen Künste gezeigt. Durch diese Ausstellungen erzielte er eine so starke Aufmerksamkeit für die Sammlung der Technischen Universität, dass sie im Jahre 1987 beinahe einen eigenen Neubau auf dem Gelände der Türkenkaserne bekommen hätte. Nach dem Scheitern dieses Projektes gelang es erst 2002, eigene Räume im Neubau der Pinakothek der Moderne zu bekommen. Aus heutiger Perspektive kann man diese Entwicklung als Glücksfall betrachten, weil sie dazu geführt hat, dass das Architekturmuseum der Technischen Universität seither im räumlichen und inhaltlichen Dialog mit den anderen im Hause vertretenen Disziplinen Kunst, Design und Grafik steht. Damit findet es in der Öffentlichkeit eine weitaus höhere Aufmerksamkeit als in einem monothematischen Haus. Zugleich bietet diese Konstellation die Möglichkeit zu interdisziplinären Projekten. Am Ende seiner räumlichen Wanderungen und einer wechselhaften Sammlungsgeschichte hat das Architekturmuseum eine räumliche und organisatorische Unterbringung gefunden, die international einzigartig ist. Die »Schaustelle«, ein temporärer Pavillon von Jürgen Mayer H., hat im Sommer 2013 gezeigt, wie das Architekturmuseum im engen Zusammenspiel mit den anderen drei Sammlungen eine tragende Rolle spielen kann, um damit auch Ideen für die Weiterentwicklung des Kunstareals zu generieren.

AUSSTELLEN UND
SAMMELN

Die Auseinandersetzung mit der Theorie und Geschichte der Architekturausstellung erlebt in den letzten Jahren eine intensive Zuwendung durch wissenschaftliche Kongresse und Publikationen. Allein im Jahre 2013 fanden zu diesem Thema mehrere Tagungen in Kopenhagen, Bozen und Yale[14] statt und für 2014 sind weitere in Berlin und an anderen Orten bereits angekündigt oder in Planung.[15] Aber auch durch die Veröffentlichung von Magazinen,[16] Dissertationen und zahlreichen Artikeln zum Themenfeld Architekturausstellung wird in den letzten Jahren deutlich, dass die Erforschung der Architekturpräsentation derzeit eine starke Aufmerksamkeit

It was precisely at this time, that under the aegis of postmodernism an attempt was being made to establish a market for architectural drawings, and the joint efforts of architectural museums intended to send the message that "important documents from the history of architecture would not be left to private collectors and speculators but would be made public property by going to museums."[13] Winfried Nerdinger had already begun cooperating with the Münchener Stadtmuseum in 1976 to present a series of exhibitions on the collections of the Technische Universität to a wide audience. Individual exhibitions were also mounted at the Bayerische Akademie der Schönen Künste (The Bavarian Academy of Fine Arts). These shows resulted in such a positive recognition of the architecture collection of the Technische Universität, that it was almost given its own new building on the site of the former Türkenkaserne in 1987. After this project fell through, the collection managed to receive its own space within the new building of the Pinakothek der Moderne in 2002. From today's perspective, this can be considered a stroke of luck, because it has led to a spatial and conceptual dialogue between the Architekturmuseum of Technische Universität and the other disciplines represented in the building: art, industrial design, and drawings. For this reason, the museum receives much more public attention than it would in its own mono-thematic building. In addition, this constellation simultaneously cultivates interdisciplinary projects. After migrating from place to place over the course of its uneven history, the collection has now found a physical and organizational home, which is unique by international comparison. A temporary pavilion designed by Jürgen Mayer H., the "Schaustelle" that was open during the summer of 2013, demonstrated to what extent the Architekturmuseum can play a fundamental role in close interaction with the other three collections in the building and thereby generate ideas for the future development of Munich's Kunstareal.

EXHIBITING AND COLLECTING

In recent years the theory and history of architectural exhibitions has been the focus of substantial attention through academic congresses and publications. Alone in 2013 there were multiple conferences on this subject, which were held in Copenhagen and Bolzano and at Yale,[14] and more have been announced or are in planning for Berlin and other locations in 2014.[15] Also

erhält. Offensichtlich hat die wissenschaftliche Erforschung der Architekturausstellung gegenüber der Aufarbeitung der Kunstausstellung erheblichen Nachholbedarf.[17] Dieses Defizit wird insbesondere vor dem Hintergrund einer steigenden Anzahl von Architekturausstellungen deutlich: So gibt es seit Einführung der ersten Architekturbiennale 1980 in Venedig inzwischen weit über ein Dutzend Architekturbiennalen und -triennalen – Tendenz steigend. Bei dieser beinahe schon inflationären Steigerung der Produktion von Architekturausstellungen muss die Rolle von Architekturmuseen hinterfragt werden. Ist das Ausstellen von Architektur eine Disziplin, die sich inzwischen unabhängig von den Architekturmuseen entwickelt? Gerade die Kombination von universitärer Forschung und die daraus zu entwickelnden Präsentationen werden in der kommenden Zeit von zentraler Bedeutung sein, um Geschichte und Theorie der Architekturausstellung aktiv voranzubringen. Das MoMA hat beim gemeinsamen Erwerb des Teilnachlasses von Frank Lloyd Wright mit der Columbia University deutlich gemacht, dass es sich von diesem akademischen Schulterschluss auch neue Perspektiven für die Zukunft erhofft. Und nur durch das Ausstellen, also die dauerhafte und konsequente Befragung der eigenen Bestände, werden sich auch Strategien entwickeln lassen, um tragfähige Antworten für die Frage nach dem weiteren Sammlungskonzepten zu gewinnen. Dass die bisherigen administrativen Strukturen in den Architekturmuseen für den Erwerb von Sammlungsgut vielfach nicht auf die heutige Geschwindigkeit der Produktion und Kommunikation ausgerichtet sind, hat Kieran Long zu der Konzeption des Rapid Response Collecting gebracht (siehe S. 172). Mit der Ausstellung *Show & Tell. Architekturgeschichte(n) aus der Sammlung* hat das Architekturmuseum der Technischen Universität München eine aktuelle Bilanz über die eigene Sammlungsgeschichte gezogen und dies zugleich zum Anlass genommen, die Sammlung durch die Schenkung bedeutender internationaler Architekten in die Zukunft zu führen. Wie das weitere Sammlungskonzept für das Architekturmuseum in München konkret aussehen wird, ist im weiteren Prozess zu definieren, die großen Herausforderungen liegen schon darin, dass die räumlichen Kapazitäten für die Lagerung voll erschöpft sind. Noch schwerer wiegt eine andere Frage. Nach der digitalen Revolution, die seit einigen Jahren die grundlegenden Planungs- und Ausführungsprozesse von Architektur radikal verändert hat, stehen die Architekturmuseen an einer epochalen Schwelle: Wie werden sie ihre Sammlungen und Archive in die Zukunft führen? Sollen oder müssen sie eigene Serverparks für die

through magazines,[16] dissertations, and numerous articles on the topic of architectural exhibitions in recent years, it has become clear that research on the presentation of architecture is currently a topic of great interest. Apparently scholarship on architectural exhibitions lags far behind that on art exhibitions.[17] This deficit is most apparent in the context of the trend toward an increasing amount of architectural exhibitions. Since the introduction of the first Architecture Biennale in Venice in 1980, over a dozen architectural biennials and triennials have emerged, and these numbers are growing. In the face of this almost inflationary increase in the production of architectural exhibitions, it becomes necessary reexamine the role of the architecture museum. Has the exhibition of architecture now become a discipline that is developing independently of architectural museums? Precisely the combination of university-level research and resulting exhibitions will be centrally important within the near future in actively taking the history and theory of architectural exhibitions forward. In acquiring a portion of Frank Lloyd Wright's papers together with Columbia University, the MoMA has recently sent a clear signal that it hopes to create new perspectives for the future by joining forces with an academic institution. Also, only by creating exhibitions, that is, by consistently and persistently interrogating its own holdings, can a museum develop strategies for sustainable approaches to furthering the development of its collections. Kieran Long's idea of Rapid Response Collecting (see p. 173) evolved from the observation that the current administrative structure of architectural museums has not been adapted to the speed of contemporary production and communication. With the exhibition *Show & Tell: Architectural (Hi)stories from the Collection* the Architekturmuseum der Technischen Universität München takes a moment to assess its own history of collecting. The exhibition also serves as occasion to look towards the future through the gifts made by important international architects. The exact shape and form of the concept guiding the future collection activities of the Architekturmuseum will need to be refined. The greatest challenge is posed by the fact that our storage capacity is physically exhausted. Another issue has major implications for the museum. Since the digital revolution, which has been radically transforming the basic planning and construction processes of architecture for a number of years, architecture museums are poised at an epochal threshold: How will they organize and administer their collections and archives in the future? Should they or must they set up their own server parks for the approaching flood of digital data? What role does the original

herannahende Flut der digitalen Daten aufbauen? Welche Rolle spielt dann hier noch das Original? Ein Aspekt ist zentral: Ein Architekturmuseum der Gegenwart, wenn es wie das der Technischen Universität München von einer zunehmend international ausgerichteten Hochschule getragen wird, muss sich auf Grundlage des Wissens um die historischen Zusammenhänge proaktiv den zeitgenössischen, globalen Fragestellungen und Aufgaben in der Architektur stellen, neue Diskurse anregen und diese auch in Forschung und Lehre nachhaltig weiter verfolgen. Nur dann wird es seine tiefere Wirksamkeit behalten.

1   Bruce Chatwin, *Utz*, Frankfurt 1991 (2002), S. 22.

2   Immer noch grundlegend: Werner Szambien, *Le Musée d'Architecture*, Paris 1988. Eine neue Darstellung der Geschichte des Architekturmuseums ist angekündigt durch Barry Bergdoll mit dem Titel *Out of Site. In Plain View. A History of Exhibiting Architecture since 1750* und erscheint etwa 2016 bei Princeton University Press,

3   Siehe hierzu Sigrid Achenbach, »Die Schinkel-Sammlung im Berliner Kupferstichkabinett«, in: *Die Hand des Architekten*, hrsg. von der Bauakademie Berlin, Köln 2002, S. 82–101, hier S. 88 f.

4   Die Liste der Mitglieder findet sich online unter http://www.icam-web.org/memberlist.php (Stand: 10.3.14).

5   Zu diesem Wettbewerb und der Idee eines Architekturmuseums für Berlin siehe Wallis Miller, »Cultures of Display. Exhibiting Architecture in Berlin 1880–1931«, in: Tim Anstey u. a. (Hrsg.), *Architecture and Authorship*, London 2007, S. 98–107.

6   Ebd., S. 102.

7   Zur Geschichte dieser Ausstellung: Terence Riley, *The International Style. Exhibition 15 and The Museum of Modern Art (Columbia Books of Architecture)*, New York 1992. Über den Versuch Philip Johnsons durch die Ausstellung *Deconstructivism* im Jahre 1989 noch einmal einen neuen Architekturstil durchzusetzen forscht Tina di Carlo in ihrer Dissertation *»Deconstructivist Architecture« as a Critical Project. Exhibition #1489 and The Museum of Modern Art*.

8   Walter Grasskamp, »Der unsichtbare Markt«, in: *Kursbuch 99. Kunst-Betrieb*, Berlin 1990, S. 97–104, hier S. 98.

9   So etwa Frederieke Taylor, Henry Urbach oder Max Protech in New York. Auch die Berliner Aedes Galerie, 1980 gegründet, hat anfangs versucht Zeichnungen zu verkaufen.

10   Ein Beispiel aus der Gegenwart ist der russisch-deutsche Architekt Sergei Tchoban, der 2013 auf der Grundlage seiner eigenen Sammlung ein eigenes Museum für Architekturzeichnungen in Berlin eröffnet hat.

11   Zur Sammlung der TU Berlin siehe Johannes Cramer, »Vom Historismus zur Moderne. Das Architektur-Museum an der Technischen Hochschule Charlottenburg«, in: *Die Hand des Architekten* (wie Anm. 3), S. 151–168 sowie Hans-Dieter Nägelke, »Baugeschichte der Jetztzeit! 125 Jahre Architekturmuseum«, in: ders. (Hrsg.), *Architekturbilder, 125 Jahre Architekturmuseum der Technischen Universität Berlin*, Berlin 2011.

12   Dieter Bechtloff (Hrsg.), *Architekturmuseen Architekturvermittlung, Kunstforum International*, Bd. 38, Mainz 1980.

13   Ebd, S.14.

14   *Dedicated to Architecture*, Dansk Arkitektur Center, Kopenhagen, 17.–19.4.2013; *Displayed Spaces. New Means of Architecture Presentations Through Exhibitions*, Bozen, 27.2.2013; *Exhibiting Architecture. A Paradox?*, J. Irwin Miller Symposium, Yale University, New Haven, Connecticut, 3.10.–5.10.2013.

15   So etwa im Mai 2014 an der Universität Navarra und zeitgleich in Berlin, Berlinische Galerie, *Architecture on Display*, in Kooperation mit dem Institut für Kunst- und Bildgeschichte der Humboldt-Universität, gefolgt von der ETH Zürich am 31.10.2014.

16   *LOG 20, Fall 2010, Curating Architecture* sowie *Oase 88. Tentoonstellingen. Architectuur tonen en produceren / Exhibitions. Showing and Producing Architecture*, Rotterdam 2012.

17   Immerhin wurden in den letzten Jahren eigene Lehrstühle an Hochschulen eingerichtet die sich verstärkt der Erforschung von Architekturausstellungen zuwenden: Felicity D. Scott als Direktorin des Programms Critical, Curatorial and Conceptual Practices in Architecture (CCCP) an der Graduate School of Architecture, Columbia University, New York. Wilfried Kühn unterrichtete bis zum Wintersemester 2012/13 an der HfG Karlsruhe Ausstellungsdesign und kuratorische Praxis.

play in this context, if any? One aspect remains key: when maintained by an increasingly internationally oriented university like the Technische Universität München, a contemporary architecture museum must use its historical knowledge as a basis for proactively engaging with the global issues and tasks facing architecture today, for generating new discourses, and for consistently pursuing these topics in research and teaching. Only then will the institution retain the depth of its impact.

1 Bruce Chatwin, *Utz* (New York, 1989), p. 20.

2 Still a seminal work: Werner Szambien, *Le Musée d'Architecture* (Paris, 1988). A new overview of the history of the architecture museum by Barry Bergdoll is forthcoming. Entitled *Out of Site: In Plain View; A History of Exhibiting Architecture since 1750* it will be published by Princeton University Press in ca. 2016.

3 See Sigrid Achenbach, "Die Schinkel-Sammlung im Berliner Kupferstichkabinett," in *Die Hand des Architekten*, ed. Bauakademie Berlin (Cologne, 2002), pp. 82–101, see pp. 88–89.

4 For a list of members, see http://www.icam-web.org/memberlist.php (last accessed on March 10, 2104).

5 On this competition and the idea of an architectural museum for Berlin, see Wallis Miller, "Cultures of Display: Exhibiting Architecture in Berlin 1880–1931," in *Architecture and Authorship*, ed. Tim Anstey et al. (London, 2007), pp. 98–107.

6 Ibid., p. 102.

7 On the history of this exhibition: Terence Riley, *The International Style: Exhibition 15 and The Museum of Modern Art*, Columbia Books of Architecture (New York, 1992). In her dissertation, *"Deconstructivist Architecture as a Critical Project": Exhibition #1489 and the Museum of Modern Art*, Tina di Carlo is studying Philip Johnson's attempt to once again assert an architectural style through the 1989 exhibition *Deconstructivism*.

8 Walter Grasskamp, "Der unsichtbare Markt," in *Kursbuch 99: Kunst-Betrieb* (Berlin, 1990), pp. 97–104, see p. 98.

9 For example, Frederieke Taylor, Henry Urbach, and Max Protech in New York. Also the Aedes Galerie in Berlin, which was founded in 1980, initially tried to sell drawings.

10 A contemporary example is the Russian-German architect Sergei Tchoban, who opened an independent museum for architectural drawings in Berlin in 2013 on the basis of his own collection.

11 On the collection of the TU Berlin see Johannes Cramer, "Vom Historismus zur Moderne. Das Architektur-Museum an der Technischen Hochschule Charlottenburg," in *Die Hand des Architekten* (see note 3), pp. 151–68; and Hans-Dieter Nägelke, "Baugeschichte der Jetztzeit! 125 Jahre Architekturmuseum," in *Architekturbilder, 125 Jahre Architekturmuseum der Technischen Universität Berlin*, ed. Hans-Dieter Nägelke (Berlin, 2011).

12 Dieter Bechtloff, ed., *Architekturmuseen Architekturvermittlung, Kunstforum International* 38, (Mainz, 1980).

13 Ibid., p.14.

14 *Dedicated to Architecture*, Dansk Arkitektur Center, Copenhagen, April 17 – 19, 2014; *Displayed Spaces: New Means of Architecture Presentations Through Exhibitions*, Bolzano, February 27, 2013; *Exhibiting Architecture: A Paradox?*, J. Irwin Miller Symposium, Yale University, New Haven, Connecticut, October 3 – 5, 2013.

15 For example in May 2014 at the University of Navarra and at the same time in Berlin at the Berlinische Galerie, *Architecture on Display*, in cooperation with the Institut für Kunst- und Bildgeschichte der Humboldt-Universität, followed by the ETH Zürich on October 31, 2014.

16 *LOG 20, Fall 2010, Curating Architecture* and *Oase 88: Tentoonstellingen; Architectuur tonen en produceren / Exhibitions; Showing and Producing Architecture*, Rotterdam 2012.

17 At universities at least a number of teaching positions have been established that are intended to support research on architectural exhibitions: Felicity D. Scott, director of the program of Critical, Curatorial and Conceptual Practices in Architecture (CCCP) at the Graduate School of Architecture, Columbia University, New York. Wilfried Kühn taught exhibition design and curatorial practice at the HfG Karlsruhe through the winter semester of 2012–13.

DER LETZTE RAUM DER
AUSSTELLUNG SHOW & TELL,
LINKS: SCHENKUNGEN
AN DAS ARCHIV ANLÄSSLICH
DER AUSSTELLUNG

THE LAST ROOM OF THE
EXHIBITION SHOW & TELL,
ON THE LEFT: DONATIONS MADE
TO THE ARCHIVE ON THE
OCCASION OF THIS EXHIBITION

SAMMELN, FORSCHEN, ZEIGEN

DIE SAMMLUNG DES ARCHITEKTURMUSEUMS DER TU MÜNCHEN ALS LEHRMITTEL, AUSBILDUNGSINSTRUMENT UND AUSSTELLUNGSOBJEKT

Das Architekturmuseum der Technischen Universität (TU) München geht in seiner heutigen Form zurück auf die Anfänge der akademischen Architektenausbildung in Bayern an der von Maximilian I. Joseph 1808 gegründeten Königlichen Akademie der Bildenden Künste in München.[1] Wie in jeder Akademie und Bauschule des 19. Jahrhunderts befand sich auch hier eine Sammlung mit Lehrmaterialien, da das Zeichnen weitgehend durch Kopieren von Vorlagenblättern und das Abzeichnen von Gipsabgüssen erlernt und eingeübt wurde.[2] Die dort verwendeten Zeichnungen bilden den Grundstock der heutigen Plansammlung des Architekturmuseums. Im Zuge der wachsenden Bedeutung der technischen gegenüber der künstlerischen Ausbildung kam es »durch die königl. allerhöchste Verordnung vom 12. April 1868« zur Eröffnung der »Königlich-Bayerischen Polytechnischen Schule zu München« mit einer »Hochbau-Abtheilung«.[3] Für den Unterricht übergab Ludwig II. den Architekturstudenten »als Vorbild und Dokument« eine Sammlung architektonischer Entwürfe aus den Beständen der Akademie. Darunter befand sich der Nachlass Carl von Fischers.[4] Dieser zählt neben Friedrich Gilly, Karl Friedrich Schinkel und Leo von Klenze zu den bedeutendsten Baumeistern des Klassizismus in Deutschland. Als Erbauer des Prinz Carl Palais hatte er sich früh einen Namen gemacht und wurde mit 24 Jahren zum ersten Lehrer an die Bauschule der Akademie der Bildenden Künste berufen. Fischers großformatige, virtuos aquarellierte Zeichnungen, seine Reisestudien sowie sein Pariser Skizzenbuch sind noch heute ein besonderer Schatz der Sammlung des Architekturmuseums.[5] Die Schenkung von 1868 umfasste auch die Zeichnungen Gottfried Sempers für das gerade in München gescheiterte Richard-Wagner-Festspielhaus (1864/65), dessen Pläne noch kurz zuvor auf der Weltausstellung 1867 in Paris ausgestellt worden waren.[6]

COLLECTING, RESEARCHING, EXHIBITING

THE COLLECTION OF THE ARCHITEKTURMUSEUM DER TU MÜNCHEN AS A LEARNING TOOL, TEACHING AID, AND EXHIBIT

IRENE MEISSNER

The Architekturmuseum der Technischen Universität (TU) München owes its current form to the beginnings of academic architectural training in Bavaria at the Königliche Akademie der Bildenden Künste, which was founded by Maximilian I Joseph in 1808.[1] Like every academy and architectural college of the nineteenth century, this institution also housed a teaching collection, since drawing was largely learned and practiced by copying existing drawings and sketching plaster casts.[2] The drawings used in this context are the basis of the Architekturmuseum's current collection of architectural plans. In the wake of the growing importance of technical over artistic training, the opening of the Königlich-Bayerische Polytechnische Schule zu München, including a department of structural design, was ordered "by his Majesty's royal decree of April 12, 1868."[3] For teaching purposes, Ludwig II donated a collection of architectural designs from the holdings of the academy to the architecture students as "models and documents." This included the papers of Carl von Fischer,[4] who, in addition to Friedrich Gilly, Karl Friedrich Schinkel, and Leo von Klenze, was considered among the most important master architects of German Classicism. Having built the Prinz-Carl-Palais, he made a name for himself at a young age and was the first instructor appointed to the Bauschule (Architectural College) of the Akademie der Bildende Künste at the age of twenty-four. Fischer's virtuosic, large-format watercolor drawings, the studies that he made during his travels, and his Paris sketchbook are still considered some of the unique treasures in the collection of the Architekturmuseum.[5] The bequest of 1868 also included drawings by Gottfried Semper for the Richard Wagner Festspielhaus (1864–65) in Munich, which was never built. The plans for the building had been exhibited at the World's Fair in Paris shortly before, in 1867.[6]

CARL VON FISCHER, KORINTHISCHES
PILASTERKAPITELL, UM 1810

CARL VON FISCHER, CORINTHIAN
PILASTER CAPITAL, CA. 1810

Die neue Polytechnische Schule war ab 1866 von Gottfried von Neureuther im Stil der Neorenaissance in prominenter Lage gegenüber der Alten Pinakothek nach dem Vorbild von Gottfried Sempers Zürcher Polytechnikum errichtet worden. In dem im Zweiten Weltkrieg zerstörten Bau befanden sich im ersten Obergeschoss die Ingenieur- und Hochbauschule. Die Sammlungen mit den Lehrgegenständen der Architekten, im Grundriss als »Hochbausammlung« bezeichnet, nahmen im südlichen Eckrisalit einen

The building of the new Polytechnische Schule began in 1866. Designed by Gottfried von Neureuther in a Neo-Renaissance style, it was constructed on a prominent site across from the Alte Pinakothek and was modeled after Gottfried Semper's Zürcher Polytechnikum. The school of engineering and structural design was on the first floor of the building, which was destroyed in World War II. Identified in the ground plan as the *Hochbausammlung* (collection of structural design), the architectural teaching collection was centrally located in the southern corner avant-corps. On the second floor, the spacious drawing studios were adjacent to the antiquities hall. In order for plaster casts to be installed in the latter, Ludwig II had granted his permission at the opening of the college "for casts to be made of the best works of sculpture from his Majesty's private collection in the Glyptothek in Munich."[7]

Six teaching collections were established for the training of architects,[8] and professors were assigned to each.[9] Until World War I, the collections were expanded by donations and purchases of drawings from architects active in Bavaria. This basis was expanded by the bequests of a number of architecture professors from the college. In addition, purchases were made of some 10,000 photographs.[10]

The collection of architectural drawing, as of 1873–74 named the *Sammlung für architectonische Constructionslehre* (the collection of architectural construction), was headed by Rudolph Gottgetreu and included approximately 100 wall panels and sample drawings as well as books and numerous photographs. Established in 1881–82, the collection of decoration and perspective was administered by Joseph Bühlmann and encompassed photographs of buildings and interiors with decorations and furnishings; the collection of modeling and sculpting, for which Konrad Knoll was responsible, included over 600 plaster casts. In addition to casts of antique sculptures in the Glyptothek, original casts made of important architectural monuments of the Renaissance, which were commissioned by the Gesellschaft San Giorgio and purchased by the Königliche Bayerische Staatministerium (Royal Bavarian Ministry of State) in 1884, were transferred to the college, among other items.[11]

Models dating from the early period of the college have not survived, and there are no drawings of these teaching materials.[12] Carl von Fischer had argued in the first curriculum of the academy from 1809, that in addition to drawing and illustration, it was necessary to teach and learn model making.[13] For the architectural collection[14] (initially the responsibility of Gottfried von Neureuther, and headed by Friedrich von Thiersch as of 1879) photographs were particularly

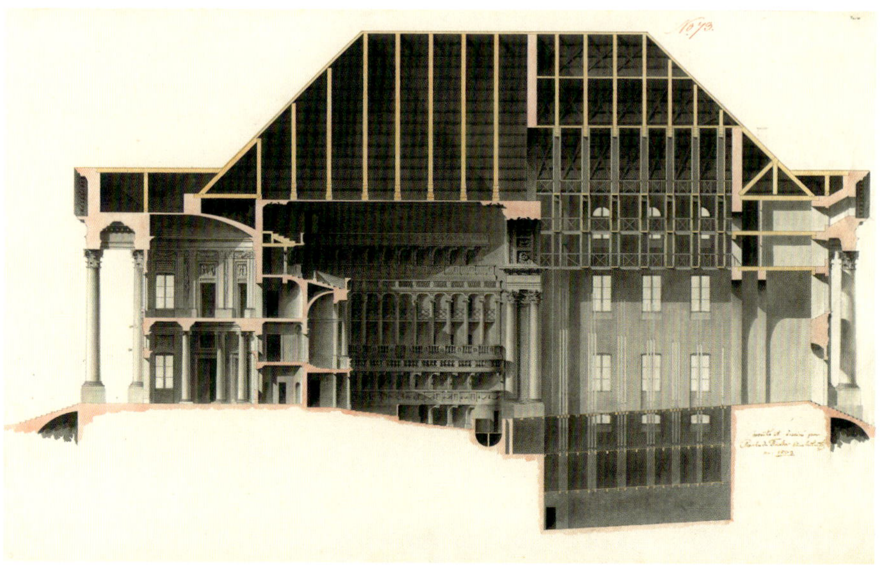

CARL VON FISCHER, STUDIENENTWURF
OPER WIEN, LÄNGSSCHNITT, 1803

CARL VON FISCHER, DESIGN FOR THE
VIENNESE OPERA, LONGITUDINAL SECTION, 1803

zentralen Ort ein. Im 2. Obergeschoss schlossen sich die großen Zeichensäle und der Antikensaal an. Damit dort Abgüsse aufgestellt werden konnten, hatte Ludwig II. mit Eröffnung der Schule die Erlaubnis erteilt, »die besten plastischen Werke aus der im allerhöchsten Privatbesitze befindlichen Glyptothek zu München abzuformen«.[7]

Für die Architektenausbildung[8] wurden zunächst 6 Lehrmittelsammlungen eingerichtet und den Professoren zugeteilt.[9] Bis zum Ersten Weltkrieg wuchsen die Sammlungen durch Schenkungen und den Ankauf von Zeichnungen von in Bayern tätig gewesenen Architekten. Dieser Grundstock wurde durch die Nachlässe einiger Architekturprofessoren der Hochschule erweitert. Außerdem wurden rund 10 000 Fotografien erworben.[10]

Die Sammlung für Bauzeichnen, ab 1873/74 Sammlung für architectonische Constructionslehre, unterstand Rudolph Gottgetreu und umfasste etwa 100 Wandtafeln und Vorlageblätter sowie Bücher und zahlreiche Fotografien; die ab 1881/82 eingerichtete Sammlung für Dekoration und Perspektive wurde von Joseph Bühlmann verwaltet und enthielt Aufnahmen von Gebäuden und Innenräumen mit Dekorationen und Ausstattungen, und die Sammlung für Modelliren und Bossiren, für die Konrad Knoll zuständig war, enthielt über 600 Gipsabgüsse. Neben den Abgüssen antiker Skulpturen

important as a means of familiarizing students with monuments of world architecture. The oldest of these images date from the beginnings of photography and were taken by photographers including Édouard Baldus, frères Bisson, Pascal Sébah, and Carlo Naya. Friedrich von Thiersch played an important role in the acquisition of photographs,[15] undertaking numerous trips to destinations including Greece, Asia Minor, Egypt, and the Near East, and returning with richly filled sketchbooks as well as photographs and glass-plate negatives.

The collection received an important addition in 1897–98, when the Moninger Collection—purchased in 1884 by the Bavarian parliament for 20,000 marks and including "2,839 drawings" by Friedrich von Gärtner and his father Andreas Gärtner as well as a number of his students, such as Friedrich Bürklein—was "finally"[16] transferred to the collection.[17] Hans Moninger was the son of Gärtner student Johann Moninger, a railway official who had wheedled the drawings from Gärtner's descendents and then had them catalogued in 1882 by the art historian Carl Albert Regnet in the manner similar to that of the Maillinger collection.[18] Friedrich von Gärtner had been taught drawing and watercolor technique by Fischer and had followed him to the Academy in 1820. Around Gärtner—a teacher and as of 1841 director of the academy—formed the famous

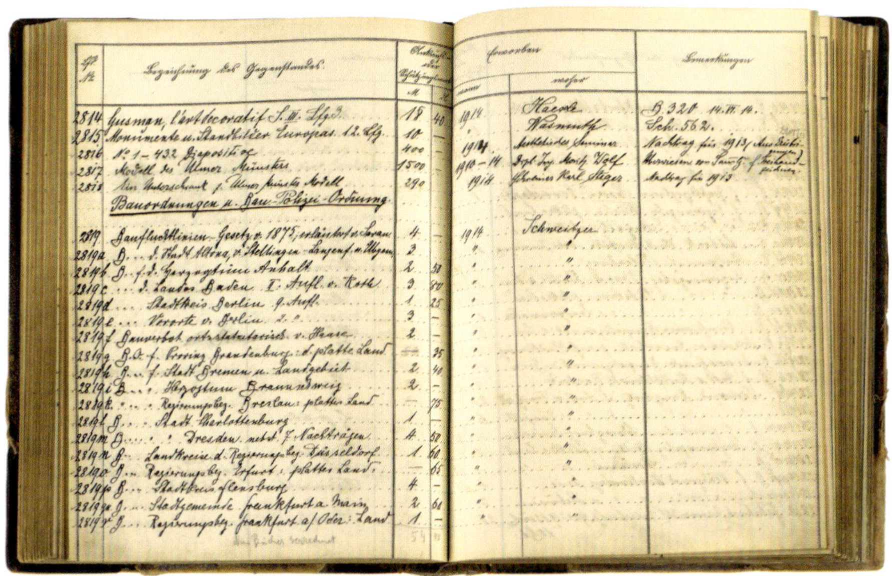

INVENTARBUCH DER
ARCHITEKTONISCHEN SAMMLUNG:
NR. 2817, EINTRAG MODELL
DES ULMER MÜNSTERS, 1910–1914

INVENTORY REGISTER OF THE
ARCHITECTURE COLLECTION; NO. 2817:
ENTRY ON THE MODEL OF
THE ULM MINSTER, 1910–14

GOTTFRIED VON NEUREUTHER,
NEUES POLYTECHNIKUM, BLICK AUF
DEN SAMMLUNGSRAUM DER
ARCHITEKTURABTEILUNG
IM 1. OBERGESCHOSS, UM 1870

GOTTFRIED VON NEUREUTHER,
NEUES POLYTECHNIKUM, VIEW OF THE
COLLECTION ROOMS OF
THE ARCHITECTURE DEPARTMENT,
FIRST FLOOR, CA. 1870

aus der Glyptothek wurden unter anderem 1884 die vom Königlich Bayerischen Staatsministerium erworbenen Originalabgüsse, welche die Gesellschaft San Giorgio von bedeutenden Baudenkmälern der Renaissance hatte fertigen lassen, der Hochschule übereignet.[11]

Modelle aus der Frühzeit sind nicht erhalten, auch existieren keine Abbildungen zu diesem Studienmaterial.[12] Carl von Fischer hatte bereits im ersten Lehrprogramm an der Akademie 1809 dargelegt, dass neben dem Erwerben der Fähigkeiten des Zeichnens und Darstellens auch der Modellbau gelehrt und gelernt werden müsse.[13] Für die architectonische Sammlung[14] (betreut zunächst durch Gottfried von Neureuther, ab 1879 dann durch Friedrich von Thiersch) waren aber insbesondere auch Fotografien von Bedeutung, damit die Studenten die Monumente der Weltarchitektur kennenlernen konnten. Die ältesten dieser Aufnahmen datieren aus den Anfängen der Fotografie und stammen unter anderem von Édouard Baldus, Bisson frères, Pascal Sébah oder auch Carlo Naya. Bei dem Erwerb der Fotografien spielte Friedrich von Thiersch eine bedeutende Rolle.[15] Er unternahm zahlreiche Reisen, unter anderem nach Griechenland, Kleinasien,

GOTTFRIED VON NEUREUTHER,
NEUES POLYTECHNIKUM,
EINGANG ZUM ZEICHENSAAL, UM 1870

GOTTFRIED VON NEUREUTHER,
NEUES POLYTECHNIKUM, ENTRANCE
TO THE DRAWING STUDIO, CA. 1870

Münchner Architekturschule, a counterpart to the Berliner Architekturschule. The Moninger collection was incorporated into "teaching aides" under the Friedrich von Gärtner collection of plans and teaching materials, for which Friedrich von Thiersch was responsible. Gärtner's drawings are some of the most beautiful of their kind, and today they are of inestimable value to the collection of the Architekturmuseum.

With the exception of the Moninger catalogue, the inventory registers of the former collections have only been preserved in a fragmentary state, which is why it is almost impossible to reconstruct the holding, new acquisitions, or possible cessions from this period.[19] When the so-called Hoffstadt-Sammlung of the Akademie der Bildenden Künste was dismantled in 1904, the architectural drawings and plaster casts of this group of works were transferred to the Technische Hochschule.[20]

Friedrich Hoffstadt was an expert in Gothic architectural drawings and lodge books. In 1840, he published the *Gotische A-B-C-Buch* (Gothic Book of A-B-Cs), a practically oriented structural geometry for artists and skilled craftsmen.[21] The Hoffstadt collection included two Gothic architectural drawings, the front elevation of a western tower by Caspar Ensinger and the plan of

LUIGI FIORELLI, PALAIS DU COMTE
ETIENNE ZIZINIA, ALEXANDRIA,
ZERSTÖRT DURCH DIE ENGLISCHE
FLOTTE AM 11. JULI 1882

LUIGI FIORELLI, PALAIS DU
COMTE ETIENNE ZIZINIA,
ALEXANDRIA, DESTROYED BY THE
BRITISH FLEET ON JULY 11, 1882

Ägypten und in den Vorderen Orient, von denen er neben reich gefüllten Skizzenbüchern auch Fotografien und Glasplattennegative mitbrachte.

Einen bedeutenden Zuwachs erhielt die Sammlung 1897/98, als die 1884 vom Bayerischen Landtag für 20 000 Mark erworbene Moninger-Sammlung mit »2 839 Zeichnungen« Friedrich von Gärtners und dessen Vaters Andreas Gärtner sowie von einigen seiner Schüler, darunter Friedrich Bürklein, »endlich«[16] übereignet wurde.[17] Hans Moninger war der Sohn des Gärtnerschülers Johann Moninger, ein Bahnbeamter, der sich die Zeichnungen von den Nachkommen Gärtners erbettelt hatte und dann von dem Kunsthistoriker Carl Albert Regnet 1882 nach Vorbild der Maillinger-Sammlung katalogisieren ließ.[18] Friedrich von Gärtner hatte bei Fischer die kunstvolle Zeichen- und Aquarelltechnik gelernt und war ihm 1820 an die Akademie gefolgt. Als Lehrer und seit 1841 Direktor der Akademie bildete sich um Gärtner die berühmte Münchner Architekturschule, das Gegenstück zur Berliner Architekturschule. Die Moninger-Sammlung wurde als *Die Friedrich von Gärtner'sche Plan- und*

a late Gothic sacristy by Burckhard Engelberg.[22] These two plans were considered lost in the wake of World War II, until they appeared on the art market in 2011 and 2012.[23] Also no longer part of the collection are the preliminary design studies, which were produced in 1888 by Emil Lange, Edwin Oppler, Albert Schmid, and Georg Bürkel for the construction of a synagogue in Munich, and which had been donated by the Jewish religious community.[24] In contrast, the extremely valuable *Codex Aureatinus* given by Prince Regent Luitpold and a collection of Baroque plans from Eichstätt by Gabriel de Gabrieli and Maurizio Pedetti are still in the possession of the Architekturmuseum.[25]

Since it was not possible to establish a well-arranged order or utilization of these valuable items due to a lack of space, in 1908 Friedrich von Thiersch suggested that "a well-lit and spacious architecture museum, which would facilitate an interesting exhibition of all materials as well as the comfortable study of individual objects" be installed in the new building that he was planning for the college.[26] A number of new purchases and donations were

FRIEDRICH VON GÄRTNER,
POMPEJANUM, ASCHAFFENBURG,
INNENRAUMPERSPEKTIVE, UM 1845

FRIEDRICH VON GÄRTNER,
POMPEJANUM, ASCHAFFENBURG,
INTERIOR VIEW, CA. 1845

Studiensammlung, für die Friedrich von Thiersch verantwortlich zeichnete, zu den »Lehrmitteln« aufgenommen. Die Zeichnungen Gärtners gehören zu den schönsten ihrer Art und stellen heute einen unschätzbaren Wert für die Sammlung des Architekturmuseums dar.

Mit Ausnahme des Moninger-Katalogs sind die Inventarbücher der einstigen Sammlungen nur noch bruchstückhaft vorhanden, deswegen können die Bestände, Neuerwerbungen oder auch etwaige Abgaben aus dieser Zeit kaum rekonstruiert werden.[19] Als an der Akademie der Bildenden Künste 1904 die sogenannte Hoffstadt-Sammlung aufgelöst wurde, gingen die zum Bestand gehörenden architektonischen Zeichnungen und Gipsabgüsse, die mit Schließung der Bauschule 1873 für die Akademie uninteressant geworden waren, in den Bestand der Technischen Hochschule über.[20]

Friedrich Hoffstadt war Kenner gotischer Baurisse und Steinmetzbücher. 1840 veröffentlichte er das *Gotische A-B-C-Buch*, eine praxisorientierte Baugeometrie für Künstler und Handwerker.[21] Zur Sammlung von Hoffstadt gehörten auch zwei gotische Baurisse auf Pergament, der Aufriss eines Westturms von Caspar Ensinger und der Riss eines spätgotischen Sakramenthauses von Burckhard Engelberg.[22] Diese beiden Pläne galten nach dem Zweiten Weltkrieg als verschollen, bis sie 2011 und 2012 im Kunsthandel angeboten wurden.[23] Ebenfalls nicht mehr in der Sammlung vorhanden sind die 1888 von der israelitischen Kultusgemeinde zugewendeten Vorprojekte für die Erbauung einer Synagoge in München von Emil Lange, Edwin Oppler, Albert Schmid und Georg Bürkel.[24] Der sehr kostbare von Prinzregent Luitpold gestiftete »Codex Aureatinus«, eine Sammlung Eichstätter Barockplanungen von Gabriel de Gabrieli und Maurizio Pedetti, befindet sich hingegen noch heute im Besitz des Architekturmuseums.[25]

Da eine übersichtliche Anordnung und Verwendung dieser Schätze aufgrund fehlender Räumlichkeiten nicht möglich war, schlug Friedrich von Thiersch 1908 vor, in dem von ihm geplanten Neubau der Hochschule »ein gut beleuchtetes geräumiges Architekturmuseum, das in gleicher Weise eine interessante Ausstellung des gesamten Materials wie ein bequemes Studium der einzelnen Objekte ermöglichen würde« einzurichten.[26] Um dieses »Architekturmuseum« ausreichend bestücken zu können, kam es zu einigen Neuerwerbungen und weiteren Schenkungen. So wurde 1912 ein Konvolut von Plänen, unter anderem zum Kloster Banz und zum Kloster Langheim aus der Bamberger Sammlung von Otto Dros, über die Galerie Helbing in München erworben, darunter Zeichnungen von Johann Dientzenhofer, Balthasar Neumann

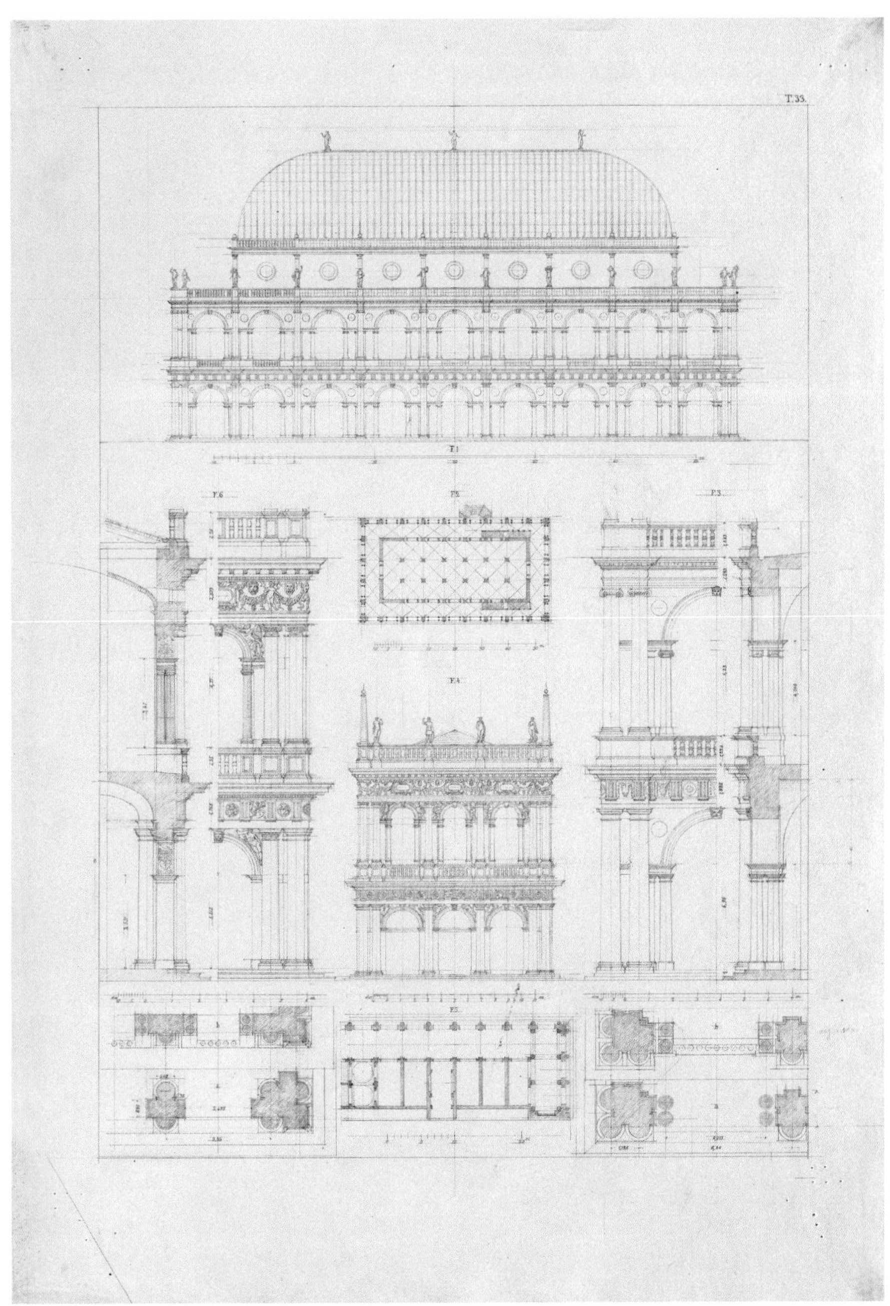

JOSEPH BÜHLMANN,
VORZEICHNUNG,
BASILIKA, VICENZA, 1896

JOSEPH BÜHLMANN,
PRELIMINARY SKETCH,
BASILICA, VICENZA, 1896

und Johann Lorenz Finck.[27] Die Familie des 1870 verstorbenen Oberbaurats August von Voit, der Gärtner 1841 an der Akademie als Lehrer gefolgt war, übergab aus dessen Nachlass eine Sammlung von Plänen und Abbildungen.[28] Insbesondere die Zeichnungen für den vorgefertigten und auf der Baustelle montierten Glaspalast, seinerzeit die größte Glas-Eisen-Konstruktion innerhalb des deutschen Staatenbundes, den Voit zusammen mit dem Ingenieur Ludwig Werder 1853/54 nach dem Vorbild des berühmten Londoner Crystal Palace am alten Botanischen Garten errichtet hatte, war für die Architektenausbildung von besonderer Bedeutung. Die bis zu 1,50 Meter breiten, farbig aquarellierten Ausführungs- und Detailpläne sind erhalten geblieben und gehören heute zu den Schätzen des Architekturmuseums.

DIE NEUEN SCHAURÄUME DER ARCHITEKTURSAMMLUNG

Die bisherigen Sammlungen wurden 1912 unter dem Namen Architektursammlung vereinigt und im Neubau entlang der Gabelsbergerstraße im 2. Obergeschoss in einer von Thiersch prachtvoll ausgestatteten Raumflucht untergebracht. Mit der Leitung wurde ein aus den Professoren bestehender Ausschuss unter einem von ihm zu wählenden Vorsitzenden berufen und mit der Verwaltung der Sammlung erstmals »ein Kustos«, der Privatdozent für Ästhetik und Kunstgeschichte Joseph Popp betraut.[29]
Die ständig wachsende Anerkennung der Architektursammlung belegt die Eröffnungszeremonie am 23. Juni 1913, bei der sich Prinzregent Ludwig zunächst den im obersten Geschoss gelegenen Übungssaal für Freihandzeichnen mit den Gipsabgüssen und dann die Räume der Architektursammlung zeigen ließ.[30] Die Aufstellung der Gipse im Übungssaal dokumentieren zwei erhaltene Fotografien sowie eine von Paul Pfann, Professor für Freihandzeichnen, im März 1912 angefertigte Zeichnung mit Eintragung der Inventarnummern.[31] Die weiteren in der Festschrift zum 50-jährigen Bestehen der Hochschule von der Architektursammlung veröffentlichten Fotografien vermitteln die Einheit des Lernens von Anschauen, Zeichnen, Studieren und Entwerfen.[32] In den von Thiersch mit Schränken und Vitrinen aus edlem Kirsch- und schwarz gebeiztem Birnbaumholz ausgestatteten Lehr- und Schauräumen befanden sich als Leihgaben auch die berühmten Korkmodelle

made in order to sufficiently equip this new "Architekturmuseum." In 1912, a convolute of plans, including those of the Banz Abbey and the Langheim Abbey from the collection of Otto Dros in Bamberg, was thus purchased via Galerie Helbing in Munich, as were drawings by Johann Dientzenhofer, Balthasar Neumann, and Johann Lorenz Finck.[27] The family of head building commissioner August von Voit, who had followed Gärtner in 1841 as a teacher at the academy and had died in 1870, bequeathed a collection of plans and images from his estate.[28] Of special significance in terms of architectural teaching materials were drawings for the glass palace, which Voit had constructed in the Alter Botanischer Garten together with engineer Ludwig Werder in 1853–54 and modeled after the famous Crystal Palace in London. The largest glass and iron construction within the union of German states at the time, the structure had been prefabricated and assembled on-site. The watercolor implementation plans plus other detailed plans, some of them 1.5 meters wide, have been preserved. Today they are among the most valued items belonging to the Architekturmuseum.

THE NEW EXHIBITION ROOMS OF THE ARCHITECTURE COLLECTION

The existing collections were unified in 1912 under the name *Architektursammlung* (architecture collection) and were housed on the second floor of a new building on Gabelsbergerstrasse in a series of rooms that had been grandly furnished by Thiersch. Overseeing the collection was a committee of professors headed by a chair appointed from their ranks. The administration of the collection was entrusted for the first time to a *Kustos,* or conservator, the assistant professor for aesthetics and art history, Joseph Popp.[29]
The growing recognition accorded to the architecture collection is reflected in the opening ceremony of June 23, 1913, at which Prince Regent Ludwig allowed himself to be guided first through the studio for free-hand drawing and then through the rooms of the architecture collection.[30] The arrangement of the plaster casts in the drawing studio is documented by two surviving photographs as well as by the drawing including inventory numbers by Paul Pfann, professor of free-hand drawing, dated March 1912.[31] Additional

ERWEITERUNGSBAU DER K. B.
TECHNISCHEN HOCHSCHULE
ZU MÜNCHEN, SCHAURÄUME
DER ARCHITEKTURSAMMLUNG,
UM 1917

EXTENSION OF THE K. B.
TECHNISCHE HOCHSCHULE
ZU MÜNCHEN, DISPLAY ROOMS OF
THE ARCHITECTURE COLLECTION,
CA. 1917

ERWEITERUNGSBAU DER K. B.
TECHNISCHEN HOCHSCHULE
ZU MÜNCHEN. ÜBUNGSSAAL
FÜR FREIHANDZEICHNEN. UM 1917

EXTENSION OF THE K. B.
TECHNISCHE HOCHSCHULE
ZU MÜNCHEN.
DRAWING STUDIO. CA. 1917

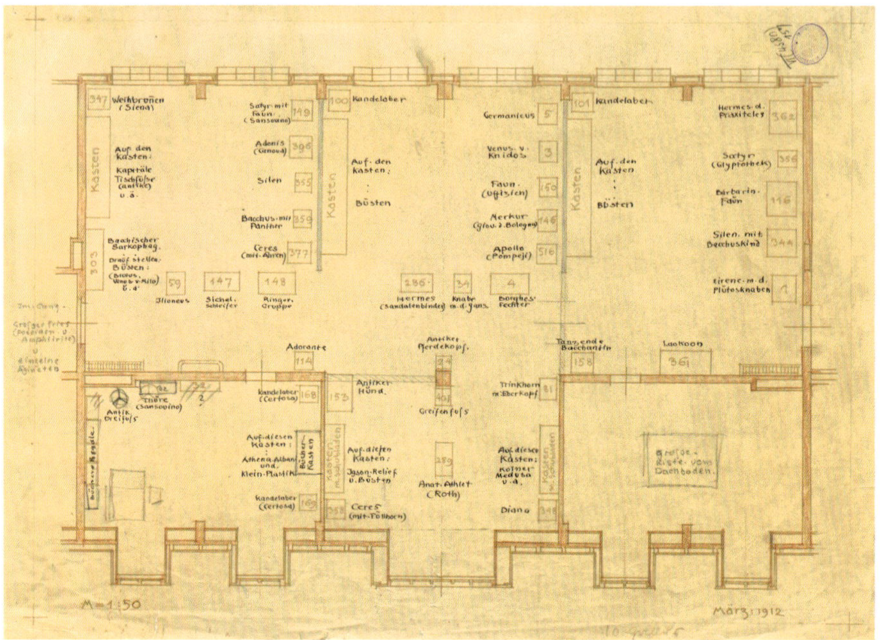

PAUL PFANN, AUFSTELLUNG DER GIPSE
IM ÜBUNGSSAAL, MÄRZ 1912

PAUL PFANN, EXHIBITION OF CASTS
IN THE STUDIO, MARCH 1912

aus der Sammlung Ludwig I.,[33] die dieser von den Korbildnern Carl May und dessen Sohn Georg hatte fertigen lassen. Die exakt erstellten Studienobjekte antiker römischer Bauten erfreuten sich in der Bevölkerung großer Beliebtheit und dienten in vielen Akademien als Lehr- und Anschauungsmaterial. Seit 1872 waren die Modelle im Königlichen Antiquarium in der Neuen Pinakothek[34] ausgestellt und fanden dort laut Popp »keine entsprechende Beachtung«, sodass sie der neu eingerichteten Architektursammlung überlassen wurden.[35] Das Prunkstück der Sammlung war das im Eingangsbereich aufgestellte, im Maßstab 1:60 gefertigte und in der Längsachse 3,12 Meter messende, imposante Modell des Kolosseums.[36] Seit ihrer Auslagerung im Zweiten Weltkrieg befinden sich die erhaltenen Modelle im Schloss Johannisburg in Aschaffenburg.

Die Architektursammlung besaß zwar nun eine repräsentative Raumfolge und die antiken Gipsabgüsse und Modelle waren gemäß der damaligen Architekturauffassung in die Ausbildung integriert, doch der seit der Jahrhundertwende wirkende Antihistorismus, die Bewegung gegen Geschichte, Ornament und Stilformen, führte kurze Zeit später zu einer grundlegenden Reform der

photographs of the architecture collection in the publication celebrating the fifty-year anniversary of the institution convey the unity of observing, drawing, studying, and designing in the curriculum.[32] In the teaching and exhibition rooms, which had been fitted by Thiersch with shelves and display cases made from precious cherry wood and black-stained pear wood, were also the famous cork models on loan from the collection of Ludwig I,[33] who had commissioned them from cork carver Carl May and his son Georg. The precisely formed models of ancient Roman buildings were very popular among the general public and were used as teaching and study materials in many academies. As of 1872, the models had been on view in the Königliches Antiquarium in the Neue Pinakothek.[34] According to Popp, they did not receive "appropriate attention" there and were thus given to the newly installed architecture collection.[35] The centerpiece of the collection was the model of the Colosseum, which was on view in the entrance area. Reconstructed in a scale of 1:60, it was an imposing 3.12 meters long.[36] Since coming out of storage after World War II, the surviving models have been on view at Schloss Johannisburg in Aschaffenburg.

The architecture collection now had a prestigious configuration of rooms at its disposal, and in accordance with the reigning concepts of architecture at the time, the ancient plaster casts and models were integrated into the educational program. However, the anti-historicism tendency that had emerged since the turn of the century, a movement against historical influences, ornament, and stylistic forms, soon led to fundamental reforms in the training of architects, in which construction and functional design consequently became increasingly important. In his lectures, Thiersch had still drawn from the "rich material of the architecture collection,"[37] but when he died in 1921, his successor, German Bestelmeyer, had the personal plans and papers of the "master of all architectural drawing"[38] removed.[39] Two-thirds were destroyed, and the remaining documents, still amounting to 10,000 drawings, sketches, and blueprints, went to the Deutsches Museum. Only many years later did they make their way back to the university (see p. 69).

The further development of the architecture collection is documented in Adolf Abel's[40] 1935 *Denkschrift über die Entstehung, das Wesen und die Aufgaben der Architektursammlung* (Memorandum on the Development, Nature, and Aim of the Architecture Collection).[41] Abel writes that since the unification of the individual teaching collections, the expansion of the collection of

Architektenausbildung, in deren Folge Konstruktion und funktionale Gestaltung immer wichtiger wurden. Thiersch hatte bei seinen Vorlesungen noch auf das »reiche Material der Architektursammlung« zurückgegriffen,[37] doch als er 1921 starb, ließ sein Nachfolger German Bestelmeyer die persönlichen Pläne und Unterlagen des »Meisters aller Architekturzeichnungen«[38] entfernen.[39] Zwei Drittel wurden vernichtet, der verbleibende Rest, immer noch 10 000 Zeichnungen, Skizzen und Pausen, ging an das Deutsche Museum und gelangte erst viele Jahre später an die Hochschule zurück (siehe S. 68).

Die weitere Entwicklung der Architektursammlung dokumentiert eine 1935 von Adolf Abel[40] verfasste *Denkschrift über die Entstehung, das Wesen und die Aufgaben der Architektursammlung*.[41] Abel schreibt, dass seit der Zusammenfassung der einzelnen Lehrmittelsammlungen ein Ausbau der Modellsammlung aufgrund des erforderlichen Raumes gescheitert wäre und auch »die glücklich begonnene Plansammlung wegen zu geringer Mittel nicht weiter geführt« werden konnte, dass aber mit der Bibliothek[42] ein wichtiges Mittel für Lehre und wissenschaftliche Arbeit entstanden sei. Um einen modernen, nicht an historischen Vorbildern orientierten Architekturunterricht zu gestalten, hatten sich die Neuerwerbungen nur noch auf die Anschaffung von Büchern, Fotografien und Projektionslichtbildern beschränkt. Die in der Bibliothek verwahrte »stattliche Anzahl von Schriften architektonischen Inhalts« wird 1922 sogar in *Meyers Reisebücher* hervorgehoben.[43]

Als Joseph Popp 1919 den Ruf als Ordinarius für Bau- und Kunstgeschichte in der Nachfolge von Karl Voll erhielt, wurde der Kunsthistoriker Hans Karlinger mit der »Wahrnehmung der Geschäfte des Konservators der Architektursammlung« betraut.[44] 1926 ging Karlinger jedoch an die Technische Hochschule Aachen. Daraufhin ernannte die Architektenabteilung als vorerst letzten Konservator vor dem Zweiten Weltkrieg den Deutsch-Schweizer Architekten Manfred Bühlmann, der als Privatdozent Geschichte der Architektur lehrte.[45] Nach der Vorstellung des Senats sollte die Stelle nun künftig mit »jungen Kunsthistorikern, im Wechsel von fünf bis sechs Jahren« besetzt werden.[46] Nach wiederholt gestellten Anträgen erhielt Bühlmann dann aber doch zum 1. April 1932 eine »etatsmäßige« Stelle.[47] Dass die Plansammlung zu dieser Zeit für die Lehre praktisch bedeutungslos geworden war, belegt einer dieser Anträge, in dem die Aufgaben des Konservators allein im Hinblick auf die Bibliothek dargelegt werden.[48] Als Bühlmann sich 1935 auf eigenen Wunsch in den Ruhestand versetzen ließ und in die Schweiz übersiedelte, übernahm Adolf Abel vertretungsweise die Geschäfte und Otto Stammhammer,

models had been unsuccessful due to a lack of space, and also "the auspicious beginning of the collection of plans [could] not be continued due to a lack of funds," but an important tool for teaching and scholarship had been established through the library.[42] In order to create a modern kind of architectural curriculum, which was not oriented toward historical models, new acquisitions had been limited to books, photographs, and slides. The "substantial number of architecture-related texts" maintained in the library was even emphasized in *Meyers Reisebücher* (Meyer's Travel Guide) from 1922.[43]

When Joseph Popp was appointed to the position of professor for the history of art and architecture in 1919, as the successor to Karl Voll, the art historian Hans Karlinger was entrusted with "administering the duties of conservator of the architecture collection."[44] However, Karlinger left for the Technische Hochschule Aachen in 1926. Subsequently the department of architecture named the German-Swiss architect Manfred Bühlmann, an assistant professor for architectural history, to his position, the last conservator prior to World War II.[45] The senate of the university deemed, however, that the position should be held by "young art historians and [reassigned] every five to six years."[46] After repeated applications, Bühlmann then did receive a "budgetary" position on April 1, 1932.[47] That the collection of plans had become practically meaningless by this time is evinced by one of these applications, in which the duties of the conservator are described solely with reference to the library.[48] When Bühlmann was retired at his own request in 1935 and moved to Switzerland, Adolf Abel temporarily assumed responsibility for the business matters of the collection, and the collection's *Präparator,* or preparator, Otto Stammhammer, took over the administration.[49] Since it was not possible to reappoint someone to the position under the National Socialist regime, at the request of the department of architecture, Friedrich Krauss oversaw the collection from 1935 to 1944 on a voluntary basis.[50] Krauss had become an architectural teaching assistant in 1934, the last year of Hubert Knackfuss's active teaching.

It was Krauss who then evacuated the collection in segments to Weihenstephan in the spring and fall of 1944 together with Annelise Eichberg, at the time a research assistant under Abel.[51]

der »Präparator« der Sammlung, die Verwaltung.[49] Da eine Stellenneubesetzung unter dem nationalsozialistischen Regime nicht möglich war, betreute auf Wunsch der Architektenabteilung Friedrich Krauss, der 1934 im letzten Lehrjahr von Hubert Knackfuß zunächst als Hilfsassistent an den Lehrstuhl für Baukunst gekommen war, von 1935 bis 1944 ehrenamtlich die Bestände.[50] Krauss war es dann auch, der im Frühjahr und Herbst 1944 zusammen mit Annelise Eichberg, damals wissenschaftliche Hilfskraft am Lehrstuhl von Abel, eine Evakuierung der Sammlung in Teilen nach Weihenstephan durchführte.[51]

NACH DEM ZWEITEN WELTKRIEG

Im Mai 1945 lag auch die Technische Hochschule mit den Sälen der Architektursammlung in Trümmern. Hans Döllgast beschreibt in seinem *Journal Retour* den Trümmerhaufen, in dem überall Schilder »off limits« aufgestellt waren, und schildert, wie er die Wiederöffnung mit einem kommissarischen Rektorat im Saal 351 erreichte – einer »Insel mitten in einer Wasserlache«.[52] Die an »5 verschiedenen Stellen« lagernde Architektursammlung war durch »Bombenschäden, Verlagerung und Diebstahl« nicht nur in ihren Beständen geschädigt worden, sondern es war auch jegliche »Ordnung, Übersicht und Kontrolle« verloren gegangen. Auch im September 1945 war die wertvolle Sammlung »teilweise immer noch dem Wetter und dem Zugriff Unbefugter ausgesetzt«.[53]

Als Krauss 1945 aus der englischen Gefangenschaft zurückkehrte, wurde ihm noch im Oktober desselben Jahres die Konservatorstelle der Architektursammlung »auf unbestimmte Zeit« übertragen.[54] »Verhältnismäßig frühzeitig« erreichte Krauss von der amerikanischen Besatzung die Freigabe der Bestände aus Weihenstephan. Auf »einer bis zwei täglichen Fahrten« mit einem »alten Lastwagen« wurden die Zeichnungen und Bücher zurück in die Stadt gebracht. Am Ende einer dieser Fahrten stellte sich Elisabeth Blume arbeitsuchend als Bibliothekarin vor und begann als studentische Hilfskraft, die Bücher zu ordnen.[55]

Krauss erhielt 1946 die Professur für Baukunst und war in den folgenden Jahren mit dem Aufbau der Lehre beschäftigt, auch verbrachte er viel Zeit auf Ausgrabungen. Während die Buchbestände allmählich von Elisabeth

LÖSCHARBEITEN AUF DEM DACH DER
TECHNISCHEN HOCHSCHULE
MÜNCHEN NACH DEM BOMBENSCHADEN
VOM 7. SEPTEMBER 1943

FIRE-FIGHTING EFFORTS ON THE
ROOF OF THE TECHNISCHE HOCHSCHULE
MÜNCHEN AFTER THE BOMB ATTACK
OF SEPTEMBER 7, 1943

AFTER
WORLD WAR II

In May 1945, the Technische Hochschule and the rooms of the architecture collection lay in rubble. In his *Journal Retour*, Hans Döllgast describes the piles of debris, where "off-limits" signs had been posted everywhere, and depicts how he managed to achieve the reopening of the college with a provisional rectorship in room 351—an "island in the midst of a pool of water."[52] Stored at "five different sites," not only had holdings of the architecture collection been reduced by "bombing damage, storage, and theft," but any and all "order, overview, and control" had been lost. In September 1945, the valuable collection "in part still remained exposed to the elements and the access of unauthorized persons."[53]

When Krauss returned from British internment in 1945, he was appointed conservator of the architecture collection for "an indeterminate period" in October of the same year.[54] "Relatively early," Krauss managed to negotiate the release of

HANS DÖLLGAST, THIERSCH-BAU
MIT UHRENTURM, UM 1945

HANS DÖLLGAST, THIERSCH BUILDING
WITH CLOCK TOWER, CA. 1945

Blume – »auf engstem Raum, umgeben von erst entstehenden Regalen und auf ein paar zusammengeflickten Tischen«[56] – sortiert wurden, lag die wertvolle Plansammlung buchstäblich in einer Ecke. 1959 schrieb Krauss, dass die Sichtung der durch die Evakuierung in Unordnung gekommenen Planbestände erst »jetzt« in Angriff genommen werden konnte, da nach »vieljähriger Pause« endlich wieder die Konservatorstelle besetzt worden sei, dass aber weder die Räume für die Aufstellung der Sammlung fertig wären noch Möbel und Mappen für die Aufbewahrung hätten angeschafft werden können.[57] Die in dem Brief von Krauss erwähnte Konservatorstelle war 1955 mit dem Architekten Otto Bauer besetzt worden, der eine wissenschaftliche

THEODOR FISCHER, VORPROJEKT
ZUR GARNISONSKIRCHE IN ULM, 1908

THEODOR FISCHER, PRELIMINARY SKETCHES
FOR THE GARNISONSKIRCHE IN ULM, 1908

the holdings from Weihenstephan with the American occupation authorities. After "one or two full-day trips" with an "old truck," the drawings and books were returned to the city. At the end of one of these journeys, Elisabeth Blume introduced herself as a librarian looking for work and subsequently began putting the books in order, working as a student research assistant.[55]

Named professor of architecture in 1946, Krauss was busy establishing the teaching program in subsequent years and also spent a great deal of time on excavations. Whereas the book holdings were gradually being sorted by Elisabeth Blume "in a very cramped space and surrounded by shelves that were in the process of being built and a few makeshift tables,"[56] the valuable

Beamtenstelle an der Architektursammlung erhalten hatte.[58]

Der erste Nachlass, der nach etwa 40 Jahren, Anfang der 1950er-Jahre, wieder an die Architektursammlung kam, waren die Zeichnungen und einige schriftliche Unterlagen von Theodor Fischer, nachdem dessen Haus, das »Laimer Schlößl« verkauft und geräumt werden musste. In Andenken an ihren verstorbenen Mann hatte Therese Fischer 1946 in dem Haus eine private Stiftung eingerichtet, wo unmittelbar nach dem Zweiten Weltkrieg ein erstes Forum für moderne Architektur entstand. Fischer hatte Generationen junger Architekten von Le Corbusier über Erich Mendelsohn und Hugo Häring bis Ernst May angezogen, und in seinem Büro hatte unter anderem Bruno Taut viele Jahre gearbeitet. Auch als Hochschullehrer besaß Fischer einen legendären Ruf, die berühmte Stuttgarter Architekturschule basierte auf seinem Wirken in Stuttgart von 1901 bis 1908.[59]

UMBAU DER ARCHITEKTURSAMMLUNG, ANFANG DER 1960ER-JAHRE

REFURBISHING THE ROOMS OF THE ARCHITECTURE COLLECTION, EARLY 1960S

Nach dem Tod von Martin Elsaesser im Jahre 1957 kam mit dessen Zeichnungen ein weiterer Nachlass an die Sammlung, da Bauer zunächst über seinen Lehrer eine Arbeit hatte schreiben wollen. Stattdessen unterstütze er aber Krauss bei der Lehre und nahm auch an dessen Grabungen teil.[60] Schließlich wurde Bauer Anfang der 1960er-Jahre der Ausbau der Sammlung mit einem Zwischengeschoss im zweiten Stock übertragen.[61] Als Krauss emeritierte, folgte 1966 Gottfried Gruben als Professor und Leiter der Architektursammlung nach.

Die folgenden Jahre gestalteten sich für die Architektursammlung wechselhaft. Im Zusammenhang mit dem 1964 gegründeten Archiv für Bildende Kunst am Germanischen Nationalmuseum Nürnberg[62] kam es zu einem

collection of plans sat—literally—in a corner. In 1959, Krauss writes that only "now" has it been possible to initiate a review of the collection of architectural plans that had come into disarray due to the evacuation, since after "many years of interruption" it was finally possible to hire a conservator, but neither had rooms for the installment of the collection been finished, nor had it been possible to purchase furnishings or portfolios for the storage of the collection.[57] The conservator position mentioned in Krauss's letter had been filled by Otto Bauer, who had been assigned an academic post at the architecture collection under a civil servant contract.[58]

In the nineteen-fifties, the first bequest donated to the architecture collection after some forty years consisted of drawings and selected papers of Theodor Fischer, after his house, the Laimer Schlössl, had been sold and needed to be cleared. To commemorate her deceased husband, Therese Fischer established a private foundation in the house in 1946, which became one of the first forums for modern architecture in the years following World War II. Fischer had mentored a generation of younger architects, from Le Corbusier to Erich Mendelsohn, Hugo Häring, and Ernst May; Bruno Taut, among others, had worked for many years for his firm. Fischer also had a legendary reputation as a professor; the famous Stuttgarter Architekturschule emerged out of his activities in Stuttgart in the years of 1901–08.[59]

After the death of Martin Elsaesser in 1957, his drawings comprised another estate added to the collection. Bauer had initially wanted to write about his teacher. Instead, he ended up helping Krauss with his teaching activities and also took part in his excavations.[60] Ultimately, Bauer was entrusted with setting up the collection in the mezzanine area on the second floor.[61] When Krauss retired, he was succeeded in 1966 by Gottfried Gruben as professor and head of the architecture collection.

The following years brought ups and downs for the architecture collection. The founding of the archive for fine arts at the Germanisches Nationalmuseum in Nuremberg[62] in 1964 resulted in a consequential agreement, which stipulated that the Nuremberg archive would receive all the written records of the Munich Architektursammlung der Technischen Hochschule and that in return Munich would receive all drawings ceded to Nuremberg as part of estates.[63] Subsequently, all written documents were transferred to the Germanisches Nationalmuseum, and in turn the architecture collection only received the teaching model of a Gothic reticulated vault dating from 1659, today the oldest model in the collection, the model of a roof

DIE BIBLIOTHEK NACH DEM
UMBAU DER SAMMLUNGSRÄUME,
1960ER-JAHRE

THE LIBRARY AFTER
THE REFURBISHMENT OF THE
COLLECTION ROOMS, 1960S

folgenschweren Vertrag, in dem vereinbart wurde, dass dem Nürnberger Archiv alle schriftlichen Unterlagen der Architektursammlung der Technischen Hochschule aus München übergeben werden und München im Gegenzug die Zeichnungen erhalten sollte, die bei der Übernahme von Nachlässen nach Nürnberg gingen.[63] Daraufhin wurden die gesamten schriftlichen Bestände an das Germanische Nationalmuseum transferiert, die Architektursammlung erhielt hingegen nur das Lehrmodell eines gotischen Netzgewölbes von 1659, das heute älteste Modell des Archivs, eine Dachstuhlkonstruktion sowie die Zeichnungen zur Nürnberger Fleischbrücke und den zeichnerischen Nachlass von Ernst May.[64]

1970 konnte dann die architekturgeschichtliche Sammlung der Landeshauptstadt München übernommen werden.[65] Diese war 1960 in der Städtischen Galerie im Lenbachhaus eingerichtet worden und wurde von Heinz Thiersch, einem Großneffen Friedrich von Thierschs und letztem Mitarbeiter Richard Riemerschmids, im »freiberuflichen Honorarvertrag« seit 1. Dezember 1961 betreut.[66] Als das Lenbachhaus wegen Platzmangel Ende der 1960er-Jahre eine Abtretung der städtischen Architektursammlung erwog, suchte Thiersch im Frühjahr 1969 Otto Bauer auf, um sich nach eventuellen Aufstellmöglichkeiten der städtischen Bestände an der Technischen Hochschule sowie um die Möglichkeit einer Planstelle oder eines Werkvertrags für ihn als Betreuer der Sammlung zu erkundigen.[67] Auch gab es Erwägungen, die Zeichnungen an das Germanische Nationalmuseum Nürnberg abzugeben. Es war der Verdienst von Gottfried Gruben und Josef A. Schmoll genannt Eisenwerth, die sich für die Angliederung der Sammlung an die Technische Hochschule aussprachen.[68] Außer dem architektonischen Teil des Nachlasses von Richard Riemerschmid umfasste der Bestand auch Zeichnungen von German Bestelmeyer, Ernst Fiechter, Peter Birkenholz und Hermann Billing.[69] Die einstige architekturgeschichtliche Sammlung der Stadt wurde nach der Übernahme in einer von der Hochschule angemieteten Wohnung an der Augustenstraße 79 untergebracht. Heinz Thiersch bekam eine Dauerstelle als wissenschaftlicher Angestellter,[70] und Otto Bauer, seit 1965 Oberkonservator, wurde zum Akademischen Direktor der Sammlung befördert.[71] Die Leitung der Architektursammlung verblieb bei Gottfried Gruben.[72] Die Bestände der Architektursammlung hatten sich durch die Übernahme auf rund 120 000 Pläne verdoppelt.[73] In den folgenden Jahren akquirierte Thiersch noch einige Zeichnungen, aber die seinerzeit noch gebündelten, in Regalen liegenden, ungeordneten Nachlässe »verstaubten« allmählich.[74]

RICHARD RIEMERSCHMID, RAUM
DER VEREINIGTEN WERKSTÄTTEN,
WANDABWICKLUNG,
WELTAUSSTELLUNG PARIS 1900

RICHARD RIEMERSCHMID,
ROOM OF THE VEREINIGTE
WERKSTÄTTEN, WALL DESIGN,
PARIS WORLD'S FAIR 1900

construction, drawings related to the so-called Fleischbrücke, or "meat bridge," and the drawings in the estate of Ernst May.[64]

In 1970, the collection obtained the history of architecture holdings from the collection of the Landeshauptstadt München (State Capital of Munich).[65] These items had been installed in the nineteen-sixties in the Städtische Galerie im Lenbachhaus and had been administered by Heinz Thiersch, a great-nephew of Friedrich von Thiersch, and Richard Riemerschmid's last assistant from December 1, 1961 onward, in accordance with a "freelance agreement."[66] When due to a lack of space the Lenbachhaus considered passing on its architectural collection in the nineteen-sixies, Thiersch approached Otto Bauer in the spring of 1969 to discuss the possible transfer of city holdings to the Technische Hochschule and the possibility of arranging a position or contract for himself as custodian of the collection.[67] Giving the drawings to the Germanisches Nationalmuseum in Nuremberg was also weighed as a possibility. It is thanks to Gottfried Gruben and Josef A. Schmoll genannt Eisenwerth that this did not occur; they argued for the incorporation of these items into the collection of the Technische Hochschule.[68] In addition to the

DIE ÄRA
WINFRIED NERDINGER

Bis Winfried Nerdinger zum Wintersemester 1975/76 als Akademischer Rat an die Architektursammlung kam, war die einstige Studiensammlung praktisch nicht bekannt. Nur der Lesesaal der Bibliothek vermittelte noch eine Ahnung von der einstigen prunkvollen Raumflucht und gerade einmal zwei Beiträge in Festschriften zum 50- und 100-jährigen Bestehen der Hochschule gaben in kurzen Abrissen Auskunft über eine der ältesten Sammlungen zur Architektur.[75]

1972 war die Unterstellung der circa 37 000 Bücher[76] umfassenden Fachbibliothek an die Hauptbibliothek erfolgt.[77] In einem Abstellbereich über dem Bibliotheksmagazin befanden sich 32 Planschränke, hinzu kam die angemietete Wohnung an der Augustenstraße mit dem Bestand der einstigen Architekturgeschichtlichen Sammlung der Landeshauptstadt München.[78] Auf einer Fläche von circa 450 Quadratmetern wurden an beiden Standorten etwa 150 000 Pläne, eine Handvoll Modelle und Reste von Gipsabgüssen aufbewahrt.[79] Archivalien waren seit der Abgabe an das Germanische Nationalmuseum nicht mehr vorhanden, Inventarisierung und Ausleihe fanden praktisch nicht statt, auch gab es keine Bestandsübersicht oder gar einen Etat. Lediglich die zweite wissenschaftliche Dauerstelle, die Heinz Thiersch seinerzeit ausgehandelt hatte, existierte auch nach dessen Eintritt in den Ruhestand weiter.[80]

Nerdinger hatte Architektur an der Technischen Hochschule studiert, 1971 bei dem Bauhäusler Gustav Hassenpflug diplomiert und anschließend bei Josef A. Schmoll genannt Eisenwerth über den Bildhauer Rudolf Belling promoviert. Neben der reinen Sammel- und Archivierungstätigkeit galt sein Interesse dem Zusammenhang zwischen Sammlung und Forschung.[81] Nerdingers Ziel war es, komplette Nachlässe oder größere Teilbestände zu übernehmen, damit das jeweilige Werk von Forschern oder Doktoranden wissenschaftlich bearbeitet werden konnte.[82] Auch war ihm wichtig, »Alltagsarchitektur« als etwas »Zeittypisches« zu erhalten, um später einmal den »heutigen Alltag« dokumentieren zu können.[83] Vor allem aber sollte die Plansammlung nun auch durch Architekturausstellungen, die damals in Deutschland noch sehr selten waren, einer breiten Öffentlichkeit sichtbar gemacht werden. Dazu vereinbarte er 1976 mit Martha Dreesbach, der Direktorin des Münchner Stadtmuseums, eine gemeinsame Ausstellungsreihe, bei der ausgehend vom

architecture-related items in Richard Riemerschmid's estate, the holdings also included drawings by German Bestelmeyer, Ernst Fiechter, Peter Birkenholz, and Hermann Billing.[69] After being taken over by the college, the former history of architecture collection of the city was housed in an apartment rented for this purpose at Augustenstrasse 79. Heinz Thiersch was given a permanent research position,[70] and Otto Bauer, the head conservator since 1965, was promoted to academic director of the collection.[71] Gottfried Gruben remained head of the architecture collection.[72] Through this transfer, the holdings of the collection doubled to some 120,000 plans.[73] In the following years, Thiersch acquired a number of other drawings, yet during this period the estate materials, neither sorted nor systematized, lay bundled on shelves and were gradually "accumulating dust."[74]

THE ERA OF
WINFRIED NERDINGER

Until Winfried Nerdinger joined the architecture collection in the winter semester of 1975–76 as an academic councilor, the former teaching collection was virtually unknown. Only the reading room of the library offered a hint of the former opulent series of rooms that it had occupied, and only two respective contributions to the publications marking the fiftieth and one-hundredth anniversaries of the university offered some brief information on one of the oldest architectural collections.[75]

In 1972, the ca. 37,000 books[76] of the departmental library were officially assigned to the main library.[77] Thirty-two drafting cabinets were held in a storage area above the library magazine, and there was also the rented apartment on Augustenstrasse with the holdings of the city's former history of architecture collection, which originated from the collection of the Landeshauptstadt München.[78] Within the some 450 square meters of these two locations, approximately 150,000 plans were preserved, as well as a handful of models and the remains of plaster casts.[79] Since the transfer of items to the Germanisches Nationalmuseum, the collection no longer contained any archival materials. There was practically no active inventory or lending process, and there was neither an overview of the holdings nor any budget. Only a second permanent academic position, which Heinz Thiersch had negotiated, continued to exist after his retirement.[80]

Bestand der Architektursammlung die süddeutsche Architektur in monografischen und Epochendarstellungen detailliert untersucht und ausgestellt werden sollte. Die komplette Finanzierung für Ausstellung und Katalog übernahm dabei das Stadtmuseum und die wissenschaftliche, konzeptionelle Erarbeitung sowie die Exponate lieferte die Architektursammlung. Bereits die erste Ausstellung über Friedrich von Thiersch, dem neben Paul Wallot bedeutendsten Vertreter des Späthistorismus in Deutschland, einer zu dieser Zeit weitgehend noch als eklektisch diskreditierten Epoche, hatte programmatischen Charakter.[84] Als Schöpfer der Architektursammlung und Lehrer der Technischen Hochschule, an der Thiersch 42 Jahre »Höhere Baukunst« unterrichtet hatte, war er in der Nachkriegszeit vollkommen in Vergessenheit geraten. Die Präsentation war von besonderer Bedeutung, um seinem

AUSSTELLUNGSPLAKAT
*FRIEDRICH VON THIERSCH.
EIN MÜNCHNER ARCHITEKT DES
SPÄTHISTORISMUS 1852–1921,*
MÜNCHNER STADTMUSEUM, 1977

EXHIBITION POSTER FOR
*FRIEDRICH VON THIERSCH. EIN
MÜNCHNER ARCHITEKT DES
SPÄTHISTORISMUS 1852–1921,*
MÜNCHNER STADTMUSEUM, 1977

Werk Anerkennung zu verschaffen. Das zur Münchner Ausstellung von Josef A. Schmoll organisierte und von der Fritz Thyssen Stiftung finanzierte Symposium lieferte einen wichtigen Beitrag zur Historismusforschung und leitete auch in Deutschland eine Neubewertung ein.

Thiersch hatte sich in Tausenden von Zeichnungen und Aquarellen eine unerreichte Fähigkeit der malerischen Architekturdarstellung erworben. Sein Nachlass lagerte am Deutschen Museum und war für die Ausstellung im Tausch gegen den an der Architektursammlung liegenden Nachlass des Geodäten Karl Maximilian von Bauernfeind, dem Gründungsrektor der Polytechnischen Hochschule, zusammen mit Zeichnungen von Peter Speeth und Franz Jakob Kreuter übereignet worden (siehe S. 54).[85] 2001 konnte der wertvolle Bestand an Thierschs Zeichnungen durch Skizzenbücher, die sich noch im Familienbesitz in der Schweiz befanden, ergänzt werden.

Nerdinger had studied architecture at the Technische Hochschule. He had completed his *Diplom* degree with Gustav Hassenpflug, a Bauhaus-trained architect, and he had subsequently completed his doctorate on sculptor Rudolf Belling with Josef A. Schmoll genannt Eisenwerth. In addition to collecting and archiving, he was also interested in the relationship between collections and research.[81] Nerdinger's aim was to take on complete estates, or larger portions of estates, which would allow a body of work to be studied by researchers or doctoral candidates.[82] It was also important to him to preserve "everyday architecture" as something "typifying an era," as a means of later documenting "the everyday life of today."[83] Above all, he wished to make the collection of architectural plans visible to a broad public through architecture exhibitions, which were still very rare in Germany at the time. Toward this purpose, in 1976 he came to an agreement with Martha Dreesbach, the director of the Münchner Stadtmuseum, to present a joint exhibition series, which would be a detailed examination and exhibition of southern German architecture based on the holdings of the architecture collection and presenting monographic materials and historical overviews. The Stadtmuseum financed the exhibition and catalogue in full, and the architecture collection provided the scholarly preparation and conception of the exhibition as well as the items for display. Even the first exhibition on Friedrich von Thiersch was programmatic in nature.[84] In addition to Paul Wallot, Friedrich von Thiersch was one of the most important figures of late historicism in Germany, a period that at the time was still discredited as being eclectic. As the founder of the architecture collection and professor at the Technische Hochschule, Thiersch, who had taught advanced architecture for forty-two years, had fallen into obscurity. Having been utterly forgotten in the postwar era, an examination of his work was of particular importance as a means of according him the recognition that he was due. The accompanying symposium, organized by Josef A. Schmoll genannt Eisenwerth and financed by the Fritz Thyssen Foundation, served as an important contribution to the study of historicism and spurred a reassessment of this period, also in Germany. Through thousands of drawings and watercolors, Thiersch had achieved unprecedented skill in architectural rendering. His estate was housed in the Deutsches Museum. On the occasion of the exhibition it was transferred to the architecture collection and exchanged for the papers of geodesist Karl Maximilian von Bauernfeind, the founding rector of the Polytechnische Hochschule, as well as drawings by Peter Speeth and Franz Jakob Kreuter (see p. 53).[85] In 2001, it was possible to complement the valuable collection

Nach dieser ersten Zusammenarbeit folgten fast jährlich Ausstellungen im Münchner Stadtmuseum über zumeist weitgehend vergessene Architektenpersönlichkeiten wie Gottfried von Neureuther (1978), Theodor Fischer (1988) oder Friedrich von Gärtner (1992), im Wechsel mit Darstellungen der gesamten Bautätigkeit einer Epoche wie *Klassizismus in Bayern und Schwaben* (1980), *Aufbauzeit* (1984) oder *Romantik und Restauration* (1987). Aber auch neue Partner für Ausstellungen wurden gewonnen. Mithilfe der 1981 gegründeten Carl-von-Fischer-Gesellschaft konnten beispielweise die Zeichnungen Carl von Fischers, dem ersten akademischen Architekturlehrer Bayerns, in der Neuen Pinakothek präsentiert werden;[86] weitere Partner kamen in den folgenden Jahren hinzu.[87] Bei allen diesen Ausstellungen ging es immer um eine kritisch analysierende Aufarbeitung des Werks und um die Einordnung in den jeweiligen Kontext; die Inhalte sollten zum Nach- und Weiterdenken anregen.[88] Die Aufarbeitung führte mehrfach zu Problemen, immer dann, wenn politische Zusammenhänge (*Die Zwanziger Jahre in München*, 1979; *Bauen im Nationalsozialismus – Bayern 1933–1945*, 1993), dynastische Interessen (*Romantik und Restauration – Architektur in Bayern zur Zeit Ludwig I.*, 1987) oder dogmatische Vorstellungen (*Geschichte der Rekonstruktion – Konstruktion der Geschichte*, 2010) in Ausstellung und Publikation berührt wurden.[89]

1980 und 1981 ergab sich durch die Finanzierung des Auswärtigen Amtes für Nerdinger die Möglichkeit, den seinerzeit noch völlig ungeordneten Nachlass des Bauhaus-Gründers Walter Gropius am Busch-Reisinger Museum in

AUSSTELLUNGSANSICHT
*ARCHITEKTURSCHULE MÜNCHEN
1868–1993. 125 JAHRE
TECHNISCHE UNIVERSITÄT MÜNCHEN*,
BAYERISCHE AKADEMIE DER
SCHÖNEN KÜNSTE, 1993,
MIT DEM HOLZMODELL EINER
KORINTHISCHEN SÄULE MIT
GEBÄLK AUS DER ARCHITEKTURSAMMLUNG

EXHIBITION VIEW,
*ARCHITEKTURSCHULE MÜNCHEN
1868–1993. 125 JAHRE TECHNISCHE
UNIVERSITÄT MÜNCHEN* AT THE
BAYERISCHE AKADEMIE DER
SCHÖNEN KÜNSTE, 1993,
INCLUDING A WOODEN MODEL
OF A CORINTHIAN COLUMN
AND ENTABLATURE FROM THE
ARCHITECTURE COLLECTION

of Thiersch's drawings with sketchbooks that had until that point been in the possession of family members in Switzerland.

After this initial cooperation, further exhibitions in the Münchner Stadtmuseum followed almost every year, for the most part on largely forgotten architectural figures, such as Gottfried von Neureuther (in 1978), Theodor Fischer (in 1988), and Friedrich von Gärtner (in 1992). These exhibitions were alternated with shows on the building activities of entire epochs, such as *Klassizismus in Bayern und Schwaben* (Classicism in Bavaria and Swabia, 1980), *Aufbauzeit* (The Era of Rebuilding, 1984) or *Romantik und Restauration* (Romanticism and Restoration, 1987). New partners were also found for the exhibitions. For example, with the help of the Carl-von-Fischer-Gesellschaft, which was founded in 1981, it was possible to present the drawings of Carl von Fischer, the first academic professor of architecture in Bavaria, in the Neue Pinakothek;[86] additional partnerships were formed in subsequent years.[87] All of these exhibitions were concerned with a critical analysis and overhaul of a body of work as a means of situating it within its given context; the content of the exhibitions was conceived to encourage reflection and the development of new ideas.[88] A number of times such reexamination led to conflicts, especially when an exhibition or publication touched on political topics, such as in *Die Zwanziger Jahre in München* (The Twenties in Munich, 1979) and *Bauen im Nationalsozialismus—Bayern 1933–1945* (Construction under National Socialism—Bavaria 1933–1945, 1993), dynastic interests, such as in *Romantik und Restauration—Architektur in Bayern zur Zeit Ludwig I.* (Romanticism and Restoration—Architecture in Bavaria during the Period of Ludwig I, 1987), or dogmatic concepts, such as in *Geschichte der Rekonstruktion—Konstruktion der Geschichte* (The History of Reconstruction—The Construction of History, 2010).[89]

In 1980 and 1981, Nerdinger was given the possibility through funding from the Auswärtiges Amt (German Federal Foreign Office) to work on the estate of Bauhaus founder Walter Gropius, which was in the possession of the Busch-Reisinger Museum at Harvard, and to subsequently present his work at the museum and in following exhibitions at the Bauhaus-Archiv in Berlin and the Deutsches Architekturmuseum in Frankfurt am Main.[90] Additional major research projects on architecture in the era of National Socialism (1993)[91] and Leo von Klenze (2000) followed.[92]

The architecture collection became known abroad through the exhibition of architectural drawings presented in 1985 at the Deutsches Architekturmuseum in Frankfurt, which subsequently travelled to what was then the *Museo*

Harvard zu bearbeiten und dessen Werk dort und anschließend am Bauhaus-Archiv in Berlin sowie am Deutschen Architekturmuseum in Frankfurt am Main zu zeigen.[90] Weitere große Forschungsprojekte über Bauen im Nationalsozialismus (1993)[91] und Leo von Klenze (2000)[92] folgten.

Über die Ausstellung zur Architekturzeichnung, die 1985 am Deutschen Architekturmuseum in Frankfurt und anschließend am damaligen *Museo Español de Arte Contemporáneo* in Madrid präsentiert wurde, fand die Architektursammlung auch im Ausland Beachtung.[93] 1993 folgte mit *Tel Aviv. Neues Bauen 1930–1939* die erste große internationale Ausstellung, die unter anderem auch in New York in der Arthur Ross Architecture Gallery (Columbia University) zu sehen war.[94] Darüber hinaus fanden fast jedes Semester Ausstellungen an der Architekturfakultät im Lesesaal und in der Immatrikulationshalle statt.

ERFASSUNG DER BESTÄNDE UND NEUERWERBUNGEN

Parallel zur Ausstellungstätigkeit begann Winfried Nerdinger mit der systematischen Erfassung der Bestände und entwickelte ein Ordnungssystem auf Karteikarten mit Fotografien. Dies war möglich, da ein Drittel des zur Fakultät gehörenden Fotolabors der Architektursammlung zugeteilt wurde. Bis zum Übergang auf die digitale Erfassung 1992 wurden über 90 000 Karteikarten erstellt, danach dann weitgehend durch studentische Hilfskräfte Hunderttausende von Datensätzen in eine Datenbank eingegeben und somit der Bestand erstmals komplett erfasst. Zugleich erhielt die Sammlung nun auch wieder zahlreiche Neuerwerbungen: 1977 gelang es mithilfe des Bundes der Freunde der TUM, Zeichnungen von Conradin Walther sowie 1979 von weiteren bedeutenden süddeutschen Baumeistern des 19. Jahrhunderts, Georg von Hauberrisser, Christian von Leins, Friedrich Laves, aber auch von Olaf Andreas Gulbransson zu erwerben. Vom Landbauamt München wurden Pläne von Leo von Klenze und von Jean Baptiste Métivier übereignet. Durch die parallel organisierten und in der Öffentlichkeit viel beachteten Ausstellungen war die Architektursammlung nun auch immer mehr für Stifter interessant. So konnten die 52 Skizzenbücher von Adolf von Hildebrand, zusammen mit zahlreichen Zeichnungen, Plänen und Fotografien, dank der Familien Braunfels und Sattler übernommen werden. Durch Übernahme großer

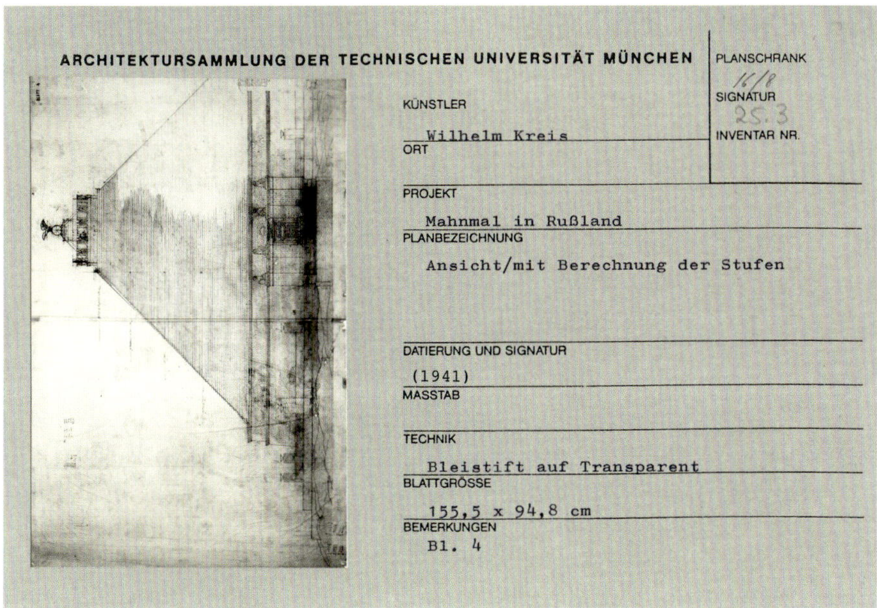

ARCHITEKTURSAMMLUNG DER TECHNISCHEN UNIVERSITÄT MÜNCHEN KARTEIKARTE »WILHELM KREIS, MAHNMAL IN RUSSLAND, 1941«, PLANSCHRANK 16/8, SIGNATUR 25.3

INDEX CARD FROM THE ARCHITECTURE COLLECTION, "WILHELM KREIS, MONUMENT IN RUSSIA, 1941," DRAFTING CABINET 16/8, SIGNATURE 25.3

Español de Arte Contemporáneo in Madrid.[93] In 1993, the first major international exhibition followed: *Tel Aviv: Neues Bauen 1930–1939 (Tel Aviv: Modern Architecture 1930–1939)*, which was presented in New York at the Arthur Ross Architecture Gallery at Columbia University, among other venues.[94] In addition, almost every semester included exhibitions in the reading room of the department of architecture and in the registration hall of the university.

CATALOGUING THE HOLDINGS AND NEW ACQUISITIONS

Parallel to these exhibition activities, Winfried Nerdinger began to systematically catalogue the collection and developed a system with file cards and photographs. This was possible since a third of the photography lab belonging to the department was reserved for the architecture collection. Until a digital record-keeping system was introduced in 1992, over 90,000 file

Fotosammlungen und Fotografenarchive, unter anderem von Hans Steinmetz und Klaus Kinold, erhielt die Architekturfotografie über die wertvollen alten Fotobestände hinaus ständig größeres Gewicht. Ebenso konnte Nerdinger neue Sammlungsgebiete systematisch erschließen: Es wurde eine Modellsammlung aufgebaut und mit den Modellen des Lehrstuhls Kurrent eine einmalige Lehrsammlung zu Wohnbauten des 20. Jahrhunderts integriert.[95]
Da sich an der Architektursammlung zahlreiche architektonische Dokumente der Architekturlehrer der Münchner Hochschule befanden, wurde dieses »Gedächtnis der Fakultät« systematisch durch Übernahmen von Nach- und Vorlässen von Josef Wiedemann, Franz Hart, Werner Eichberg, Helmut Gebhard und Gerd Albers ergänzt.[96] Ausgehend von der Übernahme der kompletten Planung für die Münchner Olympiaanlage vom Büro Behnisch & Partner wurde ein weiterer Sammlungsschwerpunkt zur Bautechnik eingerichtet. Dieser Bereich wurde mit Modellen von Ove Arup, Heinz Isler, Shigeru Ban und Thomas Herzog, aber auch durch studentische Lehrmodelle kontinuierlich weiter ausgebaut, um entscheidende Entwicklungen im Bereich der Baukonstruktion und Tragwerksplanung dokumentieren zu können. Hinzu kamen einzelne bedeutsame Planungen, beispielweise Le Corbusiers Entwurf für ein Kunstmuseum in Erlenbach am Main.[97]

AUF DEM WEG ZU EINEM EIGENEN MUSEUM

Da die Sammlung im Hochschulareal auf verschiedene Stellen verteilt war, wurde mehrfach versucht, die Bestände zusammenzufassen und an geeigneter Stelle öffentlich zugänglich zu machen. Umzugsplanungen in die Paul-Heyse-Villa an der Luisenstraße oder in ein neues »Haus der Architektur« an der Gabelsbergerstraße scheiterten Anfang der 1980er-Jahre aus Kostengründen. Auch aus Semesterarbeiten entstandene Entwürfe für einen Neubau fanden zwar Beachtung, aber es kam zu keiner konkreten Planung.[98] In den folgenden Jahren konnten schrittweise Verbesserungen erreicht werden. Aufgrund der Ablehnung eines Rufs an die McGill University in Montreal erhielt Winfried Nerdinger 1986 an der T U München eine für ihn geschaffene Professur für Geschichte der Architektur und Baukonstruktion und wurde zum Leiter der Architektursammlung ernannt. Als Anerkennung seines 12-jährigen

cards had been filled out, followed by hundreds of thousands of records being entered into databases, mostly by student assistants, and thus, for the first time, the holdings were almost completely documented. Simultaneously, the collection once again amassed numerous new acquisitions. In 1977, the collection was able to purchase drawings by Conradin Walther through the financial support of the Bund der Freunde der TU München, and in 1979 it also acquired drawings by other important southern German master architects of the nineteenth century: Georg von Hauberrisser, Christian von Leins, Friedrich Laves, and Olaf Andreas Gulbransson. Plans by Leo von Klenze and Jean Baptiste Métivier were given to the collection by the Landesbauamt (Bavarian State Building Authority) in Munich. Due to the parallel-running exhibitions that received much public attention, the architecture collection became increasingly interesting to sponsors. As a result, it was possible to acquire the fifty-two sketchbooks of Adolf von Hildebrand as well as numerous drawings, plans, and photographs through the generosity of the Braunfels and Sattler families. By accepting collections of photographs and photographic archives,

BEBAUUNG DES GELÄNDES DER EHEMALIGEN TÜRKENKASERNE IN MÜNCHEN, REALISIERUNGSWETTBEWERB 1987, 1. PREIS VON WERZ, OTTOW, BACHMANN, MARX MIT EINEM EIGENEN GEBÄUDE FÜR DIE ARCHITEKTURSAMMLUNG GEGENÜBER DER ALTEN PINAKOTHEK

DEVELOPMENT OF THE SITE OF THE FORMER TÜRKENKASERNE IN MUNICH, 1987 COMPETITION. FIRST PRIZE WENT TO WERZ, OTTOW, BACHMANN, MARX AND INCLUDED AN INDEPENDENT BUILDING FOR THE ARCHITECTURE COLLECTION ACROSS FROM THE ALTE PINAKOTHEK

Engagements wurde die Architektursammlung dank des damaligen Präsidenten der Hochschule Wolfgang
Wild in das Programm für Neubauten
der TU München und der Ludwig-
Maximilians-Universität München auf
dem Gelände der ehemaligen Türkenkaserne aufgenommen.[99] Beim Wettbewerb 1987 sahen die ersten Preisträger
Helmut von Werz und Johann-Christoph Ottow direkt gegenüber dem
Ostflügel der Alten Pinakothek ein
Gebäude für die Architektursammlung vor.[100] Aufgrund der Aussicht,
ein eigenes Museum in München zu
erhalten, erteilte Nerdinger dem Angebot, die Nachfolge von Heinrich Klotz
am Deutschen Architekturmuseum
sowie eine Professur in Frankfurt
anzunehmen, 1989 eine Absage.[101] Für

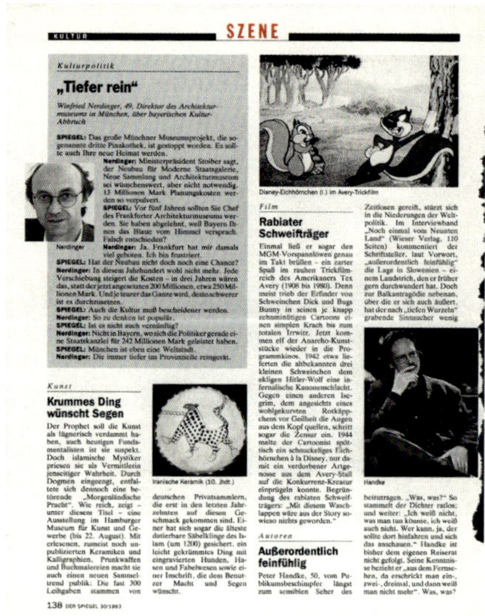

INTERVIEW MIT
WINFRIED
NERDINGER,
IN: *DER SPIEGEL*,
30, 1993,
S. 138

INTERVIEW WITH
WINFRIED
NERDINGER, IN
DER SPIEGEL,
ISSUE 30,
1993, P. 138

die Sammlung konnte er dafür erstmals einen Etat aushandeln, wovon unter
anderem für die bisher in Packpapier lagernden wertvollen Bestände säure-
freier Karton, weitere Planschränke und Computer angeschafft wurden.[102]
Zwischen 1989 und 1994 konnte Nerdinger als Präsident der International
Confederation of Architectural Museums (ICAM) wichtige Kontakte zu
anderen Museen intensivieren und weitere Partner gewinnen.
1994 kam an der TU München der Umzug im Stammgelände in Gang, da der
Rechnungshof die hohen Mietkosten der TU anmahnte. Die Räume an der Augustenstraße wurden aufgegeben und das Architekturmuseum erhielt das »Angerer-
Atelier«, eine kleine Verwaltungseinheit im 4. Obergeschoss an der Luisenstraße
sowie Räume im Haus an der Gabelsbergerstraße 43.[103] Als dann 1997 die Fakultät für Maschinenwesen nach Garching auszog, wurden per Fakultätsbeschluss
dem Museum die Räume im Thierschbau im Erd- und Untergeschoss zugespro-
chen. Die Planung war bis zur Haushaltsunterlage Bau komplett fertiggestellt,
als die Finanzmittel nicht bewilligt und der Umbau zurückgestellt wurde; nur
einzelne Büros im Erdgeschoss und die Depoträume für die Modellsammlung
im Untergeschoss konnten umgebaut und bezogen werden.

including those of Hans Steinmetz and Klaus Kinold, architectural photography gained an increasing importance above and beyond the collection's valuable photographic holdings. Nerdinger was also able to systematically expand on other aspects of the collection. He built up a collection of models, which was integrated into the models produced in the department under Professor Friedrich Kurrent, thus establishing a unique teaching collection of twentieth-century residential architecture.[95]

Since numerous architectural documents belonging to the architecture teaching staff at the university were included in the collection, this archival "memory of the department" was systematically enlarged by living and estate bequests from Josef Wiedemann, Franz Hart, Werner Eichberg, Helmut Gebhard, and Gerd Albers.[96] Upon receiving the complete planning documents for the Munich Olympic complex from the firm Behnisch & Partner, the collection developed another area of emphasis—construction technique. This area was continuously expanded by the inclusion of models by Ove Arup, Heinz Isler, Shigeru Ban, and Thomas Herzog, as well as student teaching models as a means of documenting decisive developments in the fields of building construction and support structure planning. Significant planning documents were thus added to the collection, for example Le Corbusier's design for an art museum in Erlenbach am Main.[97]

ON THE WAY TO A MUSEUM OF ITS OWN

Since the collection was divided up into various buildings belonging to the university, several attempts were made to bring the holdings together and make them open to the public at a suitable location. Plans to move the collection to the Paul-Heyse-Villa on Luisenstrasse or to a new "Haus der Architektur" on Gabelsbergerstrasse dead-ended in the nineteen-eighties due to a lack of funds. Designs for new buildings, produced by students in a semester-long project, received a good deal of attention, but no concrete plans resulted from it.[98] In the following years, gradual improvements were made. After turning down an offer to join the faculty of McGill University in Montreal, Winfried Nerdinger was appointed to professor of history of architecture and building construction at the TU München in 1986, a position that had been created for him; he also

DAS ARCHITEKTURMUSEUM SCHWABEN

Während der Umzug des Architekturmuseums der TU München in die eigenen Räume in der Pinakothek der Moderne noch einige Arbeit und Mühe bereitete,[104] war 1993 anlässlich einer Gedenkmatinee zum 100. Geburtstag von Thomas Wechs – einem der wenigen modernen Architekten der 1920er-Jahre im konservativen Süddeutschland – aus Gesprächen mit der Arno-Buchegger-Stiftung die Idee für ein Zentrum zur Erforschung, Dokumentation und Vermittlung der Architekturgeschichte Schwabens entstanden.[105] In dem wiederhergestellten Wohnhaus der Familie Buchegger im Augsburger Thelottviertel konnte 1995 eine Zweigstelle, das Architekturmuseum Schwaben, eröffnet werden. Es wird seitdem komplett von der Stiftung finanziert.[106] Gleich die erste Ausstellung stellte den seinerzeit Aufsehen erregenden Entwurf von Peter Zumthor für das Berliner Projekt »Topographie des Terrors« in den Mittelpunkt – auch um damit eine Diskussion über die Errichtung eines Dokumentationszentrums zur Geschichte des Nationalsozialismus in Bayern anzuregen.[107]

17 Jahre lang gestaltete Nerdinger in Augsburg über 80 Ausstellungen, publizierte in Katalogen, gab eine Schriftenreihe heraus und legte ein Archiv mit Nachlässen bedeutender schwäbischer Architekten an.[108] 1999 konnte auch der architektonische und künstlerische Nachlass von Thomas Wechs übernommen werden.[109] Es wurde ein eigener Thomas-Wechs-Raum eingerichtet und im Jahr 2000 mit dem Thomas-Wechs-Preis ein Architekturpreis für vorbildliche Bauten in Schwaben etabliert.[110]

DIE PINAKOTHEK DER MODERNE

Die Planung für das eigene Museum vis-à-vis der Alten Pinakothek war bereits bis zur Haushaltsunterlage Bau fertiggestellt, als Hans Zehetmair, neuer Staatsminister für Wissenschaft und Kunst, das Gelände 1989 ausschließlich für eine Museumsnutzung bestimmte. Nur Dank der Vorplanung und der gemeinsamen Initiative von Nerdinger und dem damaligen Präsidenten der TU München Otto Meitinger wurde die Architektursammlung in das Raumprogramm der Pinakothek der Moderne aufgenommen[111] und –

Mittwoch, 27. Dezember 2006 — MÜNCHEN — VUN   Süddeutsche Zeitung Nr. 297 / Seite 53

Campus München: „Architektur, wie sie im Buche steht"

Texte, die Gestalt annehmen

Für die vielgelobte Ausstellung in der Pinakothek der Moderne haben TU-Studenten Modelle nach literarischen Vorlagen gebaut

Von Martin Thurau

Jules Verne gibt in seinen Büchern nicht nur den Technik-Visionär, sondern mitunter auch den Zahlen-Fetischisten. „Standard-Island", so heißt es in der „Propellerinsel", sei ein künstliches Gebilde aus Stahlplatten, „aus 270 000 Einzelbehältern zusammengesetzt, von denen jeder 16 Meter 70 hoch und je zehn Meter lang und breit ist". Sie alle seien „durch Nieten und Bolzen miteinander verbunden" – zu einer Insel, die im Stillen Ozean schwimmt, sieben Kilometer lang und fünf Kilometer breit. Bei voller Belastung, so schreibt der detailversessene Urvater der Science Fiction weiter, tauche der Rumpf zehn Meter tief ein, dann betrage die Wasserverdrängung 259 Millionen Kubikmeter.

Einmal, zweimal, dreimal hat Stefan Ballmeier den späten, vergleichsweise unbekannten Roman von 1895 gelesen. Es ist die Geschichte einer Luxuswelt und einer Welt des technischen Fortschritts, die Geschichte einer Stadtgesellschaft, die in die verfeindeten Lager von Protestanten und Katholiken zerfällt – und schließlich untergeht. Der Student hat die Details zu Architektur und Städtebau zusammengefasst, ist im Deutschen Museum dem technischen Zeitgeist vor der Wende zum 20. Jahrhundert nachgegangen – all das, um sich ein Bild zu machen von jener Insel und der geheimnisvollen Stadt Milliard City, an der Verne das Bild der modernen US-Metropolen bricht. Ballmeier hat so gleichsam eine Topographie von Fortschritt und Zerfall entwickelt – und sie in ein Miniaturmodell aus Stahl und Kunstharz gekleidet.

schichte richte, auf die kulturhistorische Verankerung also der Architektur. Zu Beginn habe sie noch Bedenken ge- | Straßen, wenigen zentralen Anlagen und durchgängiger weitgehend identischer Blockrandbebauung und rückwärtigen | den Aufbau einer Gesellschaft, die auf kollektives Glück gerichtet ist: grundsätzliche Gleichheit ihrer Mitglieder, | ben, einem Genre, das auch trotz ihres technoiden Funkelns verschattete Visionen wie die von Vernes Propellerinsel

Lesen am Modell: Architekturstudent Stefan Ballmeier mit dem Nachbau der „Propellerinsel" (großes Bild), Miriam Knechtel und das Ministerium der Wahrheit sowie Josef Brandl (unten links) und Wolfgang Schedlbauer mit ihrer Nachbildung der „Pädagogischen Provinz".
Fotos: Andreas Heddergott

KRITIK DER AUSSTELLUNG *ARCHITEKTUR WIE SIE IM BUCHE STEHT. FIKTIVE BAUTEN UND STÄDTE IN DER LITERATUR*, IN: *SÜDDEUTSCHE ZEITUNG*, 27.12.2006

CRITIQUE OF THE EXHIBITION *ARCHITEKTUR WIE SIE IM BUCHE STEHT. FIKTIVE BAUTEN UND STÄDTE IN DER LITERATUR* IN *SÜDDEUTSCHE ZEITUNG*, DECEMBER 27, 2006

became head of the architecture collection. In recognition of his twelve years of dedication, the architecture collection was included in the plan for the new buildings of the TU München and the Ludwig-Maximilians-Universität München on the site of the former military barracks of the Türkenkaserne, thanks to Wolfgang Wild, the president of the university at the time.[99] In the competition of 1987, the winning architects Helmut von Werz and Johann-Christoph Ottow planned a building for the architecture collection across from the eastern wing of the Alte Pinakothek.[100] Given the prospects of having his own museum in Munich, Nerdinger turned down an offer in 1989 to succeed Heinrich Klotz at the Deutsches Architekturmuseum in addition to a professorship in Frankfurt.[101] As a result, he was able for the first time to negotiate a budget for the collection, from which he could purchase acid-free cardboard for valuable items that were still being stored in packing paper as well as drafting cabinets and computers.[102]

As president of the International Confederation of Architectural Museums (ICAM) between 1989 and 1994, Nerdinger was able to intensify important contacts with other museums and find additional partners.

strialisierung erfordert die Verlegung der Produktionsstätte von der Baustelle ... in die Fabrik... dadurch wird der Bau zur Montage.
Konrad Wachsmann

AUSSTELLUNGSANSICHT
EXEMPLARISCH. KONSTRUKTION
UND RAUM IN DER ARCHITEKTUR
DES 20. JAHRHUNDERTS,
ARCHITEKTURMUSEUM DER
TU MÜNCHEN, 2002

EXHIBITION VIEW,
EXEMPLARISCH. KONSTRUKTION
UND RAUM IN DER ARCHITEKTUR
DES 20. JAHRHUNDERTS,
ARCHITEKTURMUSEUM DER
TU MÜNCHEN, 2002

um den neuen Charakter einer öffentlichen Kulturinstitution zu dokumentieren – in Architekturmuseum der TU München umbenannt und Nerdinger zum Direktor ernannt. Mit den geometrischen Grundformen eines Dreiecks mit eingeschriebenem Quadrat, als architektonisches Zeichen für A und M, erhielt das Museum nun auch ein eigenes signifikantes Logo.[112]

1992 fand ein offener Realisierungswettbewerb mit internationalen Zuladungen für den Bau der Pinakothek der Moderne statt, den der Münchner Architekt Stephan Braunfels gewann.[113] Die Ausführung stellte der damalige Ministerpräsident Edmund Stoiber jedoch 1993 aus Kostengründen zurück.[114] Erst durch die Unterstützung von Bürgern und einer 1994 für den Bau der Pinakothek der Moderne gegründeten Stiftung wurde die Planung 1996 wieder aufgenommen.[115]

Mit Eröffnung der Pinakothek der Moderne am 16. September 2002[116] begann für das Architekturmuseum der TU München eine neue Epoche, die ehemalige Architektursammlung konnte erstmals seit ihrem Bestehen in eigenen Räumen öffentliche Ausstellungen zeigen.[117]

Es entstand ein großes Forum zur Vermittlung von Architektur, und die Fakultät für Architektur erhielt ein kulturelles Schaufenster, um die Architektur im Rahmen von Kunst, Grafik und Design entsprechend zu vertreten und in dem sie sich seitdem einer internationalen Öffentlichkeit präsentieren kann.[118] Aufgrund einmaliger vom Finanzministerium zugeteilter Mittel konnten Zeichnungen, unter anderem von Gunnar Asplund, Le Corbusier und Richard Buckminster Fuller angekauft werden. Auch verfügte das Museum nun über drei wissenschaftliche Mitarbeiterstellen, davon eine für das Archiv. Eine regelmäßige Ausstellungstätigkeit war aber nur

MODELLSAMMLUNG,
ARCHITEKTURMUSEUM
DER TU MÜNCHEN,
2005

MODEL COLLECTION,
ARCHITEKTURMUSEUM
DER TU MÜNCHEN,
2005

In 1994, the TU München began moving back into its original location, since the accounting office had reprimanded the university for its high outlays for rented space. The collection was removed from Augustenstrasse, and the Architekturmuseum acquired the "Angerer-Atelier," a small administrative space on the fourth floor of a building on Luisenstrasse as well as rooms in a building at Gabelsbergerstrasse 43.[103] When the department for mechanical engineering moved to Garching in 1997, a decision was made by the department of architecture to move the museum to rooms on the ground floor and basement level of the Thiersch building. Planning was completed, even down to the detailed construction budget, when the financing was not approved and the refurbishment of the building had to be put on hold. It was then only possible to outfit and move into individual offices on the ground floor and into storage spaces for the model collection on the basement level.

AUS EINEM INTERVIEW VON WOLFGANG JEAN STOCK MIT WINFRIED NERDINGER, IN: *ROTUNDE*, 1, 2007, S. 8

FROM AN INTERVIEW BETWEEN WOLFGANG JEAN STOCK AND WINFRIED NERDINGER IN *ROTUNDE*, 1, 2007, P. 8

ARCHITEKURMUSEUM SCHWABEN

While the move of the Architekturmuseum der TU München into its own space at the Pinakothek der Moderne was requiring substantial work and effort,[104] an idea was developed in discussion with the Arno-Buchegger-Stiftung in 1993 on the occasion of an anniversary event celebrating the one hundredth birthday of Thomas Wechs, one of the few modern architects in conservative southern Germany, for a center documenting and promoting the history of architecture in Swabia.[105] An offshoot of the Architekturmuseum opened in 1995 in the reconstructed home of the Buchegger family in the Thelott neighborhood of Augsburg, which has been completely financed by the

AUSSTELLUNGSANSICHT *DER ARCHITEKT.*
GESCHICHTE UND GEGENWART EINES BERUFSTANDES,
ARCHITEKTURMUSEUM DER TU MÜNCHEN, 2012

EXHIBITION VIEW, *DER ARCHITEKT.*
GESCHICHTE UND GEGENWART EINES BERUFSTANDES,
ARCHITEKTURMUSEUM DER TU MÜNCHEN, 2012

HANNS HEISS,
LEHRBOGENMODELL
EINES SPÄTGOTISCHEN
NETZGEWÖLBES, 1659

HANNS HEISS,
CENTERING MODEL FOR
CONSTRUCTION
OF A LATE GOTHIC
RETICULATED VAULT, 1659

dank der Unterstützung des Präsidenten der TU München, Wolfgang A. Herrmann, möglich, der aufgrund der Anerkennung der bisher erbrachten Leistungen persönlich einen Etat einrichtete und diesen garantierte.

Seit Eröffnung der Pinakothek der Moderne wurden bis zum Ausscheiden von Winfried Nerdinger 2012 in 42 Ausstellungen historische, biografische und aktuelle Themen mit nationalem wie internationalem Bezug behandelt.[119] Dabei sah er das Architekturmuseum immer als Einrichtung einer Hochschule mit einer ganz besonderen Aufgabe und unter der Verpflichtung des »forschenden Verstehens« (nach Johann Gustav Droysens *Historik),* zu dem für Nerdinger als Pendant die rationale und evidente Vermittlung gehört.[120] Deswegen kennzeichnen alle Ausstellungen des Architekturmuseums die Kombination von wissenschaftlicher Forschung, Lehre, didaktischer Aufbereitung und kritischer Darstellung.[121] Die Symbiose zwischen Forschung und Lehre konnte durch die Einbindung der Lehrstühle der Architekturfakultät, von Assistenten und Architekturstudenten, aber auch durch die Zusammenarbeit mit anderen Universitäten und renommierten Forschungseinrichtungen weiter intensiviert werden. Die Ausstellungsprojekte wurden zumeist über mehrere Jahre erarbeitet, viele der daraus resultierenden Kataloge sind zu Grundlagenwerken geworden.[122] Für die Präsentation der jeweils neuen komplexen Zusammenhänge wurde stets ein entsprechendes Raumkonzept entwickelt. Kritiker würdigten die »spannend aufbereiteten Themen«, die durch ihre Präsentation immer auch »ein Raumerlebnis garantieren«.[123]

foundation ever since.[106] The first exhibition that took place focused on the—at the time sensational—design by Peter Zumthor for the Berlin Topography of Terror project—also as a way of generating a discussion about setting up a documentation center on the history of National Socialism in Bavaria.[107]

Over the course of seventeen years, Nerdinger produced over eighty exhibitions, published catalogues, edited a series of journals, and established an archive including the papers of important Swabian architects.[108] In 1999, he managed to incorporate the architectural and artistic papers of Thomas Wechs into the collection.[109] A specific Thomas Wechs room was installed, and in 2000 the Thomas Wechs prize was established, an architecture award for outstanding buildings in Swabia.[110]

PINAKOTHEK DER MODERNE

The planning of an independent building for the museum across from the Alte Pinakothek had developed to the point of a detailed construction budget being presented to authorities, when Hans Zehetmair, the new state minister for science and art, set aside the property solely for use by a museum. Only thanks to the proactive planning and joint initiative of Nerdinger and Otto Meitinger, the president of the TU München at the time, was the architecture collection included in the planning of the Pinakothek der Moderne,[111] and—to confirm its new role as a public cultural institution—it was renamed the Architekturmuseum der TU München, and Nerdinger was appointed to director. Incorporating the basic geometric forms of a triangle inscribed with a square, architecturally symbolic of "A" and "M," the museum also now gained a unique and distinctive appearance.[112]

The competition for the realization of the building of the Pinakothek der Moderne took place in 1992 with invited international architects. The winner was the Munich architect Stephan Braunfels.[113] However, Bavaria's *Ministerpräsident* (Prime Minister), Edmund Stoiber, shelved the project in 1993 due to cost.[114] Only through citizen support and a foundation established in 1994 to promote the construction of the Pinakothek der Moderne was the planning process reinitiated in 1996.[115]

With the opening of the Pinakothek der Moderne on September 16, 2002,[116] a new era began for the Architekturmuseum der TU München, and for the first time since its founding, the architecture collection was able to present public exhibitions in its own rooms.[117] The museum became an important forum

FRIEDRICH VON THIERSCH,
AQUARELLSTUDIE AUS
ABYDOS, ÄGYPTEN, 1884

FRIEDRICH VON THIERSCH,
WATERCOLOR STUDY
FROM ABYDOS, EGYPT, 1884

LOUIS I. KAHN, TEMPEL DES AMUN-RE, KARNAK, SÄULENSAAL (HYPOSTYL), REISESKIZZE, ÄGYPTEN, 1951

LOUIS I. KAHN, TEMPLE OF AMUN-RE, KARNAK, HYPOSTYLE HALL, TRAVEL SKETCH, EGYPT, 1951

for promoting architecture, and the department of architecture gained a culturally-oriented presentation platform, where architecture was appropriately represented alongside art, graphics, and design, and where the department has since been able to present itself to an international public.[118] On the basis of the one-time allocation of funds from the Finanzministerium (Ministry of Finance), the museum was able to purchase drawings by Gunnar Asplund, Le Corbusier, and Richard Buckminster, among others. The museum also now benefitted from three research positions, one designated for the archive. Nevertheless, regular exhibition activities were still only possible thanks to the support of the president of the TU München, Wolfgang A. Herrmann, who personally established and guaranteed a budget on the basis of the recognition received by the collection for its past activities.

Since the opening of the Pinakothek der Moderne, forty-two exhibitions on historical, biographical, and current topics of national and international scope were mounted by the time of Winfried Nerdinger's departure in 2012.[119] Nerdinger

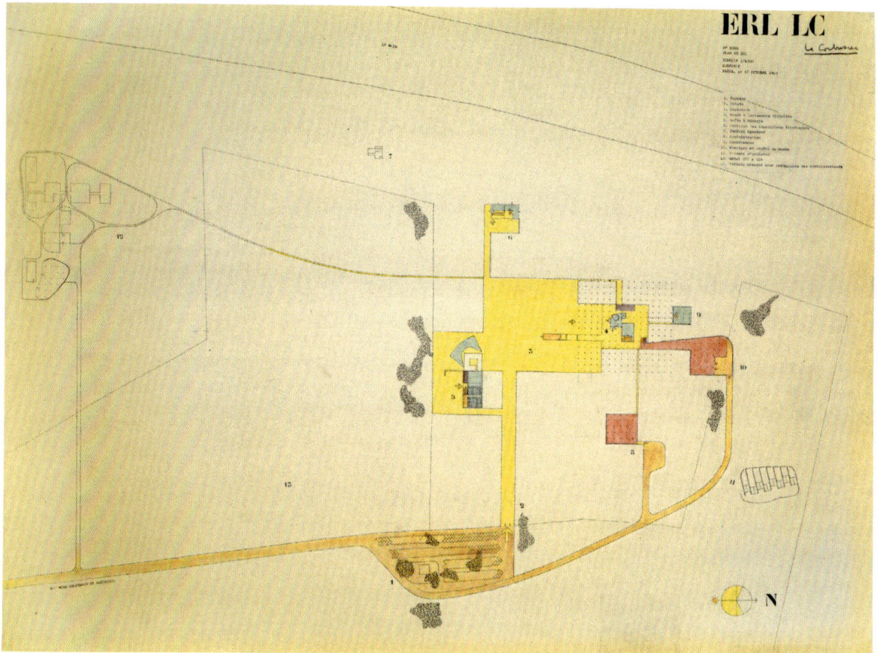

LE CORBUSIER, INTERNATIONALES
KUNSTZENTRUM IN ERLENBACH,
PLAN, 1963

LE CORBUSIER, INTERNATIONALES
KUNSTZENTRUM IN ERLENBACH,
PLAN, 1963

Für die erste Ausstellung, die in den eigenen Räumen stattfand – *Exemplarisch* –, öffnete das Architekturmuseum sein Depot und gewährte wieder einen Einblick in den reichen Sammlungsbestand.[124] Die Auswahl erfolgte dabei nach den für die moderne Architektur grundlegenden Leitbegriffen Konstruktion und Raum. Im Vorfeld stifteten zahlreiche Architekten Zeichnungen und Modelle, beispielsweise Fritz Haller das MIDI-Baukastensystem, Peter Zumthor das Porenbetonmodell des Berghotels Tschlin, Werner Sobek ein Modell seines Hauses R 128 oder Benthem Crouwel Zeichnungen und Modell des Wohnhauses Benthem, aber auch erste computergenerierte Modelle und Animationen von Kas Oosterhuis, Greg Lynn oder Asymptote Architecture kamen an die Sammlung.

Seit dieser ersten Ausstellung wurden die weiterhin wachsenden Bestände immer wieder präsentiert, zuletzt in der Abschiedsausstellung von Winfried Nerdinger *Der Architekt* (2012), bei der die große Abteilung der »Werkzeuge des Architekten« fast vollständig aus der Sammlung bestückt und auch eine exemplarische Auswahl der einst zu den Beständen zählenden Lehrbücher gezeigt werden konnte.

had always viewed the Architekturmuseum as a university institution with a special mission and commitment to an "exploratory understanding" (or as Johann Gustav Droysen describes in his *Historik,* "forschendes Verstehen"), which, for Nerdinger, included an accompanying educational dimension.[120] This is why all of the exhibitions of the Architekturmuseum are characterized by a combination of scholarly research, teaching, didactic preparation, and critically reflected presentations.[121] The symbiotic relationship between research and teaching was intensified through the involvement of various professors of the department of architecture as well as assistants and architecture students, and also through cooperations with other universities and prominent research institutions. The exhibition projects were usually developed over a number of years, and many of the resulting catalogues have come to be considered seminal publications.[122] For the presentation of the different complex relationships reflected in each exhibition, the museum always developed an individual concept for the exhibition space. Critics praised the "fascinatingly presented themes," which always "guaranteed a spatial experience" in terms of display.[123]

For the first exhibition that took place in the museum's own spaces, *Exemplarisch* (Showcase, 2002), the Architekturmuseum once again opened up its depot, thus providing an overview of its rich holdings.[124] The items selected for the exhibition were representative of the fundamental guiding notions of modern architecture: construction and space. Prior to the exhibition, many architects donated their drawings and models. For example, Fritz Haller gave his MIDI module system, Peter Zumthor the porous concrete model of his mountain hotel in Tschlin, Switzerland, Werner Sobek a model of his R128 house, and Benthem Crouwel drawings and models of their Benthem house. The first computer-generated models and animations by Kas Oosterhuis, Greg Lynn, and Asymptote Architecture also joined the collection.

Since this first exhibition, the continuously expanding collection was repeatedly presented to the public, most recently in Winfried Nerdinger's farewell exhibition, *Der Architekt* (The Architect, 2012), in which the substantial array of "architect's tools" on view was taken almost exclusively from the collection; an exemplary selection of the textbooks that once belonged to the collection was also shown.

Due to the exhibition activities of the collection, it was possible to obtain many additional drawings and models. Heinz Tesar gave the museum his large-format models and a number of watercolors. Gerkan, Marg und Partner donated their model of the reconstruction of the Olympiastadium in Berlin, and following the exhibition on Sep Ruf, the museum was able to

Mit der Ausstellungstätigkeit konnte auch eine Vielzahl weiterer Zeichnungen und Modelle für das Archiv gewonnen werden. Heinz Tesar schenkte dem Museum seine großformatigen Modelle und einige Aquarelle, Gerkan, Marg und Partner überließen ihr Modell vom Umbau des Berliner Olympiastadions, und im Zuge der Ausstellung über Sep Ruf konnten die Bestände des bedeutenden Münchner Architekten ergänzt werden.

Um die Erwerbung zahlreicher Nachlässe hat sich Nerdinger persönlich und teilweise jahrzehntelang bemüht. So war die Tochter von Roderich Fick erst nach dem Tod ihrer Mutter 2004 bereit, dessen Nachlass dem Archiv für die wissenschaftliche Aufarbeitung von Nerdingers Forschungsprojekt »Hitlers Architekten« zu übereignen.[125] Auch der Nachlass von Paul Schmitthenner gelangte erst 2008 und nach lang andauernden Verhandlungen mit Schmitthenners zweiter Ehefrau an das Museum.

Durch die Einbeziehung von Fachplanern in den modernen Architekturbürobetrieb wurden die Nachlässe immer umfangreicher; die oft mehrere Tausend Pläne umfassenden Projekte beinhalten neben Skizzen und Fotografien zunehmend auch Bauunterlagen und Korrespondenzen. Zu den größten Beständen zählt mit 23 906 Zeichnungen, 102 Modellen und 31 988 Fotografien das 2006 übereignete Material von Paul Schneider-Esleben.[126] Noch 2011 schloss Nerdinger mit dem Berliner Architekten Andreas Brandt einen Vertrag zur Übergabe von dessen Zeichnungen sowie mit Franz Kießling, dem Neffen von Hans Döllgast, eine Vereinbarung zur Übernahme des Nachlasses von dem für den Wiederaufbau bedeutenden Münchner Architekten und Hochschullehrer.[127]

Mit Mitteln der Deutschen Forschungsgemeinschaft begannen das Architekturmuseum und die Universitätsbibliothek 2009 mit der Digitalisierung der Plansammlung des Archivs. In einer zweijährigen Projektlaufzeit wurden die wertvollsten Bestände (rund 48 000 Pläne) der Architekten des 19. Jahrhunderts hochauflösend gescannt und online auf dem Multimediaserver der Universitätsbibliothek (MediaTUM) bereitgestellt.[128] Die seitdem ständig wachsende Anzahl von Nachfragen nach den Beständen zeigt das große Interesse an der Sammlung.

In 37 Jahren hat Winfried Nerdinger aus einer unbeachteten Studiensammlung ein international renommiertes Architekturmuseum in eigenen Räumen und mit reger Ausstellungs- und Publikationstätigkeit ausgebaut. Mit seinem umfangreichen und bedeutenden Planarchiv gehört das Museum heute zu einem der wichtigsten Forschungsinstitute für Architekturgeschichte in Deutschland. Über

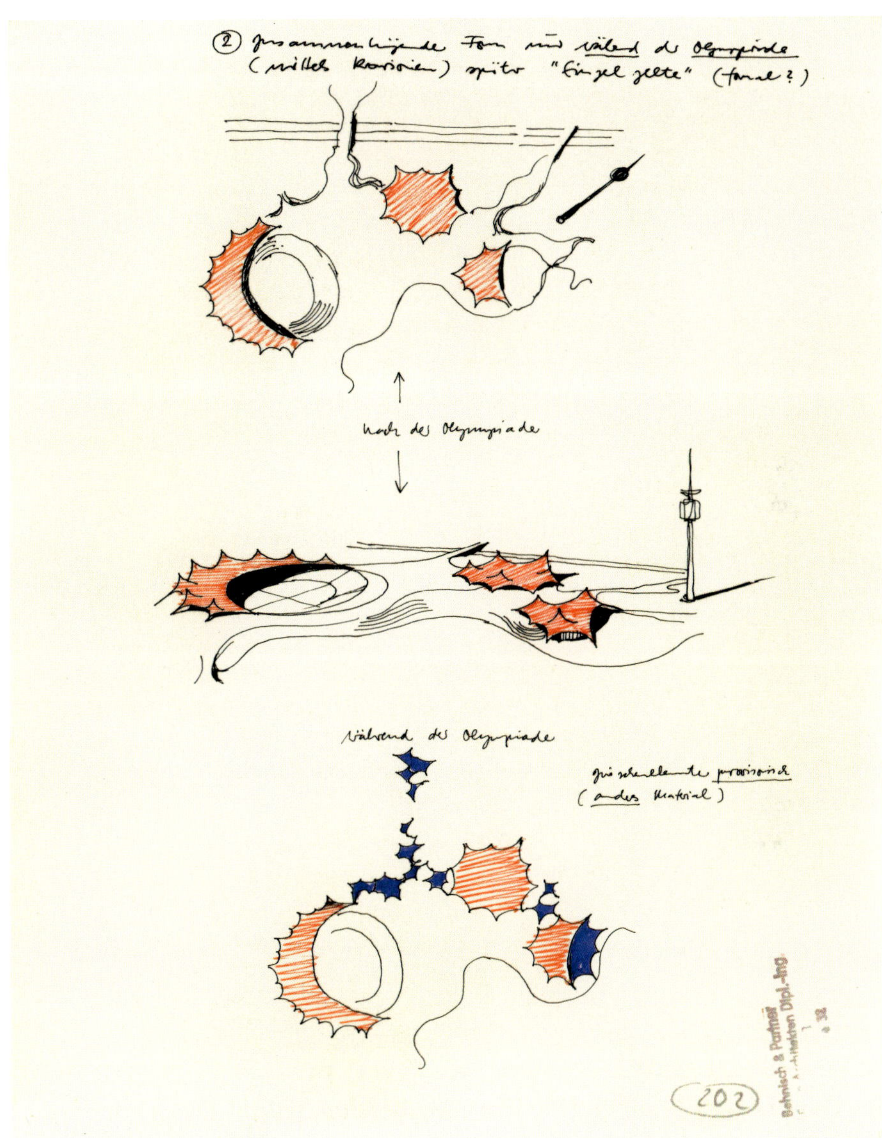

BEHNISCH & PARTNER, GÜNTER BEHNISCH, FRITZ AUER, WINFRIED BÜXEL, ERHARD TRÄNKNER, CARLO WEBER MIT JÜRGEN JOEDICKE; TRAGWERKSINGENIEUR HEINZ ISLER, BURGDORF / SCHWEIZ; WETTBEWERB FÜR DIE BAUTEN UND ANLAGEN DER XX. OLYMPISCHEN SPIELE MÜNCHEN 1972 IN MÜNCHEN, 1967, ENTWURFSSKIZZEN ZU DEN ZELTDÄCHERN, UM 1967/68 (ZEICHNUNG: CARLO WEBER)

BEHNISCH & PARTNER, GÜNTER BEHNISCH, FRITZ AUER, WINFRIED BÜXEL, ERHARD TRÄNKNER, AND CARLO WEBER WITH JÜRGEN JOEDICKE; STRUCTURAL ENGINEER HEINZ ISLER, BURGDORF / SWITZERLAND; COMPETITION OF 1967 FOR THE BUILDINGS AND GROUNDS FOR THE 1972 GAMES OF THE XX OLYMPIAD IN MUNICH, DESIGN SKETCHES FOR TENT-LIKE ROOFS, CA. 1967–68 (DRAWING: CARLO WEBER)

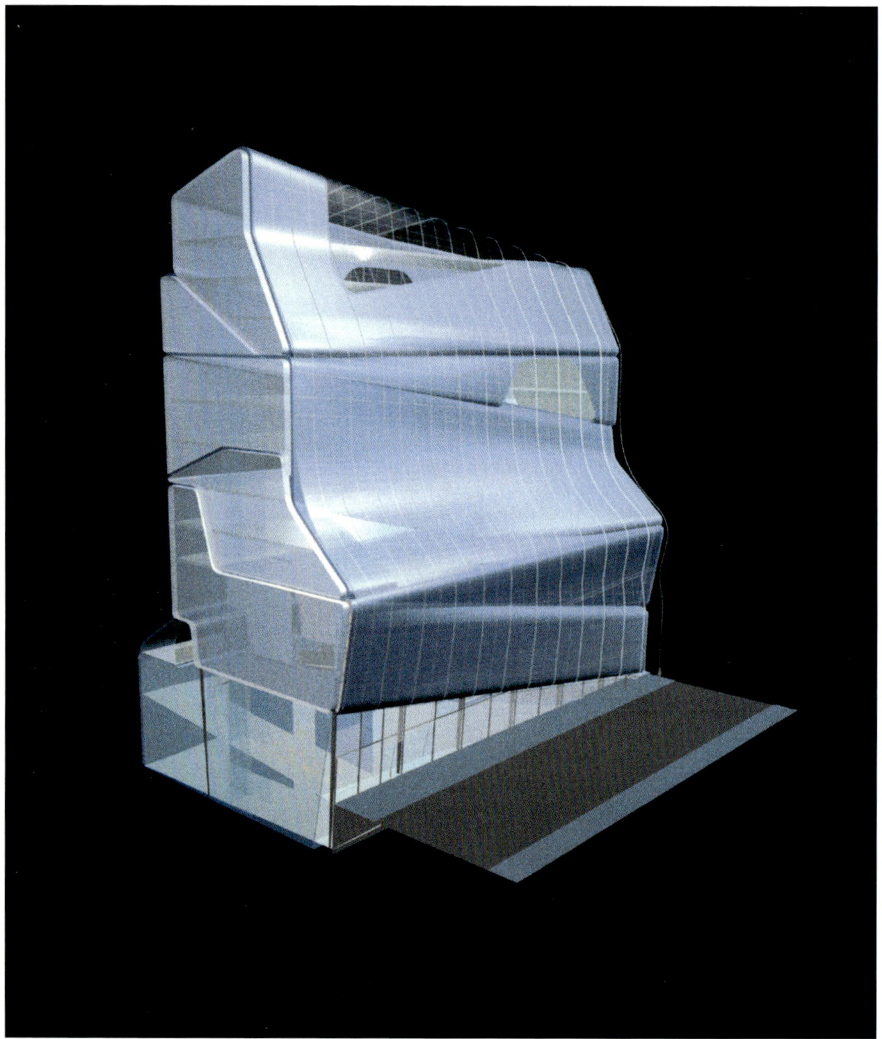

ASYMPTOTE ARCHITECTURE, EYEBEAM
MUSEUM OF ART AND TECHNOLOGY,
NEW YORK, RENDERING, 2001

die Bestände wurden zahlreiche Dissertationen[129] und wissenschaftliche Publikationen verfasst. Bei seinem Ausscheiden im September 2012 umfasste das Archiv über 550 000 Zeichnungen von 700 Architekten und 200 000 Fotografien, 1 100 Modelle, zahlreiche Stichwerke, Bauakten sowie Computeranimationen und -prints. Zum Abschied würdigten Architekturhistoriker »Winfried Nerdingers Wirken als weltweit einzigartige wissenschaftliche Leistung«.[130]

add new items relevant to this important Munich architect to its collection. Nerdinger himself made great efforts, in some cases over a period of decades, to obtain numerous bequests. For example, only after the death of her mother in 2004 was the daughter of Roderich Fick willing to donate his estate to the archive for scholarly study in the context of Nerdinger's research project "Hitler's architects."[125] The estate of Paul Schmitthenner was also only obtained by the museum in 2008, after extended negotiations with Schmitthenner's second wife.

When modern architecture firms began incorporating technical planners into their projects, such estates became increasingly comprehensive. Often including several thousand plans, individual projects also entailed sketches and photographs as well as an increasing number of construction and correspondence documents. One of the largest collections of donated materials came from Paul Schneider-Esleben in 2006 and encompassed 23,906 drawings, 102 models, and 31,988 photographs.[126] In 2011, Nerdinger even signed a contract with the Berlin architect Andreas Brandt for the transfer of his drawings to the museum, and he also signed an agreement with Franz Kiessling, the nephew of Hans Döllgast, to obtain the papers of this significant Munich architect and professor active during the postwar reconstruction era.[127]

With the help of funds from the Deutsche Forschungsgemeinschaft (German Research Foundation), the Architekturmuseum and the university library began to digitize the collection of plans in the archive in 2009. Over the course of the two-year project, the most valuable holdings (some 48,000 plans) by nineteenth-century architects were scanned in high resolution and made available online on the multimedia server of the university library (MediaTUM).[128] The steadily increasing number of requests for these materials reflects a great interest in the collection.

Over the course of thirty-seven years, Winfried Nerdinger turned an obscure teaching collection into an architectural museum of international repute, with its own space and a lively exhibition and publication program. With its extensive and important archive of architectural plans, the museum is among the most significant research institutes for the history of architecture in Germany. Numerous dissertations[129] and scholarly publications have been written about the collection. Upon his departure in September 2012, the archive included over 550,000 drawings by 700 architects, 200,000 photographs, 1,100 models, a large number of prints, construction documents, computer animations, and digital prints. On the occasion of his retirement, architectural historians lauded "Winfried Nerdinger's work as a scholarly achievement that is unique by global comparison."[130]

FRITZ HALLER, MIDI-ARMILLA,
MODELL, 1988

FRITZ HALLER, MIDI-ARMILLA,
MODEL, 1988

IRENE MEISSNER

FOLGENDE DISSERTATIONEN SIND AUS DER SAMMLUNG DES ARCHITEKTURMUSEUMS HERVORGEGANGEN

1978 Hans-Jürgen Kotzur, *Forschungen zum Leben und Werk des Architekten August von Voit*, Heidelberg

1979 Ekkehard Bartsch, *Die Prinzregentenstraße in München von 1880–1914 zwischen Prinz-Karl-Palais und Friedensengel*, München
Florian Hufnagl, *Gottfried von Neureuther (1811–1887). Leben und Werk*, München

1980 Volker Hütsch, *Der Münchner Glaspalast 1854–1931. Geschichte und Bedeutung*, Berlin

1981 Birgit Stenger, *August Thiersch (1843–1916). Geplante und ausgeführte Kirchenbauten*, München

1982 Horst K. Marschall, *Friedrich von Thiersch. Ein Münchner Architekt des Späthistorismus*, München
Ilse Springorum-Kleiner, *Carl von Fischer, 1936*, hrsg. und eingeleitet von Winfried Nerdinger, München

1984 Petra Noll, *Mauritio Pedetti, der letzte Hofbaudirektor des Hochstifts Eichstätt (1719–1799)*, München
Kristin Sinkel, *Pompejanum und Villa Ludwigshöhe in der Pfalz*, Aschaffenburg

1987 Ulrich Kerkhoff, *Theodor Fischer. Eine Abkehr vom Historismus oder ein Weg zur Moderne*, Stuttgart
Bernd-Peter Schaul, *Das Prinzregententheater in München und die Reform des Theaterbaus um 1900. Max Littmann als Theaterarchitekt*, München
Charlotte M. E. Werhahn, *Hans Schwippert (1899–1973), Architekt. Pädagoge und Vertreter der Werkbundidee in der Zeit des Wiederaufbaus*, München

1989 Elisabeth Spitzbart-Maier, *Die Kirchenbauten Martin Elsaessers und ihre Voraussetzungen in der protestantischen Kirchenbautheorie und Liturgiediskussion*, Stuttgart

1991 Cornelius Tafel, *Der Architekt Adolf Schneck. Wegbereiter der Moderne im Stuttgart der 20er Jahre*, München

1995 Elisabeth Reissinger, *Hans C. Reissinger und der evangelische Kirchenbau der 50er und 60er Jahre in Franken*, Münster

1996 Gerhard Kabierske, *Der Architekt Hermann Billing (1867–1946). Leben und Werk*, Karlsruhe
Petra S. Kühner, *Gustav Bauernfeind. Gemälde und Aquarelle*, Frankfurt am Main

PHD THESES BASED ON RESEARCH ON THE COLLECTION OF THE ARCHITEKTURMUSEUM

1978 Hans-Jürgen Kotzur, *Forschungen zum Leben und Werk des Architekten August von Voit*, Heidelberg

1979 Ekkehard Bartsch, *Die Prinzregentenstraße in München von 1880–1914 zwischen Prinz-Karl-Palais und Friedensengel*, Munich
Florian Hufnagl, *Gottfried von Neureuther (1811–1887): Leben und Werk*, Munich

1980 Volker Hütsch, *Der Münchner Glaspalast 1854–1931: Geschichte und Bedeutung*, Berlin

1981 Birgit Stenger, *August Thiersch (1843–1916): Geplante und ausgeführte Kirchenbauten*, Munich

1982 Horst K. Marschall, *Friedrich von Thiersch: Ein Münchner Architekt des Späthistorismus*, Munich
Ilse Springorum-Kleiner, *Carl von Fischer, 1936*, edited and with an introduction by Winfried Nerdinger, Munich

1984 Petra Noll, *Mauritio Pedetti, der letzte Hofbaudirektor des Hochstifts Eichstätt (1719–1799)*, Munich
Kristin Sinkel, *Pompejanum und Villa Ludwigshöhe in der Pfalz*, Aschaffenburg

1987 Ulrich Kerkhoff, *Theodor Fischer: Eine Abkehr vom Historismus oder ein Weg zur Moderne*, Stuttgart
Bernd-Peter Schaul, *Das Prinzregententheater in München und die Reform des Theaterbaus um 1900: Max Littmann als Theaterarchitekt*, Munich
Charlotte M. E. Werhahn, *Hans Schwippert (1899–1973), Architekt: Pädagoge und Vertreter der Werkbundidee in der Zeit des Wiederaufbaus*, Munich

1989 Elisabeth Spitzbart-Maier, *Die Kirchenbauten Martin Elsaessers und ihre Voraussetzungen in der protestantischen Kirchenbautheorie und Liturgiediskussion*, Stuttgart

1991 Cornelius Tafel, *Der Architekt Adolf Schneck: Wegbereiter der Moderne im Stuttgart der 20er Jahre*, Munich

1995 Elisabeth Reissinger, *Hans C. Reissinger und der evangelische Kirchenbau der 50er und 60er Jahre in Franken*, Münster

1996 Gerhard Kabierske, *Der Architekt Hermann Billing (1867–1946): Leben und Werk*, Karlsruhe
Petra S. Kühner, *Gustav Bauernfeind: Gemälde und Aquarelle*, Frankfurt am Main

1997   Hermann Rau, *Jean Baptiste Métivier. Architekt, königlich bayerischer Hofbaudekorateur und Baurat (1781–1857)*, Lassleben / Kallmünz

1998   Kay Thoss, *Hofbauintendant Andreas Gärtner (1744–1826). Architekt eines Lebens im Umbruch*, Weimar

1999   Gisela Forster, *Die rekonstruierenden Bildwelten des Kunstdidaktikers, Architekturzeichners und Architekten Joseph Bühlmann (1844–1921)*, Berg

2001   Uwe Hinkfoth, *Die evangelische Garnisonskirche von Theodor Fischer in Ulm 1905–1910 und die Bauaufgabe der Garnisonskirche in der Kaiserzeit*, Hildesheim
Christoph Hölz, *Der Civil-Ingenieur Franz Jakob Kreuter. Tradition und Moderne, 1813–1889*, Berlin und München
Sabine Klotz, *Fritz Landauer, 1883–1996. Leben und Werk eines jüdischen Architekten*, Berlin
Florian Koch, *German Bestelmeyer (1874–1942), Architekt. Tradition als Illusion der Permanenz. Der süddeutsche Kirchenbau, romantisch-retrospektiver Traditionalismus im Sakralbau der zwanziger und dreißiger Jahre*, München

2005   Ulrike Laible, *Bauen für die Kirche. Der Architekt Michael Kurz (1876–1957)*, Berlin

2005   Christiane Kaiser, *Die Fleischbrücke in Nürnberg (1596–1598)*, Cottbus

2006   Ilka Backmeister-Collacott, *Josef Wiedemann. Leben und Werk eines Münchner Architekten*, Tübingen
Sian Brehler, *Die Neue Liederhalle Stuttgart. Daten und Fakten zur Baugeschichte*, Karlsruhe

2007   Benedikt Maria Scherer, *Der Architekt Carl Sattler. Leben und Werk (1877–1966)*, München

2008   Michael Früchtel, *Der Architekt Hermann Giesler. Leben und Werk (1898–1987)*, Unterwössen
Ellen Pietrus, *Heinrich Dolmetsch. Die Kirchenrestaurierungen des württembergischen Baumeisters*, Stuttgart
Florian Seidel, *Ernst May. Städtebau und Architektur in den Jahren 1954–1970*, München

2009   Maria Wüllenkemper, *Richard Riemerschmid (1868–1957). Nicht die Kunst schafft den Stil, das Leben schafft ihn*, Regensburg

2013   Irene Meissner, *Sep Ruf 1908–1982*, Berlin und München

IM DRUCK   Lioba Schmitt-Imkamp, *Leben und Werk des Architekten Roderich Fick (1886–1955)*

1997 Hermann Rau, *Jean Baptiste Métivier: Architekt, königlich bayerischer Hofbaudekorateur und Baurat (1781–1857)*, Lassleben / Kallmünz

1998 Kay Thoss, *Hofbauintendant Andreas Gärtner (1744–1826): Architekt eines Lebens im Umbruch*, Weimar

1999 Gisela Forster, *Die rekonstruierenden Bildwelten des Kunstdidaktikers, Architekturzeichners und Architekten Joseph Bühlmann (1844–1921)*, Berg

2001 Uwe Hinkfoth, *Die evangelische Garnisonskirche von Theodor Fischer in Ulm 1905–1910 und die Bauaufgabe der Garnisonskirche in der Kaiserzeit*, Hildesheim
Christoph Hölz, *Der Civil-Ingenieur Franz Jakob Kreuter: Tradition und Moderne, 1813–1889*, Berlin and Munich
Sabine Klotz, *Fritz Landauer, 1883–1996: Leben und Werk eines jüdischen Architekten*, Berlin
Florian Koch, *German Bestelmeyer (1874–1942), Architekt: Tradition als Illusion der Permanenz: Der süddeutsche Kirchenbau, romantisch-retrospektiver Traditionalismus im Sakralbau der zwanziger und dreißiger Jahre*, Munich

2003 Ulrike Laible, *Bauen für die Kirche: Der Architekt Michael Kurz (1876–1957)*, Berlin

2005 Christiane Kaiser, *Die Fleischbrücke in Nürnberg (1596–1598)*, Cottbus

2006 Ilka Backmeister-Collacott, *Josef Wiedemann: Leben und Werk eines Münchner Architekten*, Tübingen
Sian Brehler, *Die Neue Liederhalle Stuttgart: Daten und Fakten zur Baugeschichte*, Karlsruhe

2007 Benedikt Maria Scherer, *Der Architekt Carl Sattler: Leben und Werk (1877–1966)*, Munich

2008 Michael Früchtel, *Der Architekt Hermann Giesler: Leben und Werk (1898–1987)*, Unterwössen
Ellen Pietrus, *Heinrich Dolmetsch: Die Kirchenrestaurierungen des württembergischen Baumeisters*, Stuttgart
Florian Seidel, *Ernst May: Städtebau und Architektur in den Jahren 1954–1970*, Munich

2009 Maria Wüllenkemper, *Richard Riemerschmid (1868–1957): Nicht die Kunst schafft den Stil, das Leben schafft ihn*, Regensburg

2013 Irene Meissner, *Sep Ruf 1908–1982*, Berlin and Munich

IN PRINT Lioba Schmitt-Imkamp, *Leben und Werk des Architekten Roderich Fick (1886–1955)*

1 Winfried Nerdinger wollte während seiner Zeit als Direktor des Architekturmuseums der TU München noch eine grundlegende Publikation über die Bestände der Sammlung, die er zu Dreivierteln während seiner 37-jährigen Tätigkeit zusammengetragen hatte, schreiben. Einen Teil der Texte hatte er bereits verfasst, aber aufgrund seiner Berufung zum Gründungsdirektor des NS-Dokumentationszentrums München im Frühjahr 2012, der Vorbereitung der letzten großen Ausstellungen am Architekturmuseum und weiterer Verpflichtungen konnte er das Buch nicht mehr fertigstellen. Anhand seiner zahlreichen Aufsätze und Publikationen zur Sammlung, vor allem aber aufgrund vieler Gespräche mit Winfried Nerdinger, konnte die Verfasserin den Beitrag über die Geschichte der Sammlung des Architekturmuseums schreiben. Für seine große Hilfe und Unterstützung dankt sie ihm herzlich.

2 Siehe Winfried Nerdinger, »Die Bauschule an der Akademie. Höhere Baukunst für Bayern«, in: Thomas Zacharias (Hrsg.), *Tradition und Widerspruch. 175 Jahre Kunstakademie München*, München 1985, S. 273–286; Winfried Nerdinger, »Die Bauschule an der Akademie der Bildenden Künste München 1809–1873«, in: Nikolaus Gerhart, Walter Grasskamp und Florian Matzner (Hrsg.), *200 Jahre Akademie der Bildenden Künste München. ›... kein bestimmter Lehrplan, kein gleichförmiger Mechanismus‹*, München 2008, S. 306–337.

3 »Organisation der polytechnischen Schule«, in: *Königliche Technische Hochschule zu München, Bericht über die Königl. Polytechnische Schule zu München für das Studienjahr 1868–1869*, München 1869, S. 3–5, hier S. 3; siehe auch Winfried Nerdinger, »Polytechnische Schule in München«, in: ders. und Florian Hufnagl, *Gottfried von Neureuther. Architekt der Neorenaissance in Bayern 1811–1887. Aus den Beständen der Architektursammlung der Technischen Universität München*, München 1978, S. 63–93.

4 Als Fischer 1820 starb, konnte die Akademie seinen zeichnerischen Nachlass von den Erben für die Summe von 5.900 fl erwerben; ein Großteil dieser Zeichnungen befindet sich heute in der Sammlung des Architekturmuseums der TU München und trägt auch noch die von der Akademie der Bildenden Künste vergebenen Inventarnummern, siehe Monika Meine-Schawe, *Das verschwundene Museum. Die Kunst- und Lehrsammlung der Akademie der Bildenden Künste in München. Ein vergessenes Kapitel Akademiegeschichte, erläutert auf der Grundlage eines Sammlungsverzeichnisses von 1822 und weiterer Quellen*, unveröffentlichtes Buchmanuskript (Auszug), Stand: 23.10.2013, Kopie am Architekturmuseum.

5 Siehe u. a. Winfried Nerdinger, *Carl von Fischer 1782–1820*, München 1982; Winfried Nerdinger, »Beginn der akademischen Architektenausbildung an der Münchner Akademie 180–1868«, in: ders. in Zusammenarbeit mit Katharina Blohm (Hrsg.), *Architekturschule München 1868–1993. 125 Jahre Architekturschule München*, München 1993, S. 25–35, 162; Nerdinger 1985 (wie Anm. 2); Nerdinger

2008 (wie Anm. 2); das Pariser Skizzenbuch (1806) kaufte Stephan Braunfels und schenkte es dem Architekturmuseum zur Eröffnung der Pinakothek der Moderne. Fischers Skizzenbuch galt als verschollen und war 1982 ein besonderer Fund der zum 200. Geburtstag des Architekten von Winfried Nerdinger verantworteten Ausstellung; die Rotunde der Pinakothek der Moderne ist eine Hommage von Stephan Braunfels an den jung verstorbenen Baumeister, der 1816 in seinem Entwurf für die Glyptothek eine große Rotunde im Zentrum vorsah, siehe Martina Düttmann, »Die Pinakothek der Moderne in München. Ein veritables Tageslichtmuseum«, in: *Bauwelt*, 22, 2002, S. 26–33, hier S. 26.

6 Julius Meyer, »Die bildende Kunst auf der Weltausstellung – II. Die Architektur«, in: *Zeitschrift für bildende Kunst*, 1867, Bd. 2, S. 245–249, hier S. 248.

7 Bericht 1869 (wie Anm. 3), S. 13; außerdem konnten mit Unterstützung des königl. Staatsministeriums und durch Tausch mit den königl. Preussischen Museen, der Berliner Gewerbe-Akademie und der Akademie der schönen Künste in Mailand, viele Abgüsse von antiken Kunstwerken erworben werden, siehe Königliche Technische Hochschule zu München, Bericht für das Studienjahr 1869–1870, München 1870, S. 29 f.

8 1868 gehörten 18 Studierende der »Hochbau-Abtheilung« an, siehe Bericht 1869 (wie Anm. 3), S. 15 f.; dort lehrten: Gottfried von Neureuther, Professor für Höhere Architektur und Geschichte der Baukunst, Lehre von den Baustylen und Geschichte der Baukunst; Rudolph Gottgetreu, Professor für Bauzeichnen, Baumaterialienlehre und Constructionslehre für Hochbauten; Albert Geul, Professor für bürgerliches, landwirthschaftliches und Fabrik-Bauwesen; Joseph Mozet, Professor für Ornamenten-, Figuren- und Landschaftszeichnen, siehe Bericht 1869 (wie Anm. 3), S. 6 f.; siehe auch Nerdinger 1978 (wie Anm. 3), S. 63–93, hier S. 66.

9 »Die Modellsammlung für Hochbaukunde« (Gottfried Neureuther); »Die Baumaterialien-sammlung« und »Die Sammlung für Bauzeichnen« (Rudolph Gottgetreu); »Die Sammlung für Civilbaukunde« (Albert Geul); »Die Sammlung für Planzeichnen« (Konservator Ernst Fischer, außerordentlicher Professor für Linearzeichnen, Situations- und topographisches Zeichnen); »Die kunstgeschichtliche Sammlung« (Dr. Franz Reber); »Die Sammlung für Modelliren und Bossiren« (Konrad Knoll), siehe Bericht 1869 (wie Anm. 3), S. 13 f.

10 Winfried Nerdinger, *Fotografie für Architekten. Die Fotosammlung des Architekturmuseums der TU München*, Köln 2011, S. 6–9.

11 Zur Gesellschaft San Giorgio, siehe R. [Richard] Borrmann, »Die Architektur der Renaissance in Italien«, in: *Zentralblatt der Bauverwaltung*, 97, 2.12.1911, S. 614 f.; Die Kapitelle und Ornamente in Gips konnten bei der Architektur-Sammlung

1 During his tenure as director of the Architekturmuseum der TU München, Winfried Nerdinger had wished to write a fundamental publication on the holdings of the collection, of which three-fourths had been acquired during his thirty-seven years of work. He completed a portion of the texts, but due to his appointment as founding director of the NS-Dokumentationszentrum München in the spring of 2012, the preparation of his last major exhibitions at the Architekturmuseum, and additional commitments, he was not able to complete this book. His numerous essays and publications on the collection and, above all, many conversations between Winfried Nerdinger and the author enabled the completion of this article on the history of the collection of the Architekturmuseum. The author would like to thank him most sincerely for his generous help and support.

2 See Winfried Nerdinger, "Die Bauschule an der Akademie: Höhere Baukunst für Bayern," in *Tradition und Widerspruch: 175 Jahre Kunstakademie München*, ed. Thomas Zacharias (Munich, 1985), pp. 273–86; Winfried Nerdinger, "Die Bauschule an der Akademie der Bildenden Künste München 1809–1873," in Nikolaus Gerhart et al., eds., *200 Jahre Akademie der Bildenden Künste München: "... kein bestimmter Lehrplan, kein gleichförmiger Mechanismus"* (Munich, 2008), pp. 306–37.

3 "Organisation der polytechnischen Schule," in *Königliche Technische Hochschule zu München, Bericht über die Königl. Polytechnische Schule zu München für das Studienjahr 1868–1869* (Munich, 1869), pp. 3–5, here p. 3; see also Winfried Nerdinger, "Polytechnische Schule in München," in Winfried Nerdinger and Florian Hufnagl, eds., *Gottfried von Neureuther: Architekt der Neorenaissance in Bayern 1811–1887; Aus den Beständen der Architektursammlung der Technischen Universität München* (Munich, 1978), pp. 63–93.

4 When Fischer died in 1820, the academy was able to purchase his estate from his heirs for the sum of 5,900 Guldens; a large portions of these drawings are currently found in the collection of the Architekturmuseum der TU München and still have the catalogue numbers given by the Akademie der Bildenden Künste. See Monika Meine-Schawe, *Das verschwundene Museum: Die Kunst- und Lehrsammlung der Akademie der Bildenden Künste in München; Ein vergessenes Kapitel Akademiegeschichte, erläutert auf der Grundlage eines Sammlungsverzeichnisses von 1822 und weiterer Quellen*, unpublished manuscript (excerpt), from a copy provided to the Architekturmuseum, version of October 23, 2013.

5 See the following, among other publications: Winfried Nerdinger, *Carl von Fischer 1782–1820* (Munich, 1982); Winfried Nerdinger, "Beginn der akademischen Architektenausbildung an der Münchner Akademie 1808–1868," in Winfried Nerdinger in cooperation with Katharina Blohm, eds., *Architekturschule München 1868–1993: 125 Jahre Architekturschule München* (Munich, 1993), pp. 25–35, 162; Nerdinger 1985 (see note 2); Nerdinger

2008 (see note 2); Stephan Braunfels purchased the Paris sketchbook (1806) and donated it to the Architekturmuseum upon the opening of the Pinakothek der Moderne. Fischer's sketchbook had been considered lost and represented a particular find that was shown in the exhibition organized by Nerdinger to commemorate the architect's 200th birthday; the rotunda of the Pinakothek der Moderne is Braunfels's hommage to the master architect, who died prematurely and who had placed a large rotunda at the center of his design for the Glyptothek. See Martina Düttmann, "Die Pinakothek der Moderne in München: Ein veritables Tageslichtmuseum," *Bauwelt* 22 (2002), pp. 26–33, see p. 26.

6 Julius Meyer, "Die bildende Kunst auf der Weltausstellung—II: Die Architektur," *Zeitschrift für bildende Kunst* (1867), vol. 2, pp. 245–49, see p. 248.

7 *Bericht* 1869 (see note 3), p. 13. In addition, through the help of the Königliche Staatsministerium (Royal Ministry of State) and through exchanges with the Königliche Preussische Museen, the Berlin Gewerbe-Akademie, and the Academy of Fine Arts in Milan, it was possible to acquire numerous plaster casts of antique works of art. See *Königliche Technische Hochschule zu München, Bericht für das Studienjahr 1869–1870* (Munich, 1870), pp. 29–30.

8 In 1869, there were eighteen students in the department of structural design; see *Bericht* 1869 (see note 3), p. 15–16. The instructors included Gottfried von Neureuther, professor of advanced architecture and the history of architecture; Rudolph Gottgetreu, professor for architectural drawing, building materials, and structural design; Albert Geul, professor for civil, agricultural, and factory architecture; and Joseph Mozet, professor for ornamental, figurative, and landscape drawing; see *Bericht* 1869 (see note 3), pp. 6–7. See also Nerdinger 1978 (see note 3), pp. 63–93, see p. 66.

9 The collection of models for structural design (Gottfried Neureuther); the building material collection and the collection of architectural drawings (Rudolph Gottgetreu); the collection of civil architecture (Albert Geul); the collection of technical drafting (conservator Ernst Fischer, associate professor for linear, situational, and topographic drawing; the art historical collection (Dr. Franz Reber); the collection of modeling and sculpting (Konrad Knoll); see *Bericht* 1869 (see note 3), pp. 13–14.

10 Winfried Nerdinger, *Fotografie für Architekten: Die Fotosammlung des Architekturmuseums der TU München* (Cologne, 2011), pp. 6–9.

11 On the Gesellschaft San Giorgio, see R. [Richard] Borrmann, "Die Architektur der Renaissance in Italien," in *Zentralblatt der Bauverwaltung* 97, December 2, 1911, pp. 614–15; one could order the capitals and ornaments in plaster from the architecture collection. See *Architektur-Sammlung der Kgl. Technischen Hochschule zu München, Verzeichnis einer Auswahl von Original-Abgüssen*

bestellt werden, siehe *Architektur-Sammlung der Kgl. Technischen Hochschule zu München, Verzeichnis einer Auswahl von Original-Abgüssen nach Architekturteilen aus der Zeit der Renaissance in Toskana, welche zur Vervielfältigung durch Gipsabguss bestimmt sind,* München 1900.

12 Im erhaltenem Inventarbuch der Architektur-Sammlung ist mit Nr. 2817 beispielsweise ein Modell des Ulmer Münsters eingetragen, das im Saal der Architektursammlung aufgestellt wurde, siehe Joseph Popp, »Die Architektursammlung«, in: *Die K. B. Technische Hochschule zu München. Denkschrift zur Feier ihres 50jährigen Bestehens,* München 1917, S. 128–130, Abb. 86, Tafeln. 43, 44, 45b, hier Tafel 43; siehe auch Hans Karlinger, »Architekturmodelle«, in: *Die Plastik. Illustrierte Zeitschrift für die gesamte Bildhauerei und Bildnerei und ihre Beziehungen zu Architektur und Kunstgewerbe,* hrsg. v. Alexander Heilmeyer, 10, 1921, S. 53–56, hier Tafeln 64–67.

13 Winfried Nerdinger, *Die Modellsammlung als Lehr- und Arbeitsinstrument, Internationales Kolloquium, Teil 3: Modelle und Architektur,* 7.11.2009, unveröffentlichtes Manuskript, Kopie am Architekturmuseum.

14 Bis 1869/70 »Modellsammlung für Hochbaukunde«.

15 Nerdinger 2011 (wie Anm. 10).

16 Die Sammlung wird seit 1882 in den »Berichten« der Hochschule geführt, übereignet wurde sie aber offenbar erst 1897, siehe Königliche Technische Hochschule zu München, *Bericht für das Studienjahr 1897–1898,* München 1898, S. 42.

17 Siehe Hans Moninger, *Ehrerbietigste Bittvorstellung des Bahnbeamten Hans Moninger daher in Sachen Acquirirung der Friedrich von Gärtner'schen Plan- und Studien-Sammlung durch den bayer. Staat, hier Änderung des Zahlungs-Modus für die Restkaufsumme betr. (mit 7 Beilagen),* München 1885.

18 Siehe Winfried Nerdinger (Hrsg.), *Friedrich von Gärtner. Ein Architektenleben 1791–1847,* S. 220.

19 Erhaltene Inventare: Inventar der Architektur-Sammlung, AM-TUM, Sign. oa-1463-1, oa-1463-2; Inventar der Sammlung für Modelliren & Bossiren, AM-TUM, Sign. oa-1463-3; Inventar der Sammlung für Bauzeichnen, AM-TUM, Sign. oa-1463-4; Inventar der Architektonischen Sammlung; II. Mittelalterliche Baukunst, AM-TUM, Sign. oa-1463-5; Inventar der Sammlung für architectonische Constructionslehre, AM-TUM, Sign. oa-1463-6; Inventar der Diapositiv-Sammlung der Architektenabteilung, AM-TUM, Sign. oa-1463-7; Verzeichnis der in der Architektur-Sammlung vorhandenen Photographien, AM-TUM, Sign. oa-1463-8.

20 Den Hinweis gab Monika Meine-Schawe, siehe Monika Meine-Schawe, *Die Kunst und Lehrmittelsammlung der Akademie der bildenden Künste in München. Ein vergessenes Kapitel Akademiegeschichte, erläutert auf der Grundlage*

eines Sammlungsverzeichnisses von 1822 und weiterer Quellen, unveröffentlichtes Buchmanuskript (Auszug), Kopie am Architekturmuseum: Friedrich von Thiersch und Heinrich Freiherr von Schmidt wählten von 1736 Inventarnummern 874 aus, die als Lehrmaterial für die Architekten in Frage kamen, siehe BayHStA, MK 14176, VI/208, 212, 9.2.1904, Abgaben.

21 Friedrich Hoffstadt (1802–1846), *Gotisches A-B-C Buch, das ist: Grundregeln des gothischen Styls für Künstler und Werkleute,* Frankfurt am Main 1840; siehe auch Bernd Evers, Jürgen Zimmer, Friedrich Hoffstadt (1802–1846), in: ders. [Evers] in Zusammenarbeit mit der Kunstbibliothek der Staatlichen Museen zu Berlin, *Architekturtheorie. Von der Renaissance bis zur Gegenwart,* Köln 2006, S. 410–417.

22 Der Westturm-Aufriss wurde 1924 von Rudolph Rosemann in einem Aufsatz über die Regensburger Risse im Münchner Jahrbuch als im Besitz der Architektur-Sammlung veröffentlicht, mit dem Hinweis auf einen zweiten dort befindlichen Riss eines gotischen Sakramenthauses. 1936 wird der Riss ein weiteres Mal in zwei Aufsätzen behandelt, den der Autor Otto Kletzl an der Münchner Architektursammlung zuvor studieren konnte, siehe Johann Josef Böker, Anne-Christine Brehm, Julian Hanschke und Jean-Sébastien Sauvé, *Architektur der Gotik Rheinlande. Ein Bestandskatalog der mittelalterlichen Architekturzeichnungen mit einem Beitrag von Peter Völkle über die Zeichentechnik der Gotik,* Salzburg und Wien 2013, S. 53–58.

23 Auktionshaus Nagel, Stuttgart; Johann Josef Böker, Professor für Baugeschichte an der TH Karlsruhe und Leiter des Südwestdeutschen Archivs für Architektur und Ingenieurbau (saai), informierte 2012 das Architekturmuseum. Dank der Forschungen Bökers und des Hinweises von Monika Meine-Schawe auf die Hoffstadt-Sammlung konnte die Provenienz nachgewiesen werden, seitdem wird versucht, die wertvollen Pläne für die Sammlung zurückzugewinnen. Von den weiteren überlassenen Zeichnungen der Akademie lassen sich heute noch 545 in nach Themen geordneten Mappen und Kassetten im Archiv des Architekturmuseums nachweisen, online unter http://mediatum.ub.tum. de/?id=917498 (Stand: 9.12.2013).

24 Königliche Technische Hochschule zu München, *Bericht für das Studienjahr 1888–1889,* München 1889, S. 36.

25 Der Codex Aureatinus umfasst 118 Blätter, siehe Felix Mader, »Pläne und Entwürfe der Baudirektoren Pedetti und Gabrieli«, in: *Die Kunstdenkmäler von Mittelfranken I. Stadt Eichstätt,* München 1924; von den von Mader aufgelisteten Plänen im Besitz der Architektursammlung fehlen die Blätter mit den Nummern 54, 55, 57–61, 63–68, 70–74, 83, 97 und 100–103 (alte Sign.), siehe AM-TUM, NL Krauss, schriftl. Unterlagen: Schreiben Otto Bauer an Rurik Deichsel, Kiel, v. 13.2.1963.

nach Architekturteilen aus der Zeit der Renaissance in Toskana, welche zur Vervielfältigung durch Gipsabguss bestimmt sind (Munich, 1900).

12 For example, in the surviving inventory catalogue of the architecture collection, no. 2817 is described as a model of the Ulm Cathedral, which was displayed in the room of the architecture collection. See Joseph Popp, "Die Architektursammlung," in *Die K. B. Technische Hochschule zu München: Denkschrift zur Feier ihres 50jährigen Bestehens* (Munich, 1917), pp. 128–30, fig. 86, plates 43, 44, 45b, see plate 43; see also Hans Karlinger, "Architekturmodelle," in *Die Plastik: Illustrierte Zeitschrift für die gesamte Bildhauerei und Bildnerei und ihre Beziehungen zu Architektur und Kunstgewerbe* 10 (1921), pp. 53–56, see plates 64–67. The journal was edited by Alexander Heilmeyer.

13 Winfried Nerdinger, *Die Modellsammlung als Lehr- und Arbeitsinstrument, Internationales Kolloquium, Teil 3: Modelle und Architektur,* November 7, 2009, copy of an unpublished manuscript given to the Architekturmuseum.

14 Up until 1869–70, it bore the name *Modellsammlung für Hochbaukunde* (the collection of models for structural design).

15 Nerdinger 2011 (see note 10).

16 The collection is mentioned in the *Berichten* (bulletins) of the university as of 1882, but it apparently only came into the possession of the university in 1897. See Königliche Technische Hochschule zu München, ed., *Bericht für das Studienjahr 1897–1898* (Munich 1898), p. 42.

17 See Hans Moninger, *Ehrerbietigste Bittvorstellung des Bahnbeamten Hans Moninger daher in Sachen Acquirirung der Friedrich von Gärtner'schen Plan- und Studien-Sammlung durch den bayer. Staat, hier Änderung des Zahlungs-Modus für die Restkaufsumme betr. (mit 7 Beilagen)* (Munich, 1885).

18 Winfried Nerdinger, *Friedrich von Gärtner: Ein Architektenleben 1791–1847* (Munich, 1992), p. 220.

19 Surviving inventory records: inventory of the architecture collection, AM-TUM, Sign. oa-1463-1, oa-1463-2; inventory of the collection of modeling and sculpting, AM-TUM, Sign. oa-1463-3; inventory of the collection of architectural drawing, AM-TUM, Sign. oa-1463-4; inventory of the architectural collection; II. medieval architecture, AM-TUM, Sign. oa-1463-5; inventory of the collection of architectural construction, AM-TUM, Sign. oa-1463-6; inventory of the slide collection of the architecture department, AM-TUM, Sign. oa-1463-7; index of existing photographs in the architecture department, AM-TUM, Sign. oa-1463-8.

20 This information was kindly provided by Monika Meine-Schawe. See Monika Meine-Schawe, *Die Kunst und Lehrmittelsammlung der Akademie der bildenden Künste in München: Ein vergessenes Kapitel Akademiegeschichte, erläutert auf der Grundlage eines Sammlungsverzeichnisses von 1822 und weiterer Quellen,* from a copy of an unpublished manuscript (excerpt) given to the Architekturmuseum. Friedrich von Thiersch and Heinrich Freiherr von Schmidt selected 874 of 1,736 inventoried items as potential teaching materials for architects; see BayHStA, MK 14176, VI / 208, 212, transferred on February 9, 1904.

21 Friedrich Hoffstadt (1802–1846), *Gotisches A-B-C Buch, das ist: Grundregeln des gothischen Styls für Künstler und Werkleute* (Frankfurt am Main, 1840); see also Bernd Evers et al., Friedrich Hoffstadt (1802–1846), *Architekturtheorie: Von der Renaissance bis zur Gegenwart,* ed. Bernd Evers in cooperation with the Kunstbibliothek der Staatlichen Museen zu Berlin (Cologne, 2006), pp. 410–17.

22 The elevation of the western tower was mentioned as being in the possession of the architecture department by Rudolph Rosemann in 1924 in an article in the *Münchner Jahrbuch* on Regensburg elevations. He also mentioned a second elevation of a Gothic sacristy. In 1936, the former of these two elevations was mentioned again in two essays. The author, Otto Kletzl, had been able to study this drawing beforehand at the Munich architecture collection. See Johann Josef Böker et al., *Architektur der Gotik Rheinlande: Ein Bestandskatalog der mittelalterlichen Architekturzeichnungen mit einem Beitrag von Peter Völkle über die Zeichentechnik der Gotik* (Salzburg and Vienna, 2013), pp. 53–58.

23 At the Nagel auction house in Stuttgart; Johann Josef Böker, professor of the history of building at the Karlsruher Institut für Technologie and head of the Südwestdeutsches Archiv für Architektur und Ingenieurbau (saai) provided information to the Architekturmuseum in 2012. Thanks to Böker's research and Monika Meine-Schawe's information about the Hoffstadt Collection, it was possible to prove their provenance. Since then the museum has been attempting to regain the valuable plans for the collection. Of the other drawings given to the academy, 545 are still extant and are preserved thematically in grouped portfolios and boxes in the archive of the Architekturmuseum. Available online at http://mediatum.ub.tum.de/?id=917498 (last accessed December 9, 2013).

24 Königliche Technische Hochschule zu München, ed., *Bericht für das Studienjahr 1888–1889* (Munich, 1889), p. 36.

25 The *Codex Aureatinus* encompasses 118 folios. See Felix Mader, "Pläne und Entwürfe der Baudirektoren Pedetti und Gabrieli," in *Die Kunstdenkmäler von Mittelfranken I. Stadt Eichstätt* (Munich, 1924); of the plans listed by Mader as belonging to the architecture collection, the following folios are missing: 54, 55, 57–61, 63–68, 70–74, 83, 97, and 100–103 (old signatures). See AM-TUM, NL Krauss, archive material: a letter by Otto Bauer to Rurik Deichsel, Kiel, dated February 13, 1963.

26 Friedrich von Thiersch, *Denkschrift zu dem Projekt der Erweiterungs-Bauten der K. Technischen Hochschule zu München auf dem Areal des Ostermaier-Gartens* (Munich, 1908), p. 13.

26 Friedrich von Thiersch, *Denkschrift zu dem Projekt der Erweiterungs-Bauten der K. Technischen Hochschule zu München auf dem Areal des Ostermaier-Gartens*, München 1908, S. 13.

27 Architekturpläne, Stiche und Bücher aus der ehemaligen Sammlung Dros, Bamberg. Auktion in München in der Galerie Helbing, Donnerstag, den 15. Februar 1912, Nummern 423, 424, 425, S. 18 f., 428, S. 21; siehe auch AM-TUM, Sign. oa-1463-1, Inventar der Architektonischen-Sammlung, Nrn. 2252–2260.

28 Königliche Technische Hochschule zu München, *Bericht für das Studienjahr 1912–1913*, München 1914, S. 77.

29 Ebd., S. 2 f.

30 Eröffnung der Erweiterungsbauten der Technischen Hochschule, in: *Münchner Neueste Nachrichten*, 24.6.1913, S. 4.

31 Siehe Martina Dlugaiczyk, »Gips im Getriebe. Abguss-Sammlungen an Technischen Hochschulen«, in: Charlotte Schreiter (Hrsg.), *Gipsabgüsse und antike Skulpturen. Präsentation und Kontext*, Berlin 2012, S. 333–354.

32 Popp 1917 (wie Anm. 12).

33 Siehe Bericht 1914 (wie Anm. 28), S. 77; siehe auch Popp 1917 (wie Anm. 12); Werner Helmberger und Valentin Kockel, »Herkunft und Geschichte der Aschaffenburger Korkmodellsammlung«, in: dies., *Rom über die Alpen tragen. Fürsten sammeln antike Architektur: Die Aschaffenburger Korkmodelle*, Landshut und Ergolding 1993, S. 119–126, S. 128 f.

34 Ludwig I. hatte die Modelle zunächst 1844 in den »Vereinigten Sammlungen« in den Galeriegebäuden des Hofgartens aufstellen lassen, ab 1869 wurden sie dann im ehemaligen Ausstellungsgebäude am Königsplatz gezeigt, siehe Helmberger und Kockel 1993 (wie Anm. 33), hier S. 122.

35 Popp 1917 (wie Anm. 12), hier S. 129.

36 Das heute noch erhaltene Modell ist neben dem in gleicher Größe gebauten hölzernen Rekonstruktionsmodell, das im Kolosseum aufbewahrt wird, das größte Zustandsmodell und das größte Korkmodell eines einzelnen Bauwerks überhaupt.

37 Zitat von Heinrich Lömpel, in: Heinrich Thiersch, *Friedrich von Thiersch*, München 1925, S. 70–72, hier S. 72.

38 Theodor Fischer, »Friedrich von Thiersch. Gedächtnisrede«, in: *Süddeutsche Bauzeitung*, 8, 1922, S. 37–40.

39 Horst Karl Marschall, *Friedrich von Thiersch (1852–1921). Bauten und Entwürfe*, Diss. München 1977, Vorwort, S. 7.

40 AM-TUM, NL Krauss, schriftl. Unterlagen: Adolf Abel, Denkschrift über die Entstehung, das Wesen und die Aufgaben der Architektursammlung, 26.2.1935.

41 Ebd.

42 Ebd., gemäß Abels Schätzung umfasste die Bibliothek 15 000–20 000 Bände (Einzelwerke und Zeitschriften), etwa 9 000 Fotografien und ungefähr 2 750 Projektionslichtbilder.

43 *Oberbayern und München. Innsbruck und Salzburg*, Meyers Reisebücher, 3. Aufl., Leipzig 1922, S. 115.

44 Siehe Monika Melters, »Der Lehrstuhl für Kunstgeschichte der Technischen Hochschule München (gegr. 1868): Ein Profil vor und nach 1947«, in: Iris Lauterbach, *Zentralinstitut für Kunstgeschichte, Kunstgeschichte in München 1947. Institutionen und Personen im Wiederaufbau*, München 2010, S. 19–28, S. 24 f.

45 HATUM.PA.Prof. Dr. Manfred Bühlmann.

46 Ebd., Schreiben Zenneck, Der Senat der Technischen Hochschule München an das Staatsministerium für Unterricht und Kultus, 6.7.1926.

47 Ebd., Ernennungsurkunde.

48 Ebd., Schreiben Der Vorstand der Architekten-Abteilung der Technischen Hochschule München an des Rektorat der Technischen Hochschule, 19.2.1931, unterzeichnet Robert Vorhoelzer.

49 Ebd., Schreiben Der Rektor der Technischen Hochschule an das Staatsministerium für Unterricht und Kultus, 28.12.1934; Schreiben Der Dekan der Fakultät für Bauwesen der Technischen Hochschule München an den Herrn Rektor der Technischen Hochschule München, 11.6.1934; AM-TUM, NL Krauss, schriftl. Unterlagen: Denkschrift, 26.2.1935 (wie Anm. 40); Otto Stammhammers Nachfolger war ab dem WS 1938/39 Max Hann.

50 AM-TUM, NL Krauss, schriftl. Unterlagen: Friedrich Krauss, »Verwaltung der Architektursammlung«, 24.1.1946; siehe auch HATUM.PA.Prof. Dr.-Ing. Friedrich Krauss: Professor Adolf Abel, München, Technische Hochschule Architektur-Abteilung an seine Magnifizenz den Herrn Rektor der Technischen Hochschule München, 8.9.1945, Betreff: Architektursammlung.

51 Ebd., Krauss schreibt, dass er sich ausschließlich um die Sicherstellung des »Abteilungsbesitzes« gekümmert habe, seine eigenen wertvollen wissenschaftlichen Unterlagen seien bei der Zerstörung des Neureuther-Altbaus unwiederbringlich verloren gegangen. In einer Bestätigung, die Krauss 1946 Julius Schulte-Frohlinde ausstellte, schrieb er hingegen, dass dieser die Sicherstellung seines »unersetzlichen wissenschaftlichen Materials« persönlich unterstützt und ihm die Unterbringung in seinem Privathaus ermöglicht habe. (AM-TUM, NL Krauss, Bestätigung, 12.9.1946); siehe auch HATUM. PA.Prof. Dr.-Ing. Friedrich Krauss (wie Anm. 50).

52 Hans Döllgast, *Journal Retour*, München 1973, Bd. 1, S. 12 f.; siehe auch Martin Pabst, »Neuaufbau aus dem Trümmerfeld«, in: Wolfgang A. Herrmann (Hrsg.), *Technische Universität München. Die*

27 Architectural plans, engravings, and books from the former Dros collection, Bamberg. Auction in Munich at the Galerie Helbing on Thursday, February 15, 1912, nos. 423, 424, 425, pp. 18–19, 428, p. 21. See also AM-TUM, Sign. oa-1463-1, inventory of the architecture collection, nos. 2252–2260.

28 Königliche Technische Hochschule zu München, *Bericht für das Studienjahr 1912–1913* (Munich, 1914), p. 77.

29 See *Bericht* 1914 (see note 28), pp. 2–3.

30 See the report on the opening of the additions to the Technische Hochschule in *Münchner Neueste Nachrichten*, June 24, 1913, p. 4.

31 See Martina Dlugaiczyk, "Gips im Getriebe: Abguss-Sammlungen an Technischen Hochschulen," in Charlotte Schreiter, ed., *Gipsabgüsse und antike Skulpturen: Präsentation und Kontext* (Berlin, 2012), pp. 333–54.

32 Popp 1917 (see note 12).

33 See *Bericht* 1914 (see note 28), p. 77; see also Popp 1917 (see note 12); Werner Helmberger and Valentin Kockel, "Herkunft und Geschichte der Aschaffenburger Korkmodellsammlung," in *Rom über die Alpen tragen: Fürsten sammeln antike Architektur; Die Aschaffenburger Korkmodelle* (Landshut and Ergolding, 1993), pp. 119–26, 128–29.

34 Ludwig I initially had the models installed in the unified collections in the gallery spaces of the Hofgarten in 1844. From 1869 onward, they were on view in a former exhibition hall on Königsplatz. See Helmberger and Kockel 1993 (see note 33), see p. 122.

35 Popp 1917 (see note 12), see p. 129.

36 Apart from a wooden model reconstruction of the same size and on view at the Colosseum, this surviving model is the largest reconstructive model of the Colosseum, and it is the largest existing cork model of a single building.

37 Quoted by Heinrich Lömpel in Heinrich Thiersch, *Friedrich von Thiersch* (Munich, 1925), pp. 70–72, see p. 72.

38 Theodor Fischer, "Friedrich von Thiersch: Gedächtnisrede," *Süddeutsche Bauzeitung* 8 (1922), pp. 37–40.

39 Horst Karl Marschall, "Vorwort," in *Friedrich von Thiersch (1852–1921): Bauten und Entwürfe* (PhD diss., TU München, 1977), p. 7.

40 AM-TUM, NL Krauss, archive material: Adolf Abel, *Denkschrift über die Entstehung, das Wesen und die Aufgaben der Architektursammlung*, dated February 26, 1935.

41 Ibid.

42 Ibid. By Abel's estimation, the library encompassed 15,000–20,000 volumes (individual books and magazines), some 9,000 photographs, and approximately 2,750 slides.

43 *Oberbayern und München: Innsbruck und Salzburg, Meyers Reisebücher*, vol. 3 (Leipzig, 1922), p. 115.

44 See Monika Melters, "Der Lehrstuhl für Kunstgeschichte der Technischen Hochschule München (gegr. 1868): Ein Profil vor und nach 1947," in Iris Lauterbach, ed., *Zentralinstitut für Kunstgeschichte, Kunstgeschichte in München 1947: Institutionen und Personen im Wiederaufbau* (Munich, 2010), pp. 19–28, 24–25.

45 HATUM.PA. Prof. Dr. Manfred Bühlmann.

46 Ibid. A letter from Zenneck, a member of the senate of the Technische Hochschule München, to the Staatsministerium für Unterricht und Kultus (State Ministry for Education and Culture), dated July 6, 1926.

47 Ibid. Letter of appointment.

48 Ibid. Letter from the board of the architecture department of the Technische Hochschule München to the rector of the Technische Hochschule, dated February 19, 1931 and signed by Robert Vorhoelzer.

49 Ibid. Letter from the rector of the Technische Hochschule to the Staatsministerium für Unterricht und Kultus (State Ministry for Education and Culture), dated December 28, 1934; letter from the dean of the school of architecture at the Technische Hochschule München to the rector of the Technische Hochschule München, dated June 11, 1934; AM-TUM, NL Krauss, archive material: memorandum, dated Febrary 26, 1935 (see note 40); Otto Stammhammer's successor as of winter semester 1938–39 was Max Hann.

50 AM-TUM, NL Krauss, archive material: Friedrich Krauss, "Verwaltung der Architektursammlung" (January 24, 1946); see also HATUM.PA. Prof. Dr.-Ing. Friedrich Krauss: letter from Prof. Adolf Abel, Munich, department of architecture of the Technische Hochschule to the rector of the Technische Hochschule München (here and traditionally addressed as *"seine Magnifizenz"*), dated September 8, 1945, re: the architecture collection.

51 Ibid. Krauss writes that he exclusively took pains to secure the "physical property of the department," and that his own valuable research and archival documents were irretrievably lost with the destruction of the historical Neureuther building. However, in a clearance certificate (a document of the postwar denazification program) issued to Julius Schulte-Frohlinde by Krauss in 1946, he wrote that he personally facilitated the safekeeping of the "irreplaceable scholarly and archival materials" and enabled it to be stored in his home. (AM-TUM, NL Krauss, clearance certificate, dated September 12, 1946); see also HATUM.PA. Prof. Dr.-Ing. Friedrich Krauss: letter of Prof. Adolf Abel, Munich (see note 50)

52 Hans Döllgast, *Journal Retour*, vol. 1 (Munich, 1973), pp. 12–13.; see also Martin Pabst, "Neuaufbau aus dem Trümmerfeld," in Wolfgang A. Herrmann, ed., *Technische Universität München: Die Geschichte eines*

Geschichte eines Wissenschaftsunternehmens, München
und Berlin 2006, S. 353–392, hier S. 353, 386 f.

53 HATUM.PA.Prof. Dr.-Ing. Friedrich Krauss: Abel,
8.9.1945 (wie Anm. 51).

54 AM-TUM, NL Krauss, schriftl. Unterlagen:
Dienstvertrag, 24.1.1946.

55 Ebd., Friedrich Krauss, Rede des Leiters der
Architektursammlung, gehalten bei der Totenfeier
für die Bibliothekarin der Sammlung Fräulein
Elisabeth Blume vor der Einäscherung in München
am 30.7.1964 und der nachfolgenden Überführung
nach Worpswede.

56 Ebd.

57 AM-TUM, NL Heinz Thiersch, schriftl. Unterlagen,
Sign. thie_he-1-2: Schreiben Friedrich Krauss an
Architekt Heinz Thiersch, 15.1.1959.

58 Aufgrund einer schweren Kriegsversehrtheit –
1953 wurde aufgrund der großen Zahl der
Kriegsversehrten, das »Gesetz über die Beschäftigung
Schwerbeschädigter« geschaffen – erhielt Bauer
die Stelle, siehe u. a. AM-TUM, Gottfried Gruben,
schriftl. Unterlagen: Werdegang und Laufbahn des
Akad. Oberrats Dipl.Ing. O. Bauer, geb. 5.10.1919
zu Wunsiedel/Ofr., v.13.10.1970; Ebd., NL Krauss,
schriftl. Unterlagen: Facharztliche Bescheinigung,
Dr. med. Gerd Mielert, München, 12.1.1971.

59 Vgl. Winfried Nerdinger, »Le Corbusier in
Deutschland«, in: *arch +*, 90/91, 1987, S. 80–86;
siehe auch AM-TUM, Sign. fis_t-346-224: Brief
von Le Corbusier an Theodor Fischer, 18.4.1932,
Übersetzung in: Winfried Nerdinger, *Theodor Fischer.
Architekt und Städtebauer 1862–1938*, Berlin 1988,
S. 90.

60 AM-TUM, Gottfried Gruben, schriftl. Unterlagen:
Dipl.Ing. Otto Bauer, Oberkonservator
Architektursammlung Techn. Hochschule München,
München, 1.4.1968.

61 Die Bücher fanden Aufstellung in sich eng
aneinanderreihenden Regalen, auf der Galerie wurde
die Plansammlung in offenen Stahlrohrgestellen
untergebracht, siehe AM-TUM, NL Krauss, schriftl.
Unterlagen: Aufstellung Planarchiv 1962.

62 Seit 2008 Deutsches Kunstarchiv; zum Archiv
für Bildende Kunst siehe u. a.: Ludwig Veit, »Das
Historische Archiv und das Archiv für Bildende
Kunst«, in: Bernward Deneke und Rainer Kahsnitz
(Hrsg.): *Das Germanische Nationalmuseum
Nürnberg 1852–1977. Beiträge zu seiner Geschichte*,
München und Berlin 1978, S. 521–545 (mit
älterer Literatur: siehe S. 1167); Birgit Jooss,
»Das Deutsche Kunstarchiv im Germanischen
Nationalmuseum«, in: *Kunstchronik. Monatsschrift
für Kunstwissenschaft, Museumswesen und
Denkmalpflege*, 61, 7, 2008, S. 346 f.

63 AM-TUM, schriftl. Unterlagen Architekten A-Z:
Vereinbarung über Abgrenzung des Sammlungs-
Programms zwischen der Architektursammlung,
Herrn Prof. Dr. Gruben und dem Germanischen

Nationalmuseum Nürnberg, Dr. Ludwig Veit,
Archivdirektor, 29.5.1973.

64 AM TUM, NL Heinz Thiersch, schriftl. Unterlagen:
Arbeitsbericht Heinz Thiersch an Herrn Prof.
Gruben.

65 Siehe u. a.: AM-TUM, NL Heinz Thiersch, schriftl.
Unterlagen: Architekturgeschichtliche Sammlung
der Städt. Galerie im Lenbachhaus, Beschluß
der Stadtratsvollversammlung, 7.10.1970; Heinz
Thiersch, »Die Architekturgeschichtlichen
Sammlungen der Landeshauptstadt München in
der Städtischen Galerie des Lenbachhauses«, in:
Bauspiegel, 12, 1963, 181 f.

66 Siehe AM-TUM, NL Heinz Thiersch, schriftl.
Unterlagen: Verträge, Korrespondenz.

67 AM-TUM, Gottfried Gruben, schriftl. Unterlagen:
Schreiben Prof. Dr.-Ing. G. Gruben an den
Kulturreferenten der Stadt München Herrn Dr. H.
Hohenemser, 21.1.1970.

68 Friedbert Ficker, »Münchens architekturgeschichtliche Sammlung. Durch Übergabe an den
Staat soll die Zukunft des wertvollen Materials
gesichert werden«, in: *Bayerischer Staatsanzeiger*,
24.4.1970, siehe auch AM-TUM, NL Heinz Thiersch,
schriftl. Unterlagen (wie Anm. 65).

69 »Städtische Galerie gibt Architektursammlung ab«,
in: *Münchner Stadtanzeiger*, 13.11.1970, S. 6.

70 AM-TUM, NL Heinz Thiersch, schriftl. Unterlagen
(wie Anm. 66).

71 AM-TUM, schriftl. Unterlagen (Person), Schreiben
Prof. Dr.-Ing. G. Gruben an den Herrn Rektor der
TU München, 23.10.1970; Otto Bauer ging 1975 in
den vorzeitigen Ruhestand und verstarb 1979.

72 Siehe u. a. AM-TUM, NL Heinz Thiersch, schriftl.
Unterlagen: Niederschrift über den Lokaltermin bei
der Architektursammlung in der Augustenstraße 79/
III am 23.3.1973: Leiter der Architektursammlung,
Prof. Dr. Gruben, Direktor der Sammlung Dipl.-Ing.
Bauer, Wissenschaftl. Angestellter der Sammlung
Herr Thiersch.

73 Wie Anm. 66.

74 Winfried Nerdinger, »Sammeln und Forschen am
Architekturmuseum«, in: Koldewey-Gesellschaft.
Vereinigung für Baugeschichtliche Forschung e. V.,
*Bericht über die 41. Tagung für Ausgrabungswissenschaft
und Bauforschung*, hrsg. v. Adolf Hoffmann u. a.,
Stuttgart 2002, S. 9 –17, hier S. 10.

75 Popp 1917 (wie Anm. 12); Oswald Hederer,
»Die Architektursammlung«, in: *Technische
Hochschule München 1868–1968*, München 1968,
S. 239–241.

76 AM-TUM, Gottfried Gruben, schriftl. Unterlagen:
Schreiben Gottfried Gruben an den Herrn Rektor
der TU München v. 23.10.1970.

77 Eberhard Dünninger und Irmela Holtmeier,
*Handbuch der historischen Buchbestände in
Deutschland*, Bd. 10, Hildesheim 1996, S. 154,

Wissenschaftsunternehmens (Munich and Berlin, 2006), pp. 353–92, see pp. 353, 386–87.

53 HATUM.PA. Prof. Dr.-Ing. Friedrich Krauss: Abel, dated September 8, 1945 (see note 51).

54 AM-TUM, NL Krauss, archive material: employment contract, dated January 24, 1946.

55 Ibid. Friedrich Krauss, speech given by the director of the architecture collection on July 30, 1964 at the memorial ceremony for Miss Elisabeth Blume, the librarian of the collection, before her cremation and subsequent burial in Worpswede.

56 Ibid.

57 AM-TUM, NL Heinz Thiersch, archive material, Sign. thie_he-1-2: letter of Friedrich Krauss to architect Heinz Thiersch, dated January 15, 1959.

58 Bauer was granted the position due to a severe disability incurred by military service—due to the large number of disabled veterans, the law for the employment of the severely disabled was passed in 1953. See, among other documents, AM-TUM, Gottfried Gruben, archive material: employment and career of Akad. Oberrat (academic senior councilor) Dipl.Ing. O. Bauer, born October 5, 1919 in Wunsiedel / Oberfranken and died October 13, 1970; AM-TUM, NL Krauss, archive material: medical certification, Dr. med. Gerd Mielert, dated Munich, January 12, 1971.

59 See Winfried Nerdinger, "Le Corbusier in Deutschland," *arch* + 90–91 (1987), pp. 80–86; see also AM-TUM, Sign. fis_t-346-224: letter from Le Corbusier to Theodor Fischer, dated April 18, 1932. A translation is found in Winfried Nerdinger, *Theodor Fischer: Architekt und Städtebauer 1862–1938* (Berlin, 1988), p. 90.

60 AM-TUM, Gottfried Gruben, archive material: Dipl.Ing. Otto Bauer, senior conservator of the architecture collection, Technische Hochschule München, dated April 1, 1968, Munich.

61 The books were placed on shelves that were set up in rows with narrow aisles. The collection of plans was placed in open racks made of steel tubing. See AM-TUM, NL Krauss, archive material: installation of the archive of plans, 1962.

62 Since 2008, the Deutsches Kunstarchiv; on the Archiv für Bildende Kunst, see, among other sources, Ludwig Veit, "Das Historische Archiv und das Archiv für Bildende Kunst," in *Das Germanische Nationalmuseum Nürnberg 1852–1977: Beiträge zu seiner Geschichte* (Munich and Berlin, 1978), pp. 521–45 (and for references to older sources, see p. 1167); Birgit Jooss, "Das Deutsche Kunstarchiv im Germanischen Nationalmuseum," *Kunstchronik: Monatsschrift für Kunstwissenschaft, Museumswesen und Denkmalpflege* 61, vol. 7 (2008), pp. 346–47.

63 AM-TUM, archive material Architekten A-Z: agreement on the delineation of the collection program between the architecture collection, Prof. Dr. Gruben, and the Germanisches

Nationalmuseum Nürnberg, Dr. Ludwig Veit, archive director, May 29, 1973.

64 AM-TUM, NL Heinz Thiersch, archive material: work report by Heinz Thiersch addressed to Prof. Gruben.

65 See, among other documents, AM-TUM, NL Heinz Thiersch, archive material: collection of the history of architecture of the Städtische Galerie im Lenbachhaus, resolution of the plenary meeting of the city council on October 7, 1970; Heinz Thiersch, "Die Architekturgeschichtlichen Sammlungen der Landeshauptstadt München in der Städtischen Galerie des Lenbachhauses," *Bauspiegel* 12 (1963), pp. 181–82.

66 AM-TUM, NL Heinz Thiersch, archive material: contracts, correspondence.

67 AM-TUM, Gottfried Gruben, archive material: letter of Prof. Dr.-Ing. G. Gruben to the Kulturreferent der Stadt München (municipal cultural officer), Dr. H. Hohenemser, dated January 21, 1970.

68 Friedbert Ficker, "Münchens architekturgeschichtliche Sammlung: Durch Übergabe an den Staat soll die Zukunft des wertvollen Materials gesichert werden," *Bayerischer Staatsanzeiger* (April 24, 1970). See also AM-TUM, NL Heinz Thiersch, archive material (see note 65).

69 "Städtische Galerie gibt Architektursammlung ab," *Münchner Stadtanzeiger,* November 13, 1970, p. 6.

70 AM-TUM, NL Heinz Thiersch, archive material (see note 66).

71 AM-TUM, archive material (in folder "Person"), letter from Prof. Dr.-Ing. G. Gruben to the rector of the TU München, dated October 23, 1970; Otto Bauer went into early retirement in 1975 and died in 1979.

72 See, among other documents, AM-TUM, NL Heinz Thiersch, archive material: protocol of the on-site meeting at the architecture collection at Augustenstrasse 79 / III on March 23, 1973 with the head of the architecture collection, Prof. Dr. Gruben, director of the collection, Dipl.-Ing. Bauer, and researcher, Mr. Thiersch.

73 See note 66.

74 Winfried Nerdinger, "Sammeln und Forschen am Architekturmuseum," in Adolf Hoffmann et al., eds., *Bericht über die 41. Tagung für Ausgrabungswissenschaft und Bauforschung,* proceedings of the conference organized by the Koldewey-Gesellschaft Vereinigung für Baugeschichtliche Forschung e. V. (Stuttgart, 2002), pp. 9–17, see p. 10.

75 Popp 1917 (see note 12); Oswald Hederer, "Die Architektursammlung," in *Technische Hochschule München 1868–1968* (Munich, 1968), pp. 239–41.

76 AM-TUM, Gottfried Gruben, archive material: letter from Gottfried Gruben to the rector of the TU München, dated October 23, 1970.

77 Eberhard Dünninger and Irmela Holtmeier,

online unter http://fabian.sub.uni-goettingen.
de/?Technische_Universitaet_%28Muenchen%29
(Stand: 14.1.2014); Die Räume der »Teilbibliothek
Architektur« blieben im zweiten Obergeschoss
(Thierschbau) bis zum Umzug in das Hauptgebäude
2008 bestehen.

78 AM-TUM, NL Krauss, schriftl. Unterlagen (wie
Anm. 61); Die ehemalige »Architekturgeschichtliche
Sammlung« zog 1978 in das Nachbarhaus
Augustenstraße 77, Rückgebäude, drittes
Obergeschoss, um.

79 Zu den wenigen Modellen gehören die Lehrmodelle
eines gotischen Netzgewölbes (AM-TUM, Sign. heiss-1-1)
und einer Dachstuhlkonstruktion (AM-TUM, Sign.
oa-14-1) sowie das Kugelhaus von Peter Birkenholz
(AM-TUM, Sign. bir-282-1); die Gipsabgüsse wurden
zum größten Teil entsorgt, siehe Winfried Nerdinger,
»Architekturmuseum«, in: Fakultät für Architektur
Technische Universität München, *Jahrbuch / Yearbook
2012*, München 2012, S. 252–263, hier S. 256.

80 Es ist bis heute die einzige feste wissenschaftliche
Dauerstelle am Architekturmuseum. Von 1974
bis 2005 hatte Birgit Verena Karnapp und seit
2005 die Verfasserin (seit 2001 wissenschaftliche
Mitarbeiterin am Architekturmuseum der TU
München) diese Stelle inne.

81 Nerdinger 2002 (wie Anm. 74).

82 Gespräch mit Winfried Nerdinger, Dezember 2013.

83 Zur Person: »Winfried Nerdinger im Gespräch mit
Wilfried Dechau und Ursula Baus«, in: *db, deutsche
bauzeitung*, 4, 1995, S. 34–36, hier S. 34.

84 Winfried Nerdinger, *Friedrich von Thiersch. Ein
Münchner Architekt des Späthistorismus 1852–1921*,
München 1977; Horst Karl Marschall, *Friedrich
von Thiersch 1852–1921. Ein Münchner Architekt des
Späthistorismus*, hrsg. v. der Architektursammlung
der Technischen Universität München, Winfried
Nerdinger, München 1982; siehe auch Monika
Steinhauser, »Die formale Gleichheit vor dem
Recht. Friedrich Thiersch, ein Münchner Architekt
der Gründerzeit. Ausstellung in München«, in:
Frankfurter Allgemeine Zeitung, 2.7.1977, S. 23.

85 Die Zeichnungen von Thiersch wurden zur
Bearbeitung der Dissertation von Horst
Karl Marschall zunächst als Leihgabe der
Architektursammlung übergeben.

86 Nerdinger 1982 (wie Anm. 5).

87 Siehe Nerdinger 2011 (wie Anm. 10), S. 137–140.

88 Nerdinger 1995 (wie Anm. 83).

89 Beispielsweise kam bei der Ausstellung über die
Architektur zur Zeit Ludwigs I., dessen intensive
Bautätigkeit als künstlerisches Mäzenatentum
verklärt wurde, heraus, dass Ludwigs Privatschatulle
aus Staatsgeldern bestand und dass er Bauten von
einzelnen Gemeinden erpresst hatte. Mythos und
Wirklichkeit waren für München seinerzeit eine
Provokation. Aber auch Nachlassgeber verursachten
Probleme, wie dies bei der Aufarbeitung von dem

Werk von Wilhelm Kreis, der Fall war: Der Erbe
war über die korrekte historische Darstellung in
der Monografie derart empört, dass er die restlichen
Zeichnungen aus dem Nachlass verweigerte, siehe
Nerdinger 2002 (wie Anm. 74), hier S. 12.

90 Winfried Nerdinger, *Der Architekt Walter Gropius.
Zeichnungen, Pläne, Fotos, Werkverzeichnis*, Berlin
1985, 2. Aufl., 1996, Italienische Ausgaben: *Walter
Gropius. Opera completa*, Mailand 1988; *Walter
Gropius 1883–1969*, Mailand 2005; Ausstellung
Busch-Reisinger Museum / Harvard University
Art Museums, Cambridge / Massachusetts 26.9.–
10.11.1985, Bauhaus-Archiv, Berlin 16.12.1985–
10.2.1986, Deutsches Architekturmuseum, Frankfurt
am Main 1.3.–30.4. 1086.

91 Gefördert von der Deutschen
Forschungsgemeinschaft, siehe Winfried Nerdinger
(Hrsg.), *Bauen im Nationalsozialismus. Bayern
1933–1945*, München 1993; Ausstellung Münchner
Stadtmuseum 24.9.1993–9.1.1994.

92 Gefördert von der Ernst von Siemens Kunststiftung
und der Gerda Henkel Stiftung, siehe Winfried
Nerdinger (Hrsg.), *Leo von Klenze. Architekt
zwischen Kunst und Hof 1784–1864*, München
2000; Ausstellung Münchner Stadtmuseum 12.5.–
3.9.2000, Altes Museum Berlin 24.2.–29.4.2001.

93 Winfried Nerdinger, *Die Architekturzeichnung. Vom
barocken Idealplan zur Axonometrie. Zeichnungen aus
der Architektursammlung der Technischen Universität
München*, München 1985, 2. Aufl. 1986, 3.Aufl.
1987, Spanische Ausgabe: Dibujos de Arquitectura.
Del diseño ideal barroco a la axonometria, Madrid
1987; Ausstellung Deutsches Architekturmuseum,
Frankfurt am Main, 14.12.1985–23.2.1986, *Museo
Español de Arte Contemporáneo*, Madrid,
12.11.–13.12.1987.

94 Winfried Nerdinger, Institut für
Auslandsbeziehungen Stuttgart,
Architekturmuseum der TU München (Hrsg.),
Tel Aviv. Neues Bauen 1930–1939, Tübingen und
Berlin 1993, Englische Ausgabe: *Tel Aviv. Modern
Architecture 1930–1939*, Tübingen und Berlin 1994,
Ausstellung: Forum für Kulturaustausch, Institut
für Auslandsbeziehungen, Stuttgart 9.6.–25.7.1993,
Bauhaus-Archiv, Museum für Gestaltung, Berlin
28.9.–28.11.1993, ifa-Galerie, Bonn, Institut
für Auslandsbeziehungen 4.5.–11.6.1994,
Wanderausstellung u. a. in Zürich, Wien, Grenoble,
New York und Ankara von 1994 bis 2001.

95 Univ.-Prof. Friedrich Kurrent, Lehrstuhl für
Entwerfen, Raumgestaltung und Sakralbau,
Technische Universität München, 1973–1998;
zu den Modellen, siehe u. a. Friedrich Kurrent,
Raummodelle. Wohnhäuser des 20. Jahrhunderts,
Salzburg 1995; Ausstellung im Aktionsforum
Praterinsel 19.6.–4.8.1996.

96 Siehe u. a. Winfried Nerdinger, »Das
Architekturmuseum der Technischen Universität
München«, in: Stiftung Pinakothek der Moderne,
Detlev von der Burg, *Pinakothek der Moderne. Eine
Vision*, München 1995, S. 18 f.

Handbuch der historischen Buchbestände in Deutschland, vol. 10 (Hildesheim, 1996), p. 154. Available online at http://fabian.sub.uni-goettingen.de/?Technische_Universitaet_%28Muenchen%29 (last accessed January 14, 2014); the *Teilbibliothek Architektur,* or departmental library, remained on the second floor (Thiersch building) until it was moved into the main building in 2008.

78 AM-TUM, NL Krauss, archive material (see note 61); the former collection of architectural history was moved to the third floor of the rear building at the neighboring address of Augustenstrasse 77 in 1978.

79 Among the few models was the teaching model of a reticulated Gothic vault (AM-TUM, Sign. heiss-1-1) and a roof construction (AM-TUM, Sign. oa-14-1) as well as the Kugelhaus, an orb-shaped construction by Peter Birkenholz (AM-TUM, Sign. bir-282-1); the plaster casts were largely discarded. See Winfried Nerdinger, "Architekturmuseum," in *Jahrbuch / Yearbook 2012,* a publication of the school of architecture at the TU München (Munich, 2012), pp. 252–63, here p. 256.

80 Even today this remains the only full-time permanent position at the Architekturmuseum. From 1974 to 2005, this position was held by Birgit Verena Karnapp, and since 2005 it has been held by the author (who has been a member of the research staff at the Architekturmuseum der TU München since 2001).

81 Nerdinger 2002 (see note 74).

82 Conversation with Winfried Nerdinger, December 2013.

83 On his persona, see "Winfried Nerdinger im Gespräch mit Wilfried Dechau und Ursula Baus," in *db, deutsche bauzeitung* 4 (1995), pp. 34–36, see p. 34.

84 Winfried Nerdinger, *Friedrich von Thiersch: Ein Münchner Architekt des Späthistorismus 1852–1921* (Munich, 1977); Horst Karl Marschall, *Friedrich von Thiersch 1852–1921: Ein Münchner Architekt des Späthistorismus,* eds. the Architektursammlung der TU München / Winfried Nerdinger (Munich, 1982); see also Monika Steinhauser, "Die formale Gleichheit vor dem Recht: Friedrich Thiersch, ein Münchner Architekt der Gründerzeit; Ausstellung in München," in *Frankfurter Allgemeine Zeitung,* July 2, 1977, p. 23.

85 The drawings were first provisionally loaned to the architecture collection for the dissertation work of Horst Karl Marschall.

86 Nerdinger 1982 (see note 5).

87 See Nerdinger 2011 (see note 10), pp. 137–40.

88 Nerdinger 1995 (see note 83).

89 For example, it was revealed through the exhibition on architecture under the reign of Ludwig I, whose activities as a patron of the arts had traditionally been glorified, that his private stash of funds consisted of state money, and that he had extorted money from individual communities for his building projects. This clash of myth and reality was considered a provocation at the time of the exhibition. Donors of estates and papers also caused problems, as in the case of the research done on the work of Wilhelm Kreis. His heir was so outraged by the correct portrayal of historical events that he refused to hand over the remaining drawings of the estate. See Nerdinger 2002 (see note 74), see p. 12.

90 Winfried Nerdinger, *Der Architekt Walter Gropius: Zeichnungen, Pläne, Fotos, Werkverzeichnis* (Berlin, 1985). A second edition was published in 1996. The Italian editions: *Walter Gropius: Opera completa* (Milan, 1988); and *Walter Gropius 1883–1969* (Milan, 2005). Exhibitions: Busch-Reisinger Museum / Harvard University Art Museums, Cambridge, Massachusetts, September 26–November 10, 1985; Bauhaus-Archiv, Berlin December 16, 1985–February 10, 1986; Deutsches Architekturmuseum, Frankfurt am Main March 1–April 30, 1986.

91 Funded by the Deutsche Forschungsgemeinschaft. See Winfried Nerdinger, ed., *Bauen im Nationalsozialismus: Bayern 1933–1945* (Munich, 1993). Exhibition at the Münchner Stadtmuseum, September 24, 1993–January 9, 1994.

92 Sponsored by the Ernst von Siemens Kunststiftung and the Gerda Henkel Stiftung; see Winfried Nerdinger, ed., *Leo von Klenze: Architekt zwischen Kunst und Hof 1784–1864,* (Munich, 2000). Exhibitions: Münchner Stadtmuseum, May 12–September 3, 2000; Altes Museum Berlin, February 24–April 29, 2001.

93 Winfried Nerdinger, *Die Architekturzeichnung: Vom barocken Idealplan zur Axonometrie; Zeichnungen aus der Architektursammlung der Technischen Universität München* (Munich, 1985). A second edition was published in 1986 and a third in 1987. Spanish edition: *Dibujos de Arquitectura: Del diseño ideal barroco a la axonometria* (Madrid, 1987). Exhibitions: Deutsches Architekturmuseum, Frankfurt am Main, December 14, 1985–February 23, 1986; *Museo Español de Arte Contemporáneo,* Madrid, November 12–December 13, 1987.

94 Winfried Nerdinger et al., eds., *Tel Aviv: Neues Bauen 1930–1939* (Tübingen and Berlin, 1993). English edition: *Tel Aviv: Modern Architecture 1930–1939* (Tübingen and Berlin, 1994). Exhibitions: Forum für Kulturaustausch, Institut für Auslandsbeziehungen, Stuttgart, June 9–July 25, 1993; Bauhaus-Archiv, Museum für Gestaltung, Berlin, September 28–November 28, 1993; ifa-Galerie, Bonn, Institut für Auslandsbeziehungen, May 4–June 11, 1994; from 1994 to 2001 the exhibition traveled to Zurich, Vienna, Grenoble, New York, and Ankara.

95 University professor Friedrich Kurrent, chair for design, interior design, and sacral architecture, TU München, 1973–1998. On the models, see, among other sources, Friedrich Kurrent, *Raummodelle: Wohnhäuser des 20. Jahrhunderts* (Salzburg, 1995). Exhibition: Aktionsforum Praterinsel, June 19–August 4, 1996.

97 Siehe u. a. »Corbusier-Museum. Eckige Schnecke«, in: *Der Spiegel*, 12,1962, S. 86, 89 f.; *Musee labyrinthe, Bulletin. Internationales Kunstzentrum e.V. Erlenbach am Main*, Erlenbach 1963.

98 Wie Anm. 82; siehe u. a. Walter Voss u. a., Architektursammlung der TU München, *Umbau und Erweiterung der Gabelsbergerstraße 49. Studienarbeiten am Lehrstuhl für Entwerfen, Raumgestaltung und Sakralbau, TU München, 1-semestriger Entwurf im Sommersemester 1982, Ausstellung im Lesesaal der Architektursammlung [...] vom 28. Juni bis 8. Juli 1983*, München 1983.

99 Siehe u. a. Nerdinger 1995 (wie Anm. 83).

100 Martin Pabst, »Von der Überlastbewältigung zum wettbewerbsfähigen Wissenschaftsunternehmen«, in: Herrmann 2006 (wie Anm. 52), S. 601–810, hier S. 637; »Zwei Universitäten – ein Bauplatz«, in: *TUM-Mitteilungen*, 6, 1987, S. 8; zum Wettbewerb, siehe »Münchens jüngster Universitätsbau. Wettbewerb um die Bebauung des Roncalli-Platzes«, in: *Baumeister*, 12, 1987, S. 9; »Realisierungswettbewerb Bebauung des Geländes der ehemaligen Türkenkaserne in München«, in: *Wettbewerbe aktuell*, 12, 1987, S. 697–710, hier S. 697–699.

101 Siehe u. a. »›Tiefer rein‹. Winfried Nerdinger, 49, Direktor des Architekturmuseums in München, über bayerischen Kultur-Abbruch«, in: *Der Spiegel*, 30, 1993, S. 138; online unter http://www.emeriti-of-excellence.tum.de/index.php?id=71 (Stand: 14.1.2014).

102 Wie Anm. 82.

103 AM-TUM, schriftl. Unterlagen: Umzug Augustenstraße, Angerer-Atelier, 1994.

104 Siehe u. a. *Der Spiegel* 1993 (wie Anm. 101); »Eine einzige Peinlichkeit«. Die Sammlung soll in der Pinakothek der Moderne gezeigt werden, doch bis jetzt fehlen dafür alle Voraussetzungen. Michael Grill, »Interview mit Winfried Nerdinger, dem Direktor des Architekturmuseums der Technischen Universität«, in: *Münchner Merkur*, 4.7.2000, S. L1.

105 Siehe Ernst Berschet, Arno-Buchegger-Stiftung, Winfried Nerdinger, Architekturmuseum Schwaben, in: ders., *Thomas Wechs 1893–1970. Architekt der Moderne in Schwaben*, Berlin 2005, S. 7.

106 Die Stiftung finanziert seit 1995 umfassend das Museum, stellt die aufwendig renovierte Buchegger-Villa sowie zwei größere Depots zur Verfügung, trägt die Kosten für Ausstellungen, Veranstaltungen und für Mitarbeiter (am Anfang eine halbe wissenschaftliche Stelle, heute zwei), fördert Forschungsprojekte und Publikationen, siehe Architekturmuseum Schwaben, *Zehn Jahre Architekturmuseum Schwaben 1995–2005*, 25, Augsburg 2005; siehe auch Winfried Nerdinger, »Architekturmuseum der Technischen Universität München. Architekturmuseum Schwaben Augsburg«, in: Fakultät für Architektur, Technische Universität München, *Jahreskatalog 1995. Architekturfakultät, Technische Universität*

München, München 1996, S. 42–45: Weitere Ausstellungsflächen und Archivräume sollte ein Neubau bieten, für den 1995 ein Wettbewerb durchgeführt wurde, der dann aber nicht zur Ausführung kam.

107 Architekturmuseum Schwaben, *Peter Zumthor. Stabwerk*, 1, 1996; Ausstellung 24.5.– 28.7.1996.

108 Siehe u. a. ub [Ursula Baus], »Architekturmuseum Schwaben«, in: *db, deutsche bauzeitung*, 1, 1995, S. 34; siehe auch AM Schwaben, online unter http://www.architekturmuseum.de/index.php?id=129 (Stand: 14.1. 2014); die Mitarbeiter des Architekturmuseums von 1975–2012 sind genannt in: Winfried Nerdinger (Hrsg.), *Architektur ausstellen / Exhibiting Architecture. Architekturmuseum der TU München 2007–2012*, München 2012, S. 165.

109 Siehe Nerdinger 2005 (wie Anm. 105).

110 Siehe online unter http://www.thomaswechspreis.de/ (Stand: 14.1. 2014).

111 Gerhard Matzig, »Die Bau-Geschichte von Zimmer 2327. Das Münchner Architekturmuseum soll in die Pinakothek der Moderne«, in: *Süddeutsche Zeitung*, 12.7.1995, S. 13.

112 Das Erscheinungsbild des Architekturmuseums gestaltete der Grafiker Hagen Nerdinger.

113 Zum Wettbewerb siehe »Realisierungswettbewerb Museumsbauten auf dem Gelände der ehemaligen Türkenkaserne in München«, in: *Wettbewerbe aktuell*, 7, 1992, S. 27–44; zum feriggestellten Gebäude u. a. »Wettbewerbe weiterverfolgt: Pinakothek der Moderne in München«, in: *Wettbewerbe aktuell*, 7, 2002, S. 87–92; Düttmann 2002 (wie Anm. 5).

114 Siehe u. a. Peter M. Bode, »Kunst-Kahlschlag in München. Stimmen des Protests gegen Stoiber wegen der Verzögerung des Neubaus der Staatsgalerie«, in: *Abendzeitung München*, 2.7.1993, S. 15; Wolfgang Jean Stock, »Abbruch statt Aufbau. Sparzwang in der TU: Die Architekturausbildung verliert den internationalen Anschluß«, in: *Süddeutsche Zeitung*, 16.7.1993.

115 Zur Planungsgeschichte der Pinakothek der Moderne, siehe u. a. Staatliches Hochbauamt München, *Pinakothek der Moderne*, München 2002.

116 Die offizielle Eröffnung fand am Freitag und Samstag, den 13./14.9.2002 statt, für die Besucher war das Haus ab Montag, den 16.9.2002 geöffnet.

117 Siehe u. a. Gottfried Knapp, »Trauriges aus der Druckkulisse, Münchens dritte Pinakothek: Wie Politik und Behörden jahrelang dem Projekt zugesetzt haben, dessen sie sich jetzt rühmen«, in: *Süddeutsche Zeitung*, 14./15.9.2002, S. 13; Robert Huber, »München steht Schlange. Der erste Tag: Schon 35 000 Besucher waren in der Pinakothek der Moderne – gratis«, in: *Abendzeitung München*, 18.9.2002, S. 23; Tanja Rest, »Die Pinakothek der Moderne: Der erste Tag fürs Volk – Tausende

96 See, among other sources, Winfried Nerdinger, "Das Architekturmuseum der Technischen Universität München," in Stiftung Pinakothek der Moderne and Detlev von der Burg, eds., *Pinakothek der Moderne: Eine Vision* (Munich, 1995), pp. 18–19.

97 See, among other sources, "Corbusier-Museum: Eckige Schnecke," *Der Spiegel* 12 (1962), pp. 86, 89–90.; *Musee labyrinthe, Bulletin: Internationales Kunstzentrum e.V. Erlenbach am Main* (Erlenbach, 1963).

98 See note 82; see, among other sources, Walter Voss et al. and the Architektursammlung der TU München, *Umbau und Erweiterung der Gabelsbergerstraße 49. Studienarbeiten am Lehrstuhl für Entwerfen, Raumgestaltung und Sakralbau, TU München, 1-semestriger Entwurf im Sommersemester 1982, Ausstellung im Lesesaal der Architektursammlung [. . .] vom 28. Juni bis 8. Juli 1983* (Munich, 1983).

99 See, among other sources, Nerdinger 1995 (see note 83).

100 Martin Pabst, "Von der Überlastbewältigung zum wettbewerbsfähigen Wissenschaftsunternehmen," in Herrmann 2006 (see note 52), pp. 601–810, see p. 637; "Zwei Universitäten—ein Bauplatz," *TUM-Mitteilungen* 6 (1987), p. 8. On the competition, see "Münchens jüngster Universitätsbau: Wettbewerb um die Bebauung des Roncalli-Platzes," *Baumeister* 12 (1987), p. 9; "Realisierungswettbewerb Bebauung des Geländes der ehemaligen Türkenkaserne in München," *Wettbewerbe aktuell* 12 (1987), pp. 697–710, see pp. 697–99.

101 See, among other sources, "'Tiefer rein': Winfried Nerdinger, 49, Direktor des Architekturmuseums in München, über bayerischen Kultur-Abbruch," *Der Spiegel* 30 (1993), p. 138; http://www.emeriti-of-excellence.tum.de/index.php?id=71 (last accessed January 14, 2014).

102 See note 82.

103 AM-TUM, archive material: move, Augustenstrasse, Angerer-Atelier, 1994.

104 See, among other sources, *Der Spiegel* 1993 (see note 101); "Eine einzige Peinlichkeit": Die Sammlung soll in der Pinakothek der Moderne gezeigt werden, doch bis jetzt fehlen dafür alle Voraussetzungen. Michael Grill, "Interview mit Winfried Nerdinger, dem Direktor des Architekturmuseums der Technischen Universität," *Münchner Merkur* (July 4, 2000), L1.

105 See Ernst Berschet et al., *Thomas Wechs 1893–1970: Architekt der Moderne in Schwaben*, eds. Ernst Berschet et al. (Berlin, 2005), p. 7.

106 The foundation has comprehensively financed the museum since 1995. It provided the Buchegger Villa, which had been renovated at great cost, as well as two larger depots. It covers the costs of the exhibitions, events, and staff (initially a half-time research position, now two), and it also supports research projects and publications. See *Zehn Jahre Architekturmuseum Schwaben 1995–2005*, no. 25 (Augsburg, 2005); see also Winfried Nerdinger, "Architekturmuseum der Technischen Universität München: Architekturmuseum Schwaben Augsburg," in *Jahreskatalog 1995: Architekturfakultät, Technische Universität München* (Munich, 1996), pp. 42–45. Additional exhibition spaces and rooms for the archive were intended to be provided by a new building, for which a competition was held in 1995 but which was never built.

107 Architekturmuseum Schwaben, *Peter Zumthor: Stabwerk*, vol. 1 (1996); exhibition May 24–July 28, 1996.

108 See, among other sources, ub [Ursula Baus], "Architekturmuseum Schwaben," *db, deutsche bauzeitung* 1 (1995), p. 34; see also the museum website: http://www.architekturmuseum.de/index.php?id=129 (last accessed January 14, 2014); the staff members of the museum from 1975–2012 are named in Winfried Nerdinger, ed., *Architektur ausstellen / Exhibiting Architecture: Architekturmuseum der TU München 2007–2012* (Munich, 2012), p. 165.

109 See Berschet et al. 2005 (see note 105).

110 See http://www.thomaswechspreis.de (last accessed January 14, 2014).

111 Gerhard Matzig, "Die Bau-Geschichte von Zimmer 2327: Das Münchner Architekturmuseum soll in die Pinakothek der Moderne," *Süddeutsche Zeitung*, July 12, 1995, p. 13.

112 The image of the museum was conceived by graphic designer Hagen Nerdinger.

113 On the competition, see "Realisierungswettbewerb Museumsbauten auf dem Gelände der ehemaligen Türkenkaserne in München," *Wettbewerbe aktuell* 7 (1992), pp. 27–44; on the completed building see, among other sources, "Wettbewerbe weiterverfolgt: Pinakothek der Moderne in München," *Wettbewerbe aktuell* 7 (2002), pp. 87–92; Düttmann 2002 (see note 5).

114 See, among other sources, Peter M. Bode, "Kunst-Kahlschlag in München: Stimmen des Protests gegen Stoiber wegen der Verzögerung des Neubaus der Staatsgalerie," *Abendzeitung München*, July 2, 1993, p. 15; Wolfgang Jean Stock, "Abbruch statt Aufbau. Sparzwang in der TU: Die Architekturausbildung verliert den internationalen Anschluss," *Süddeutsche Zeitung*, July 16, 1993.

115 On the history of the planning of the Pinakothek der Moderne, see, among other sources, Staatliches Hochbauamt München, *Pinakothek der Moderne* (Munich, 2002).

116 The official opening took place on Friday and Saturday, September 13 and 14, 2002. The building was open to the public as of Monday, September 16, 2002.

117 See, among other sources, Gottfried Knapp,

nutzen die Chance für einen Besuch. Ein Haus füllt sich mit Menschen. Am ersten Eröffnungstag Riesenansturm auf Münchens jüngstes Kunstmuseum – Die Besucher sind begeistert von der Atmosphäre«, in: *Süddeutsche Zeitung*, 18.9.2002, S. 51; Ulrike Knöfel, »Feierliches Labyrinth. In München wird der größte deutsche Museumsneubau der vergangenen Jahre, die Pinakothek der Moderne, eingeweiht – nach einer langen Geschichte von Pleiten, Pech und Pannen«, in: *Der Spiegel*, 37, 2002, S. 178 f.

118 In der Pinakothek der Moderne sind vier voneinander unabhängige Museen vereint, während die Bayerische Staatsgemäldesammlung, die Staatliche Graphische Sammlung und die Neue Sammlung – The International Design Museum Munich zu den staatlichen Museen des Freistaats Bayern gehören, ist das Architekturmuseum eine universitäre Einrichtung.

119 Über die Ausstellungen Nerdingers der vergangenen 35 Jahre informiert die Reihe »Architektur ausstellen«, siehe Winfried Nerdinger, Bd. 2, 2002–2007, München 2007, Bd. 1, 1977–2002, München 2011, Bd. 3, 2007–2012, München 2012. Die drei Bände dokumentieren nicht nur die Ausstellungstätigkeit, sondern sie zeigen auch die ganze Bandbreite des Themas Architektur ausstellen, wie lässt sich Architektur im Museum präsentieren, siehe auch Winfried Nerdinger, »Architektur im Museum«, in: *Bauen, Sammeln, Zeigen: Winfried Nerdinger, Christ & Gantenbein; Max Dudler, Architekturvorträge der ETH Zürich*, hrsg. v. Departement Architektur der ETH Zürich, Andreas Tönnesmann, 6, Zürich 2008, S. 8–47.

120 Winfried Nerdinger Rede zur Eröffnung der Ausstellung *Der Architekt*, 26.9.2013, unveröffentlichtes Manuskript, Kopie am Architekturmuseum.

121 »›Das Museums als Wissensspeicher‹. Interview Wolfgang Jean Stock mit Winfried Nerdinger«, in: Stiftung Pinakothek der Moderne, *Rotunde*, 1, 2007, S. 8 f.

122 U. a. *Gottfried Semper 1803–1879. Architektur und Wissenschaft*, Zürich und München 2003; *Frei Otto. Leicht Bauen, natürlich gestalten*, Basel 2005; *Ort und Erinnerung. Nationalsozialismus in München*, München 2006; *Architektur wie sie im Buche steht. Fiktive Bauten und Städte in der Literatur*, Salzburg 2007; *100 Jahre Deutscher Werkbund 1907–2007*, München 2007; *Geschichte der Rekonstruktion. Konstruktion der Geschichte*, München 2010; *Der Architekt. Geschichte und Gegenwart eines Berufsstandes*, München 2012.

123 Hanskarl von Neubeck, »Wie stellt man Architektur im Museum aus? Winfried Nerdinger weiß es«, in: *Schwäbisches Tagblatt*, 25.9.2012.

124 Siehe u. a. Wolfgang Jean Stock, »Hinter den Fassaden. Die Pinakothek der Moderne in München glänzt auch durch das Architekturmuseum – doch dessen Etat ist ungesichert«, in: *Süddeutsche Zeitung*, 30.11./1.12.2002; Winfried Nerdinger (Hrsg.), *Exemplarisch – Konstruktion und Raum in der Architektur des 20. Jahrhunderts. Beispiele aus der Sammlung des Architekturmuseums der Technischen Universität München*, München u. a. 2002.

125 »Hitlers Architekten: Troost, Speer, Fick und Giesler. Historisch-kritische Studien zur Regimearchitektur des Dritten Reiches«: Das seit 2007 von der DFG geförderte Projekt wird von Prof. Dr.-Ing. Winfried Nerdinger / TU München und Prof. Dr. phil. Raphael Rosenberg / Universität Wien durchgeführt, online unter http://kunstgeschichte.univie.ac.at/forschungsprojekte/abgeschlossene-projekte/hitlers-architekten-troost-speer-fick-und-giesler/ (Stand: 14.1. 2014).

126 Nerdinger hatte Schneider-Esleben (1915–2005) auf seinem Gut Engelsberg im bayerischen Fischbachau über viele Jahre immer wieder besucht und dabei wertvolle Erkenntnisse zu seinem architektonischen Werk gewinnen können; derzeit wird vom Architekturmuseum eine Ausstellung und Publikation zum 100. Geburtstag des Architekten vorbereitet.

127 Siehe AM-TUM, schriftl. Unterlagen Architekten A-Z.

128 Online unter http://mediatum.ub.tum. de/?id=647610 (Stand: 14.1.2014).

129 Dissertationen, siehe S. 98, 100.

130 »Vergötterter Gestalter, Anmoderation Ernst Grandits nach Werner Oechslins Laudatio zum 65. Geburtstag von Winfried Nerdinger, am 25.9.2009«, in: *Kulturzeit extra, Sehnsucht Stadt – wie wollen wir leben?*, 14.11.2012.

"Trauriges aus der Druckkulisse, Münchens dritte Pinakothek: Wie Politik und Behörden jahrelang dem Projekt zugesetzt haben, dessen sie sich jetzt rühmen," *Süddeutsche Zeitung*, September 14–15, 2002, p.13.; Robert Huber, "München steht Schlange: Der erste Tag; Schon 35 000 Besucher waren in der Pinakothek der Moderne—gratis," *Abendzeitung München*, September 18, 2002, p. 23; Tanja Rest, "Die Pinakothek der Moderne: Der erste Tag fürs Volk—Tausende nutzen die Chance für einen Besuch; Ein Haus füllt sich mit Menschen; Am ersten Eröffnungstag Riesenansturm auf Münchens jüngstes Kunstmuseum—Die Besucher sind begeistert von der Atmosphäre," *Süddeutsche Zeitung*, September 18, 2002, p. 51; Ulrike Knöfel, "Feierliches Labyrinth: In München wird der größte deutsche Museumsneubau der vergangenen Jahre, die Pinakothek der Moderne, eingeweiht—nach einer langen Geschichte von Pleiten, Pech und Pannen," *Der Spiegel* 37 (2002), pp. 178–79.

118 Four independent museums have been brought together in the Pinakothek der Moderne. Whereas the Bayerische Staatsgemäldesammlung, the Staatliche Graphische Sammlung, and the Neue Sammlung—The International Design Museum Munich belong to the state museums of Bavaria, the Architekturmuseum is a university institution.

119 For information on the exhibitions organized by Nerdinger over the past thirty-five years, see the publication series "Architektur ausstellen," see Winfried Nerdinger, vol. 2, 2002–07 (Munich, 2007), vol. 1, 1977–2002 (Munich, 2011), vol. 3, 2007–12 (Munich, 2012). The three volumes not only document his exhibitions but also reflect the full spectrum of topics relevant to architecture, and they demonstrate how architecture can be presented in a museum context. See also Winfried Nerdinger, "Architektur im Museum," in Departement Architektur der ETH Zürich and Andreas Tönnesmann, eds., *Bauen, Sammeln, Zeigen: Winfried Nerdinger, Christ & Gantenbein; Max Dudler, Architekturvorträge der ETH Zürich*, no. 6 (Zurich, 2008), pp. 8–47.

120 Winfried Nerdinger's speech at the opening of the exhibition *Der Architekt* on September 26, 2013, copy of an unpublished manuscript in the collection of the Architekturmuseum.

121 Stiftung Pinakothek der Moderne, ed., "'Das Museum als Wissensspeicher'. Interview Wolfgang Jean Stock mit Winfried Nerdinger," *Rotunde*, vol. 1, (2007), pp. 8–9.

122 Among other sources, *Gottfried Semper 1803–1879: Architektur und Wissenschaft* (Zurich and Munich, 2003); *Frei Otto: Leicht Bauen, natürlich gestalten* (Basel, 2005); *Ort und Erinnerung: Nationalsozialismus in München* (Munich, 2006); *Architektur wie sie im Buche steht: Fiktive Bauten und Städte in der Literatur* (Salzburg, 2007); *100 Jahre Deutscher Werkbund 1907–2007* (Munich, 2007); *Geschichte der Rekonstruktion. Konstruktion der Geschichte* (Munich, 2010); *Der Architekt: Geschichte und Gegenwart eines Berufsstandes* (Munich, 2012).

123 Hanskarl von Neubeck, "Wie stellt man Architektur im Museum aus? Winfried Nerdinger weiß es," *Schwäbisches Tagblatt*, September 25, 2012.

124 See, among other sources, Wolfgang Jean Stock, "Hinter den Fassaden: Die Pinakothek der Moderne in München glänzt auch durch das Architekturmuseum—doch dessen Etat ist ungesichert," *Süddeutsche Zeitung*, November 30–December 1, 2002; Winfried Nerdinger, ed., *Exemplarisch—Konstruktion und Raum in der Architektur des 20. Jahrhunderts: Beispiele aus der Sammlung des Architekturmuseums der Technischen Universität München* (Munich et al., 2002).

125 "Hitlers Architekten: Troost, Speer, Fick und Giesler: Historisch-kritische Studien zur Regimearchitektur des Dritten Reiches." Funded by the DFG since 2007, the project is being conducted by Prof. Dr.-Ing. Winfried Nerdinger / TU München and Prof. Dr. phil. Raphael Rosenberg / University of Vienna, see http://kunstgeschichte.univie.ac.at/forschungsprojekte/abgeschlossene-projekte/hitlers-architekten-troost-speer-fick-und-giesler/ (last accessed January 14, 2014).

126 Nerdinger repeatedly visited Schneider-Esleben (1915–2005) at his Engelsberg estate in the Bavarian town of Fischbachau over the course of many years and was able to thus gain valuable insights into his body of work; the Architekturmuseum is currently planning an exhibition and publication to commemorate the one hundredth birthday of the architect.

127 See AM-TUM, archive material Architekten A-Z.

128 See http://mediatum.ub.tum.de/?id=647610 (last accessed January 14, 2014).

129 Dissertations, see p. 99, 101.

130 "Vergötterter Gestalter, Anmoderation Ernst Grandits nach Werner Oechslins Laudatio zum 65. Geburtstag von Winfried Nerdinger, am 25.9.2009," in *Kulturzeit extra, Sehnsucht Stadt—wie wollen wir leben?* (November 14, 2012).

DIE ARCHITEKTURSAMMLUNG DES MUSEUM OF MODERN ART

Architekturausstellungen waren durchaus nichts Neues, als der 27-jährige Kunsthistoriker Alfred H. Barr, Jr. den Trustees des geplanten Museum of Modern Art 1929 vorschlug, das neue Museum nicht wie andere amerikanische Kunstmuseen zu organisieren, sondern sich vielmehr von den Aktivitäten des fortschrittlichen Bauhaus inspirieren zu lassen. Doch bis zu diesem Zeitpunkt unterstanden die meisten Architekturmuseen entweder einer Architekturhochschule oder einem Berufsverband wie dem Royal Institute of British Architects (RIBA) oder sie dienten als Freilichtmuseen – wie das Skansen-Museum in Stockholm – der Darstellung der nationalen Bautradition. Derartige Beispiele schwebten vermutlich auch der Familie Rockefeller vor, als sie Ende der 1920er-Jahre unter dem Namen Colonial Williamsburg große Teile der Stadt Williamsburg in Virginia restaurieren ließ. Die zu dieser Zeit an dem ebenfalls von der Familie Rockefeller finanzierten Museum of Modern Art (MoMA) in New York geführte Diskussion über ein geeignetes Konzept für die Präsentation von Architektur blieb von diesem Engagement allerdings völlig unberührt.[1]

Die von Barr vorgeschlagene Architekturabteilung sollte die erste ihrer Art im Rahmen eines Kunstmuseums sein, vielleicht mit Ausnahme des kurzlebigen Architekturmuseums, das Mitte des 19. Jahrhunderts im Londoner South Kensington Museum beheimatet war, dem heutigen Victoria and Albert Museum. Gleichzeitig war es Barrs erklärtes Ziel, das Kunstschaffen der Gegenwart und der jüngeren Vergangenheit gleichermaßen respektvoll und sorgfältig zu präsentieren und zu erforschen, wie es das Metropolitan Museum und das Brooklyn Museum mit den Alten Meistern zu tun pflegten. Nach Barrs Vorstellung sollten im MoMA mit Abteilungen für Fotografie, Film, Industriedesign und Architektur auch diejenigen Disziplinen vertreten sein, die in einem Kunstmuseum traditionell nicht vorgesehen waren. Diese Abteilungen sollten ihre Arbeiten genauso sammeln und ausstellen wie bisher jene für Gemälde, Skulpturen, Zeichnungen und druckgrafische Werke. Als das Museum 1929 in einer vorläufigen Unterkunft eröffnete, gab

COLLECTING AND EXHIBITING ARCHITECTURE AT THE MUSEUM OF MODERN ART

BARRY BERGDOLL

Architecture exhibitions were anything but a novelty in 1929, when the twenty-seven-year-old art historian Alfred H. Barr, Jr. proposed to the trustees of the Museum of Modern Art (MoMA), then in formation, that the museum should be structured not on the organizational plans of other American art museums but rather on the types of activities practiced in the avant-garde Bauhaus. But museums and galleries of architecture were largely, up until that point, either associated with the professional training of architects—in schools or associations like the Royal Institute of British Architects (RIBA)—or took the form of national collections meant to save vernacular architecture as national heritage in outdoor museums: the Skansen museum in Stockholm is a key example. These were models that the Rockefeller family would emulate in the creation of Colonial Williamsburg, Virginia, in the late nineteen-twenties, even as the discussion on what a museum department of architecture might be was underway at that other focus of the family's patronage of the arts, the new Museum of Modern Art in New York City.[1]

The Department of Architecture that Barr proposed would have been the first devoted to architecture within the walls of an art museum—with the possible exception of the short-lived architecture museum inside London's South Kensington Museum (now the Victoria and Albert Museum) in the mid-nineteenth century—and with the set mission, moreover, of establishing the art of the moment and the recent past as worthy of the same esteem, attention, and scholarly study as that of the old masters honored locally in the galleries of the Metropolitan and Brooklyn museums. Barr proposed a departmental plan for MoMA, which he hoped would take on a whole range of arts not traditionally within the purview of an art museum—photography, film, industrial art, and architecture—and develop strategies for collecting and exhibiting them, which could rival the traditional departments of painting and sculpture, drawings, and prints. None of these departments, in which arts tinged with commerce and industry or even serial replication mixed with artistic expression, was created when the museum opened its door in temporary

es jedoch noch keine einzige der geplanten Abteilungen, in denen sich die Kunst mit dem Handel und der Industrie verbinden und sogar Massenprodukte gezeigt werden sollten. Die Trustees waren vielmehr daran interessiert, das amerikanische Publikum mit der Malerei seit dem Impressionismus und mit der Bildhauerei seit Auguste Rodin bekannt zu machen. Barr ließ sich davon jedoch nicht beirren. Kaum ein Jahr nach der Eröffnung des Museum of Modern Art beauftragte er zwei junge Männer, die sich besonders gut mit der europäischen Avantgardearchitektur auskannten: Der Kunsthistoriker Henry-Russell Hitchcock und der Ästhet Philip Johnson sollten eine Ausstellung entwickeln, welche die Bereitschaft des amerikanischen Publikums testen sollte, sich die Entwürfe, Skizzen und Pläne bedeutender Architekten im Museum anzusehen. Diese Testausstellung sollte die Entwicklung der europäischen Architektur der vergangenen 10 Jahre beleuchten, mit der sich Hitchcock bereits in seinem ehrgeizigen Buchprojekt *Modern Architecture. Romanticism and Reintegration* (1929) intensiv auseinandergesetzt hatte. Sie trug den Titel *Modern Architecture. International Exhibition* und war vom 10. Februar bis zum 23. März 1932 in New York zu sehen, bevor sie durch mehrere US-Städte tourte und zuletzt in Bullock's Wilshire Department Store in Los Angeles Station machte. Die Ausstellung war so erfolgreich und beeinflusste so unmittelbar den Diskurs, der jetzt plötzlich in dem von der Depression gebeutelten Amerika über Fragen des architektonischen Stils und der Moderne entbrannte, dass die MoMA-Trustees noch vor Ende des Jahres dafür stimmten, eine eigene Architekturabteilung einzurichten: das Department of Architecture. Mit der Leitung betrauten sie den erst 26 Jahre alten Philip Johnson.[2]

Das Ausstellungskonzept der ersten Architekturausstellung des MoMA ging von der Annahme aus, dass die üblichen Entwurfs- und Planzeichnungen ohnehin nur einem Fachpublikum verständlich seien, das sich etwa bei den Jahresausstellungen der New Yorker Architectural League versammelte. Deshalb waren in dieser Ausstellung, die auch unter dem Titel »International Style« große Bekanntheit erreichte, vornehmlich Fotografien und Modelle zu sehen. Bei dieser prägnanten Bezeichnung der Ausstellung handelt es sich eigentlich um den Titel des von Hitchcock und Johnson herausgegebenen Begleitbuchs, der schließlich einer ganzen Stilrichtung ihren bis heute gebräuchlichen Namen gab. Die Schau etablierte zugleich einen Standard, der sich mithilfe der museumseigenen Abteilung für Wanderausstellungen leicht auf Tour schicken ließ. Tatsächlich oblag es dieser

quarters in 1929; the trustees were focusing their attention on educating the American public in appreciating developments in painting and sculpture since the Impressionists and since Auguste Rodin. But Barr was not dissuaded. Within a year of the opening of the new MoMA, he invited two young enthusiasts for European avant-garde architecture, the art historian Henry-Russell Hitchcock and the aesthete Philip Johnson, to research and stage an exhibition that would test the receptiveness of the public to architecture exhibited in a museum. The test exhibition would highlight developments in European architecture within the last ten years, which Hitchcock had sought to document and categorize in an ambitious 1929 book, *Modern Architecture: Romanticism and Reintegration.* The resulting exhibition, *Modern Architecture: International Exhibition,* held between February 10 and March 23, 1932, before traveling throughout the country, ending its tour at Bullock's Wilshire department store in Los Angeles, was so successful, and had such an immediate impact on the discussion of architectural style and modernism in depression-era America, that the trustees voted to establish a Department of Architecture under the direction of the twenty-six-year-old Philip Johnson by the end of the year.[2]

With its emphasis on photographs and models, as well as on the assumption that architectural drawings were comprehensible only to a professional audience who gathered together in such settings as the Architectural League of New York's annual exhibitions, MoMA's first architectural exhibition—remembered as the "International Style" show for the term it helped coin and for the highly influential book that Hitchcock and Johnson published that year—established an agenda for exhibitions that could be widely circulated with the help of the museum's Department of Circulating Exhibitions, a division whose mission was to create easy-to-install exhibitions (largely on panels and very didactic) that could be sent to smaller museums and even to schools around the country. Not only were the photographic reproductions that comprised the show—mostly panels all at the same height to create a clean horizon for hanging—robust enough to travel and subject to easy reconfiguration for different types of spaces from museums to universities to event-holding department stores, but the goal of Johnson and Hitchcock to change American taste in architecture made it a natural ally of the museum's missionary branch. Hitchcock, advising Johnson, hoped the Department of Architecture might devote itself to a program that would alternate shows on contemporary designers, approved as models for current and future practice,

Classrooms
Workshops

AUSSTELLUNGSANSICHT
MODERN ARCHITECTURE.
INTERNATIONAL EXHIBITION,
THE MUSEUM OF MODERN ART,
NEW YORK, 1932

INSTALLATION VIEW,
MODERN ARCHITECTURE.
INTERNATIONAL EXHIBITION,
THE MUSEUM OF MODERN ART,
NEW YORK, 1932

AUSSTELLUNGSANSICHT
MODERN ARCHITECTURE.
INTERNATIONAL EXHIBITION,
THE MUSEUM OF MODERN ART,
NEW YORK, 1932

INSTALLATION VIEW,
MODERN ARCHITECTURE.
INTERNATIONAL EXHIBITION,
THE MUSEUM OF MODERN ART,
NEW YORK, 1932

Abteilung, auf der Basis von Schautafeln und in einem dezidiert didakti-schen Stil leicht installierbare Ausstellungen zu entwickeln, die man an kleinere Museen und sogar an Universitäten im ganzen Land verschicken konnte. Die Fotoreproduktionen, aus denen das Anschauungsmaterial im Wesentlichen bestand – meist gleich große Schautafeln, die sich an der Wand in geschlossenen Reihen hängen ließen –, waren robust genug, um sie auf Reisen zu schicken. Außerdem ließen sie sich je nach Ausstellungsraum – ob Museum, Universität oder Kaufhaus – immer wieder neu arrangie-ren. Doch damit nicht genug: Da Johnson und Hitchcock den Architek-turgeschmack des amerikanischen Publikums verändern wollten, hatte die Abteilung auch die Funktion, die »missionarischen Aktivitäten« des Museums zu unterstützen. Hitchcock, der als Johnsons Berater fun-gierte, hoffte, dass sich die Ausstellungen des Architekturabteilung nicht nur den Beispielen zeitgenössischer Architekten widmen würde, die als Vorbilder für die derzeitige und zukünftige Praxis dienten, sondern im Wechsel auch immer wieder den für die Moderne grundlegenden archi-tektonischen Leistungen der vergangenen 150 Jahre. Allerdings fiel der historische Aspekt dieses Konzepts, der etwa in einer Ausstellung über die Chicagoer Schule im späten 19. Jahrhundert vorgestellt wurde, schon bald dem missionarischen Impuls zum Opfer.[3] Doch das lag durchaus nicht allein daran, dass Johnson und Hitchcock unbedingt neue Stil-vorstellungen für die Moderne durchsetzen wollten. Vielmehr gab es da noch die – häufig übersehene – junge Catherine Bauer, die im Kreis der damaligen amerikanischen Wohnungsbautheoretiker und -reformer eine führende Rolle spielte und in den ersten 10 Jahren nach Gründung des MoMA im Department of Architecture als Beraterin tätig war. Bauer ver-folgte eine Politik, die in deutlichem Gegensatz zu Johnsons Bemühen stand, die Architektur und den Städtebau um jeden Preis vor staatlicher Bevormundung zu schützen, während er sich selbst gleichzeitig politisch immer weiter nach rechts orientierte. Die Presse war dagegen von Bauers Konzept sehr angetan. So erschien zum Beispiel 1938 – als das Museum gerade im Begriff stand, in dem von Philip R. Goodwin und Edward Durell Stone entworfenen Gebäude in der 53. Straße die ersten eigenen Ausstellungsräume zu beziehen – im Magazin *Fortune* ein Bericht über das Department. Darin hieß es, dass es der MoMA-Abteilung gelungen sei, »ein durch und durch unprätentiöses und lebendiges Ausstellungs-konzept zu entwickeln. Diese Vorgehensweise erlaubt es, die Dinge so zu

with shows that would gradually define the contours of the last century-and-a-half of architecture leading up to the modern movement. But the historical side of this agenda, pursued in a show on the Chicago School in the late nineteenth century, for instance, was soon abandoned in favor of the missionary agenda.[3] This was not confined to Johnson and Hitchcock's determination to create a new stylistic idiom for modernity. It is too often forgotten that in the first decade of the department, the young Catherine Bauer, one of the leading housing reformers and theorists in America, served as curator in the Department of Architecture, pursuing an engaged agenda quite at odds with Johnson's studied avoidance of linking architecture to government, even as he himself became more and more engaged in right-wing politics. The press responded particularly favorably, *Fortune* magazine writing in 1938—as the museum was preparing to open its first galleries in a building designed by Philip R. Goodwin and Edward Durell Stone on Fifty-Third Street in 1939—that the Department of Architecture had "perfected an informal and dramatic technique for exhibiting and explaining things in a way that makes people want to look at them, an example being a housing exhibition in 1934 in which actual rooms, even to the cockroaches, of an old-law New York tenement house were set up for comparison with a low-priced modern interior."[4] That exhibition actually yielded changes in the city's housing laws and policies. Housing indeed would remain a theme for years to come, with Bauer's *Architecture in Government Housing* (1936), and, more recently, Terence Riley's *The Un-Private House* (1999) as well as my own *Foreclosed: Rehousing the American Dream* (2012 with Reinhold Martin).

Some of the most well-known of these were the series of model houses built in the museum's sculpture garden.[5] Even as early as 1940, Frank Lloyd Wright had hoped to include a full-scale Usonian House—his new concept of an easy-to-build house for the everyman—in the garden as the culmination of his retrospective exhibition *Frank Lloyd Wright: American Architect,* which was held on the museum's ground floor galleries overlooking the new sculpture garden. But both exhibition catalogue and 1:1 scale house—meant to counter the traditional taste of the latest version of model houses, such as those on view at New York's 1939–40 World's Fair—were ultimately cancelled as planning slipped behind schedule and funding fell short.[6] In 1941, Buckminster Fuller was able to show off his ideals with a Dymaxion Deployment Unit, a prefabricated cylindrical structure adapted from a grain storage unit to a living space, with furnishings borrowed from Bloomingdale's. But the most

zeigen und zu erklären, dass die Leute sie auch tatsächlich sehen wollen. Ein gutes Beispiel ist etwa die Wohnungsbauausstellung von 1934, in der Originalzimmer – inklusive Kakerlaken – aus einem alten Mietshaus mit einer preiswerten zeitgenössischen Wohnungseinrichtung verglichen wurden.«[4] Diese Ausstellung hatte tatsächlich bewirkt, dass die Wohnungsbaupolitik und die Bauvorschriften der Stadt New York modifiziert wurden. Der Wohnungsbau spielte aber auch in späteren Jahren weiter eine Rolle, etwa in Catherine Bauers *Architecture in Government Housing* (1936) sowie in jüngerer Zeit in Terence Rileys *The Un-Private House* (1999) und in meiner eigenen (gemeinsam mit Reinhold Martin konzipierten) Ausstellung *Foreclosed. Rehousing the American Dream* (2012).

Zu den wohl bekanntesten Exponaten gehören in diesem Zusammenhang die Modellhäuser, die im Laufe der Zeit im Skulpturengarten des Museums entstanden.[5] Bereits 1940 hatte Frank Lloyd Wright für seine Retrospektive *Frank Lloyd Wright. American Architect,* die 1940 im Erdgeschoss des Museums – mit Blick auf den neuen Skulpturengarten – stattfand, ein komplettes Usonian House geplant. Es sollte der Höhepunkt seiner Schau werden und sein neues Konzept eines einfachen Hauses im Selbstbauverfahren präsentieren. Doch letztendlich kamen aus finanziellen Gründen, aber auch aus Zeitnot, weder der Ausstellungskatalog noch das in Originalgröße geplante Modell zustande, das in der Retrospektive eigentlich als Alternative zu den traditionellen Modellhäusern gedacht war, die fast gleichzeitig auf der New Yorker Weltausstellung (1939/40) zu sehen waren.[6] 1941 konnte Richard Buckminster Fuller dann seine Dymaxion Deployment Unit zeigen, eine ursprünglich als Getreidespeicher konzipierte zylindrische Konstruktion, die er in einen Wohncontainer umgestaltet und mit Möbeln von Bloomingdale's ausgestattet hatte. In der Nachkriegszeit erregten dann vor allem die Modelle suburbaner Häuser Aufmerksamkeit, die sich als Alternative zu den Häusern präsentierten, die in Massenproduktion für Levittown gebaut oder als Fertighaus von der Lustron Corporation damals in großen Stückzahlen auf den Markt gebracht wurden und die in den späten 1940er-Jahren auf reges Interesse stießen. Marcel Breuers *House in the Garden* (1949) gehörte in USA zu den populärsten Architekturausstellungen der Jahrhundertmitte. Sie zog Tausende von Besuchern an und bot auch ein Forum für jene Haushaltseinrichtungen und -geräte, die das MoMA jetzt unter der Leitung von Edgar Kaufmann, Jr. regelmäßig in seinen *Good-Design*-Ausstellungen der Abteilung für Industriedesign zeigte.

famous examples were models for postwar suburban living, which research has now shown were meant to counter the appeal of such mass-produced houses as those of Levittown and the prefabricated Lustron Houses that were gaining attention in the late nineteen-forties. Marcel Breuer's *House in the Garden* (1949) was one of the most popular architectural exhibitions mounted in mid-century America. Visited by thousands, it served as the most convincing showplace for the types of furnishings and household appliances the MoMA was now regularly endorsing through the Good Design exhibitions staged by Edgar Kaufmann, Jr. in the Department of Industrial Design, which merged with Architecture in 1949 to become today's Department of Architecture and Design.[7] It was followed in 1950 by a one-story house designed by Los Angeles architect Gregory Ain, bringing the new California style of living with nature to the East Coast. Ironically enough, the *House in the Garden* series reached a crescendo of popularity not with modern building but with the unexpected decision of the museum's newly appointed director of archi-

FRANK LLOYD WRIGHT, FALLINGWATER,
EDGAR KAUFMANN HOUSE,
BEAR RUN, PENNSYLVANIA, 1935–1937,
MODELL, 1984

FRANK LLOYD WRIGHT, FALLINGWATER,
EDGAR KAUFMANN HOUSE,
BEAR RUN, PENNSYLVANIA, 1935–37,
MODEL, 1984

Diese Abteilung verschmolz 1949 mit derjenigen für Architektur, seither bilden sie gemeinsam das Department of Architecture and Design.[7] Schon 1950 folgte dann ein von dem Architekten Gregory Ain aus Los Angeles entworfenes einstöckiges Haus, das den naturnahen neuen Wohn- und Lebensstil aus Kalifornien an der Ostküste bekannt machte. Den größten Anklang fanden jedoch nicht etwa die im Rahmen der *House-in-the-Garden*-Reihe gezeigten Exponate der Moderne, sondern ein japanisches Bauwerk, das Arthur Drexler als neuer Leiter der Architekturabteilung 1953 in einer Ausstellung vorstellte. Drexler, der eine Vorliebe für japanische Architektur hatte, beauftragte Junzõ Yoshimura mit dem maßstabsgetreuen Nachbau eines authentischen japanischen Tempels aus dem 17. Jahrhundert, der schon bald allgemein als japanisches Haus bezeichnet wurde. 1955 wurde er in den Fairmount Park in Philadelphia überführt und ist noch heute beliebt.

In den Nachkriegsjahren blieben die Architekturausstellungen des MoMA vielseitig und experimentell in ihren Annäherungen an die Frage, wie Architektur innerhalb der Galerieräume präsentiert werden kann. Aber das Inszenieren von Ausstellungen hatte Vorrang vor dem Aufbau einer Sammlung, die etwa mit den Abteilungen für Malerei, Skulptur, Druckgrafik, Buchillustration oder auch der fortschrittlichen Filmabteilung konkurrieren kann. Die *House-in-the-Garden*-Ausstellungen umgingen die Frage nach dem Daseinszweck einer solchen Sammlung von vornherein, indem die Exponate im Maßstab 1:1 im Freien aufgebaut und am Ende entfernt oder zerstört wurden. Das gilt sogar noch für die von mir kuratierte Ausstellung *Home Delivery. Fabricating the Modern Dwelling* (2008), die sich mit den Techniken und Herausforderungen der heutigen Fertigbauweise auseinandersetzte. Auch nach dieser Schau wurden die Exponate abtransportiert. Andere Ausstellungen machten dagegen die Ausstellungseinrichtung selbst zu Architektur. Beispielsweise die erste monografische Schau, die sich 1947 Ludwig Mies van der Rohe widmete. Philip Johnson war bereits seit der »International-Style«-Ausstellung ein großer Bewunderer des Architekten, von dem auch seine eigenen Entwürfe etwa für das Glas House in New Canaan, Connecticut, und für die University of St. Thomas in Houston, Texas, unmittelbar beeinflusst waren. Während der Vorbesprechungen zeichnete Mies einen freien Grundriss, ein für ihn typischen Innenraum wie ihn aber seit der Zerstörung des Barcelona-Pavillons rund 20 Jahre zuvor kaum jemand mehr gesehen hatte.[8] Mit großformatigen

tecture, Arthur Drexler, in 1953, to act on his great enthusiasm for Japan by commissioning Junzō Yoshimura to design and orchestrate the shipping of a full-scale reproduction of a seventeenth-century temple, dubbed the Japanese House in the Garden, which is still popular in Philadelphia's Fairmount Park where it was moved in 1955.

Into the postwar years, architectural exhibitions at MoMA remained varied and experimental in their approach to the problem of exhibiting architecture in the spaces of the gallery. But staging events took precedence over any focus on forming a collection for posterity to rival those being pursued in the Departments of Painting and Sculpture and of Prints and Illustrated Books, or in the pioneering Film Library. While the *House in the Garden* series sidestepped the issue of what would constitute a collection of architecture by commissioning a full-scale demonstration architecture to be erected out of doors and demolished or moved with the conclusion of the display—an approach returned to in 2008 in my own exhibition examining the techniques and stakes of contemporary prefabrication, *Home Delivery: Fabricating the Modern Dwelling*—other exhibitions turned the installation itself into a new architecture. Such was notably the case in 1947 with the first monographic exhibition ever devoted to Ludwig Mies van der Rohe, an architect whom Philip Johnson had been championing since the so-called International Style show and whom he was soon to emulate quite literally in his own early architectural designs, such as the Glass House in New Canaan, Connecticut and the design of the University of St. Thomas in Houston, Texas. Mies designed the pinwheel plan of his exhibition, which was an interior of a sort few had experienced since the demolition of the Barcelona Pavilion nearly twenty years earlier.[8] With large-scale photographic reproductions, Mies explored a new exhibition technique pioneered by Herbert Bayer a decade earlier in Germany and in MoMA's own 1938 Bauhaus exhibition, but now conceived to simulate the experience of entering buildings otherwise inaccessible: for example, the Barcelona Pavilion or Villa Tugendhat, with its dramatic glazed curtain wall leading to its garden, a building available to few now that it was sequestered behind what Winston Churchill had dubbed in 1945 the "Iron Curtain," separating Brno in what was then Czechoslovakia from the West. No less inaccessible were Mies van der Rohe's own drawings, for they had been moved by his office assistants in Berlin to a farmhouse for safekeeping during the war, only to find, after the war, that the farmhouse now lay within the Soviet sector. Mies, there-

Fotoreproduktionen testete Mies eine innovative Ausstellungstechnik, wie sie Herbert Bayer 10 Jahre zuvor in Deutschland verwendet und auch bereits 1938 in der *Bauhaus*-Ausstellung des MoMA eingesetzt hatte. Die Besucher sollten über diese Großfotos die zu dieser Zeit nicht mehr zugänglichen Gebäude in ihrer Vorstellung betreten können. Also beispielsweise den Barcelona-Pavillon oder die Villa Tugendhat in Brünn mit ihren gläsernen Vorhangfassaden, wobei der Barcelona-Pavillon eben schon längst nicht mehr existierte und die Villa Tugendhat seit 1945 hinter dem – von Winston Churchill so bezeichneten – Eisernen Vorhang lag. Ebenso unerreichbar waren aber auch Mies van der Rohes Entwürfe und Zeichnungen. Seine Berliner Mitarbeiter hatten die Pläne im Krieg in einem Bauernhaus auf dem Land in Sicherheit gebracht, und die Gegend lag inzwischen in der sowjetischen Besatzungszone. Daher musste Mies seine erste Einzelausstellung ohne Zugriff auf seine Zeichnungen und Materialien gestalten. Erst in den 1960er-Jahren gelang es ihm mit Unterstützung des US-Außenministeriums, sein Archiv aus der DDR in die USA zu überführen, wo er seinen Nachlass dem Museum of Modern Art übergab.[9]

So gelangte fast das gesamte Archiv des Architekten (rund 19 000 Entwurfszeichnungen und Pläne, die gesamte Geschäftskorrespondenz sowie zahlreiche Fotografien) in den Besitz des MoMA, während die private Korrespondenz 1969 nach seinem Tod der Library of Congress in Washington, D. C. übereignet wurde. Tatsächlich trug dieser kostbare Besitz dazu bei, dass das Interesse an Entwurfszeichnungen und Bauplänen deutlich zunahm und sich die Ausrichtung und die Aktivitäten des Department of Architecture and Design radikal änderten. Es erreichte damit seine Reife als wissenschaftliche Sammlung. Als Le Corbusier dem MoMA 1932 handkolorierte Abzüge seines für die Cité international universitaire de Paris entworfenen Schweizer Pavillons zugeschickt hatte, ließ das Museum die Bilder noch einmal abfotografieren, damit sie besser zu den anderen Fotos in der betreffenden Ausstellung passten. Die Originale wurden eingelagert, da die Architekturabteilung vor allem damit beschäftigt war, sich um die Einrichtung einer »Phototeque« zu kümmern, auf welche die US-Massenmedien und -Fachpresse Zugriff hatten. Im Lager wurden die Le-Corbusier-Abzüge dann zusammen mit den Modellen der Villa Savoye und diversen Bauhaus-Materialien zu Studienzwecken verwahrt. Später sollten die Objekte den Anfang einer Sammlung markieren, die vor allem vormalige Exponate umfasste.

fore, would need to envision his first-ever solo exhibition without access to his own materials. By the nineteen-sixties, with the intervention of the US Department of State, Mies had finally been successful in having his office archive sent from the GDR to Chicago and had been persuaded to entrust it to the Museum of Modern Art. [9]

The arrival of the Mies van der Rohe archive—some 19,000 drawings, as well as Mies's office correspondence (the personal correspondence was left to the Library of Congress in Washington after Mies's death in 1969) and photographs—helped to catalyze a gathering interest in architectural drawings that would radically transform the mission and activities of the Department of Architecture and Design as it entered its maturity. In 1932, when Le Corbusier had sent hand-colored prints of his latest project, the Pavillon Suisse at the Cité universitaire, they had been re-photographed by MoMA to match those that dominated the installation. The originals were placed in storage, and the department focused on developing a *phototeque* for use by the country's mass and professional press. In storage, Le Corbusier's prints joined the models of the Villa Savoye and of the Bauhaus, which were kept as study material, only later to make up the beginnings of a collection largely formed by the residue of the architecture of installations. In 1947 this began to change, as the department formerly assigned acquisition numbers to the Le Corbusier prints along with an important composition by Theo van Doesburg, *Contra-Construction Project, Axonometric* (1923), the gift of design curator Edgar Kaufmann, Jr. While elsewhere archives filled with drawings of all sorts—sketches, technical drawings, and even travel sketches were principle activities of the museums of architecture that had been set up by professional organizations like the RIBA in London or, after the war, by national governments, such as museums of architecture in Finland and Sweden—MoMA turned only slowly toward this trend. Even then, the principle was established to seek the single salient work, the masterpiece of architectural drawing related to a project, one that could be displayed as a singular work of art, an assimilation of architecture with painting and sculpture. This confirmed a point of cross-influence long studied by Henry-Russell Hitchcock, notably in his seminal book *Painting Toward Architecture* of 1948, a theory he sought in particular to explore in relationship to developments in Latin American architecture, painting, and town and landscape painting, expressly in the highly colorful representations done by Roberto Burle Marx and by Oscar Niemeyer for

Das änderte sich erst, als die Le-Corbusier-Abzüge 1947 zusammen mit Theo van Doesburgs Komposition *Contra-Construction Project, Axonometric* (1923) inventarisiert wurden, einem Geschenk des Designkurators Edgar Kaufmann, Jr.

Andere Architekturarchive sammelten zu dieser Zeit bereits eifrig Bauzeichnungen: Entwurfsskizzen, Baupläne, ja sogar Reiseskizzen. Das galt in der Nachkriegszeit zum Beispiel für Einrichtungen wie das RIBA in London, aber auch für die staatlichen Architekturmuseen in Finnland und Schweden. Das MoMA dagegen machte sich diese Praxis erst relativ spät zu Eigen. Doch selbst dann galt das Prinzip, nach herausragenden Entwurfszeichnungen (tatsächlich realisierter Bauten) Ausschau zu halten, die auch als eigenständige Kunstwerke – als Verschmelzung von Architektur, Malerei und Skulptur – gelten konnten. Mit diesen Zusammenhängen beschäftigte sich auch Henry-Russell Hitchcock in seinem bedeutenden Buch *Painting Toward Architecture* (1948) und zwar vor allem im Hinblick auf die lateinamerikanische Architektur, auf Stadt- und Landschaftsarchitektur. Sein Hauptinteresse galt dabei den farbintensiven Entwurfszeichnungen, die Roberto Burle Marx und Oscar Niemeyer für Projekte wie den Ibirapuera-Park in Saõ Paulo oder das nicht gebaute Tremaine House im kalifornischen Santa Barbara angefertigt hatten. Die meisterhaften Zeichnungen, die die beiden Männer in diesem Zusammenhang angefertigt hatten, konnte das MoMA für seine Architektursammlung erwerben.[10]

Erst in den 1960er-Jahren setzte sich im MoMA allmählich eine neue Einstellung gegenüber der Architekturzeichnung durch. Den Anstoß gab vor allem Arthur Drexlers bahnbrechende Ausstellung *Visionary Architecture* (1960). Erst jetzt gab das MoMA die seit Hitchcock und Johnson kultivierte Bevorzugung gebauter gegenüber hypothetischer Architektur auf, da die Verantwortlichen endlich den Eigenwert visionärer Ideen und Entwürfe erkannten. In den 1930er-Jahren hatte das MoMA seine Aufgabe noch darin gesehen, das konservative amerikanische Publikum mit der modernen Architektur vertraut zu machen, die damals im Begriff stand, das Alltagsleben und das Erscheinungsbild der Städte in Europa nachhaltig zu verändern. Die andere Seite der modernen Architektur als einer Bewegung mit radikalen und unrealisierbaren Visionen wurde dabei unterdrückt. Doch inzwischen betrachtete die Öffentlichkeit die Sterilität des von großen Konzernen dominierten Städte- und Wohnungsbaus mit einer gewissen Beunruhigung. Deshalb schlug Drexler vor, dem Publikum ebenso die visionären

ROBERTO BURLE MARX UND OSCAR NIEMEYER, IBIRAPUERA-PARK, SÃO PAULO, PROJEKTSKIZZE, 1953

ROBERTO BURLE MARX AND OSCAR NIEMEYER, IBIRAPUERA PARK, SÃO PAULO, PROJECT SKETCH, 1953

projects like the Ibirapuera Park in São Paulo or the unbuilt project for the Tremaine House in Santa Barbara, California, which entered the collection in these years as master drawings.[10]

Attitudes toward drawing began to shift at MoMA in the nineteen-sixties, notably with the staging of Arthur Drexler's landmark *Visionary Architecture* exhibition (1960), the first time that MoMA, which had held doggedly to Hitchcock and Johnson's preference for built work over hypothetical proposals, focused on the capacity of drawings to project an architecture without precedent. In the nineteen-thirties the museum had been concerned to portray to conservative American tastes that modern architecture was a phenomenon that was changing daily life and cityscapes in Europe, rather than a radical movement of unrealizable visions. But now in the face of the increased sense of the sterility of postwar corporate architecture, Drexler proposed to celebrate not only new visionary proposals for whole cities and for megastructures, but also the prehistory of such thinking back to the work of Étienne-Louis Boullée, Claude Nicolas Ledoux, and their contemporaries in Enlightenment France. But even here the show was comprised primarily of photographic reproductions of famous proposals, despite the fact that in its

neuen Entwürfe für ganze Städte und Megastrukturen vorzustellen wie die historischen Vorläufer dieser Konzepte, also etwa Étienne-Louis Boullée, Claude Nicolas Ledoux und ihre Mitstreiter während der französischen Aufklärung. Obwohl in der Ausstellung selbst vor allem nur Fotoreproduktionen berühmter Entwürfe zu sehen waren, begann das Department of Architecture zu dieser Zeit allmählich auch mit dem Erwerb von Originalzeichnungen. Die Entstehung der Sammlung ging also mit der Zunahme des Interesses an der Architekturzeichnung der Architekten selbst einher, die sie als kritische Form oder auch als Medium zur Erforschung von Alternativen zu den Orthodoxien der Moderne erkannten und damit auch die repräsentative Kraft der Zeichnung bestätigten.

Als sich das Museum schließlich im öffentlichen Bewusstsein als Flaggschiff der Moderne etabliert hatte, setzte bereits die Postmoderne ein und das Interesse an der Zeichnung nahm wieder deutlich zu. Im Jahr 1966 brachte das MoMA Robert Venturis *Komplexität und Widerspruch in der Architektur* heraus. Dieses Buch veränderte grundlegend die Einstellung zur Geschichte und zur Quellenforschung als auch zum Bauen selbst als Ausdruck eines technokratischen Unterfangens. Im gleichen Jahr wurden Mies van der Rohes gerade erst erworbenen Zeichnungen erstmals öffentlich ausgestellt. In den 1970er-Jahren erreichte die Bewunderung für die Zeichnung dann einen neuen Höhepunkt und das nicht erst seit dem Erscheinen des Buches *Five Architects. Eisenman, Graves, Gwathmey, Hejduk, Meier,* welches die axonometrische Erkundung bislang beispielloser Formen in den Vordergrund rückte. Besonders wichtig wurden zwei Ausstellungen von 1975: In seiner ebenso zukunftsweisenden wie umstrittenen Ausstellung *The Architecture of the Ecole des Beaux-Arts* stellte Drexler studentische Entwurfszeichnungen aus dem 19. Jahrhundert vor, die er im Archiv der Pariser Hochschule entdeckt hatte. Die Schau ließ sich durchaus als Kritik an zahlreichen Aspekten der Architektur der Moderne verstehen, etwa an der Tendenz zur Vernachlässigung des Standorts, der räumlichen Abfolge und der städtebaulichen Komponente – ein Defizit, das Drexler auf die Vorliebe der zeitgenössischen Architektur für das Spanplattenmodell und die axonometrische Zeichnung zurückführte.[11]

Im Frühjahr desselben Jahres organisierten Emilio Ambasz und Barbara Jakobson in der Mitgliederlounge des MoMA eine Verkaufsausstellung von Architekturzeichnungen; sie markierte den Beginn einer rund 15 Jahre dauernden Periode, in der Architekturzeichnungen plötzlich Einzug in

aftermath the collecting of drawings by the Department of Architecture and Design slowly got underway. In this, the growth of the collection paralleled, in ways that need still to be studied fully, the rise of interest in architectural drawings as exhibitable works of art, notwithstanding decades of a modernist belief in the drawing as document or information.

Even as the museum was considered to be the leader of the fleet in flying the modernist banner, the signs of emerging postmodernism and a renewed interest in the art of drawing began to accumulate. In 1966, MoMA published a book destined to have a wide impact on attitudes toward the past, toward sources, and toward architecture as a technocratic enterprise, Robert Venturi's *Complexity and Contradiction in Architecture.* In the same year, the newly acquired drawings of Mies van der Rohe began to be displayed. The nineteen-seventies were the heyday of a renewed appreciation of drawing, and not only with the publication of *Five Architects: Eisenman, Graves, Gwathmey, Hejduk, Meier,* with its renewed sense of axonometric exploration of unprecedented form generation. Most notable were two exhibitions of 1975: On the one hand, Drexler's seminal exhibition *The Architecture of the Ecole des Beaux-Arts* brought the large-scale nineteenth-century student competition drawings from the Parisian School's archive to a controversial display on the walls of the museum that was poised as a critique of many aspects of the modern movement, not the least the tendency toward abstraction from place, from spatial sequence, and from urban values that Drexler thought to find in contemporary architecture's allegiance to chipboard models and to axonometric drawings.[11] On the other hand, the sales exhibition of architectural drawings staged in the Members' Lounge at the MoMA in the spring of that year by Emilio Ambasz and Barbara Jakobson announced a decade-and-a-half in which architectural drawings would take their place in the world of art galleries—New York's fashionable and cutting-edge Castelli Gallery began with them in a key show of 1977—at the same time as architects were developing new sensual and experimental means of representation through drawing.

MoMA's collection would grow to include well over a thousand drawings, not including the Mies van der Rohe archive, in the next forty years under the direction of Arthur Drexler, of Stuart Wrede, and of Terence Riley. A windfall came with the acquisition of the Howard Gilman Collection, focused on visionary and utopian drawings of the nineteen-sixties and seventies, a collection of over two hundred drawings—notably by Archigram, Superstudio, Yona Friedman, Aldo Rossi, and many others—assembled by Pierre Apraxine

die Kunstgalerien erhielten. So hatte die angesagte New Yorker Castelli Gallery solche Zeichnungen beispielsweise erstmals 1977 in einer Ausstellung präsentiert – zu einer Zeit also, als die Architekten gerade ganz neue zeichnerische Darstellungsmittel entwickelten. Unter Arthur Drexlers, Stuart Wredes und Terence Rileys Leitung wuchs die MoMA-Sammlung dann in den folgenden 40 Jahren auf deutlich über 1 000 Zeichnungen, die umfangreichen Materialien des Mies van der Rohe Archives nicht berücksichtigt. Einen besonderen Zugewinn bedeutete der Erwerb der Sammlung Howard Gilman, die hauptsächlich visionäre und utopische Zeichnungen aus den 1960er- und den 1970er-Jahren umfasste, insgesamt über 200 Blatt – vor allem von Archigram, Superstudio, Yona Friedman, Aldo Rossi und vielen mehr. Diese Arbeiten hatte Pierre Apraxine zwischen 1976 und 1980 zusammengetragen, also auf dem Höhepunkt der Nachfrage nach derartigen Architekturzeichnungen. Sie wurden jedoch nicht nur von Architekten gesammelt, sondern auch von etlichen neuen Architekturmuseen, etwa dem Canadian Centre for Architecture, dem Getty Research Institute der J. Paul Getty Foundation in Los Angeles und dem Deutschen Architekturmuseum in Frankfurt am Main, die allesamt in der Blütezeit der Postmoderne entstanden waren.

Am MoMA gingen Wrede (1988–1992) und Riley (1992–2006) in diesen Jahren zusehends dazu über, möglichst ganze projektbezogene Konvolute von Plänen zu erwerben, da sie wussten, dass es für einen angemessenen Eindruck von der ganzen Komplexität eines Gebäudes und seines Kontexts mehr braucht als eine einzelne Ansicht. Als ich selbst 2007 die Position des Chefkurators übernommen habe, habe ich diesen Ansatz in unserer Sammlungspolitik sogar noch weiter ausgebaut. So bestehen die einzelnen Konvolute heute möglichst aus Zeichnungen – und gegebenenfalls Modellen –, die nicht nur die konstruktiven Aspekte des jeweiligen Bauwerks beleuchten, sondern auch die wesentlichen planerischen Schritte. Wir unterscheiden nunmehr sorgfältig zwischen der eigenhändigen Architektenzeichnung und der eines Renderers, also eines Präsentations- oder Auftragszeichners, eine Differenzierung, die in historischen Sammlungen so oft nicht gegeben ist – dort werden die Pläne sämtlicher Entwurfs- und Ausführungsphasen häufig dem jeweiligen Architekten selbst zugeschrieben, auch wenn sie gar nicht persönlich von ihm gezeichnet wurden oder auch erst im Nachhinein entstanden sind.

LUDWIG MIES VAN DER ROHE,
FARNSWORTH HOUSE, FOX RIVER, PLANO,
ILLINOIS, ENTWURFSZEICHNUNG, 1945

LUDWIG MIES VAN DER ROHE,
FARNSWORTH HOUSE, FOX RIVER,
PLANO, ILLINOIS, DRAWING, 1945

between 1976 and 1980 during the heyday of the craze for architectural drawings, not only among architects projecting possible architects, but among a new generation of architectural museums, including the Canadian Centre for Architecture, the Getty Research Institute at the J. Paul Getty Foundation in Los Angeles, and the Deutsches Architekturmuseum in Frankfurt, all founded during the period of the rise of postmodernism. At MoMA, Wrede (from 1988–92) and Riley (from 1992–2006) increasingly moved to a policy of collecting clusters of drawings related to a single project whenever possible, realizing that rarely did a single view provide a full understanding of any work of architecture in its full complexity and in relationship to its setting. When I assumed the position of chief curator in 2007, I expanded this approach, and clusters grew to include, whenever possible, an array of drawings—and, if possible, models—that showed not only a project in all its built aspects but also its salient developments. Distinctions are now drawn between the hand of the architect and that of the renderer, something that has rarely been attended to in the formation of historical collections, where most drawings tend to be catalogued as the work of the architect no matter what hand is really at work and in what stage of the project, from preliminary to a posteriori, is represented.

Most importantly, with the addition of permanent departmental galleries from the nineteen-sixties—architecture had previously been shown, for the

AUSSTELLUNGSANSICHT 194X–9/11:
AMERICAN ARCHITECTS IN THE CITY,
THE MUSEUM OF MODERN ART,
NEW YORK, 2011/12
INSTALLATION VIEW, 194X–9/11:
AMERICAN ARCHITECTS IN THE CITY,
THE MUSEUM OF MODERN ART,
NEW YORK, 2011–12

AUSSTELLUNGSANSICHT *194X–9/11.
AMERICAN ARCHITECTS IN THE CITY*,
THE MUSEUM OF MODERN ART,
NEW YORK, 2011/12

INSTALLATION VIEW, *194X–9/11:
AMERICAN ARCHITECTS IN THE CITY*,
THE MUSEUM OF MODERN ART,
NEW YORK, 2011–12

Besonders wichtig war, dass das Department of Architecture and Design seit den 1960er-Jahren eigene Galerieräume beziehen konnte, in denen es neben einer Dauerausstellung auch immer wieder kleinere Einzelausstellungen mit Exponaten aus den eigenen Beständen zeigen konnte. Diese waren bis dahin nur in Sonderausstellungen oder integriert in Themenausstellungen wie Alfred H. Barrs *Cubism and Abstract Art* (1936) zu sehen. Der neuen Ausstellungspraxis lag die Annahme zugrunde, dass sich die Besucher vor allem einen Überblick über die wichtigsten historischen Entwicklungen im Bereich der Architektur, der grafischen Gestaltung und des Möbel- und des Industriedesigns verschaffen wollten. Viele Jahre wurden in diesen Sonderausstellungen, deren Exponate aus der eigenen Sammlung stammten, vor allem hochwertige Entwürfe als Meisterwerke gezeigt. Schon seit Terence Rileys Zeiten, verstärkt aber seit meinem Amtsantritt befassen sich unsere Sonderausstellungen sowohl mit historischen als auch mit zeitgenössischen Themen und zielen darauf ab, die Kontinuitäten zwischen diesen beiden Aspekten sichtbar zu machen. Dabei stehen zwar bisweilen neue Erwerbungen im Vordergrund, häufiger sind jedoch thematische Ausstellungen wie jene, die Andres Lepik (von 2008 bis 2011 Kurator in unserer Abteilung) unter dem Titel *Dreamland. Architectural Experiments since the 1970s* (2008/09) entwickelt hat. Eher konzeptionell angelegt war auch die von mir selbst kuratierte Ausstellung *194X–9/11. American Architects and the City* (2011/12), die sich mit den wichtigsten städtebaulichen Konzepten zwischen der frühen Nachkriegszeit und der Zerstörung des New Yorker World Trade Center 2001 befasste. Von einem ähnlichen Erkenntnisinteresse war auch Pedro Gadanhos Ausstellung *9 + 1 Ways of Being Political. 50 Years of Political Stances in Architecture and Urban Design* (2012/13) geleitet, ebenso seine Auseinandersetzung mit der Collage in *Cut 'n' Paste. From Architectural Assemblage to Collage City* (2013/14).

In den sechseinhalb Jahren, in denen ich hier am MoMA eine leitende Funktion wahrnehme, hat der Umfang unserer Sammlung deutlich zugenommen. So haben wir beispielsweise nicht nur zwei komplette Kücheneinrichtungen erworben: eine Frankfurter Küche (Margarete Schütte-Lihotzky, 1926) und eine Küche aus der Unité d'habitation in Marseille (Charlotte Perriand und Le Corbusier, 1947), sondern auch Konvolute mit Plänen und Modellen bedeutender Bauwerke von Architekten wie Mahmoud Bodo Rasch, Jean Tschumi, Ricardo Porro, Sauerbruch Hutton, Steven Holl, Rem Koolhaas, Paulo Mendes da Rocha und Weiss / Manfredi. Nach dem großen

REM KOOLHAAS,
DREAMLAND
PROJECT, CONEY
ISLAND, NEW YORK,
ENTWURFS-
ZEICHNUNG, 1976

REM KOOLHAAS,
DREAMLAND
PROJECT, CONEY
ISLAND,
NEW YORK,
DRAWING, 1976

most part, in either specialized temporary exhibitions or in integrated hangings such as Barr's *Cubism and Abstract Art* (1936)—smaller-scale installations of selections from the permanent collection became part of the department's regular exhibition. It was assumed that just as visitors to the museum could expect to walk through a historical survey of modern painting and sculpture, so in galleries of architecture and design could they witness key milestones in the development of architecture as well as graphic, furniture, and industrial design. For many years, these rotations of works in the museum's collection were largely examples of fine design, but in recent years—beginning under Terence Riley and then definitively during my tenure—these were used to create thematic installations that could engage both historic and contemporary themes, and often underscore the continuity between the two. Sometimes these installations highlight recent acquisitions, but more frequently the architecture curators choose themes, such as in the installations *Dreamland: Architectural Experiments since the 1970s* (2008–09) by Andres Lepik, curator in the department from 2008 to 2011, my own *194X–9/11: American Architects and the City* (2011–12), which looked at urban propositions from the era of postwar urban renewal to the debates ensured by the tragedy at New York's World Trade Center site in 2001, and Pedro Gadanho's look at

Erfolg der Ausstellung *Groundswell. Constructing the Contemporary Landscape* (2005) begannen wir zudem, Entwurfszeichnung und Pläne bedeutender Landschaftsarchitekten zu sammeln. Unsere größte Errungenschaft war jedoch die Übernahme des Frank Lloyd Wright Archives und der Taliesin Fellowship im Jahre 2012/13, die das MoMA in Zukunft gemeinsam mit den Columbia University Libraries betreuen wird. Diese großartige Erwerbung umfasst nicht nur Tausende von Zeichnungen, die in Wrights langem Berufsleben entstanden sind, sowie zahlreiche Modelle (von denen viele schon 1940 in seiner MoMA-Ausstellung zu sehen waren), diverse Gebäudedetails, experimentelle Baustoffe, sondern auch Tausende von Fotografien und die gesamte Korrespondenz des großen Architekten. Der Wright-Nachlass ist damit aber auch das erste Experiment des Museums im Bereich der Architektur mit einer gemeinschaftlichen Erwerbung. Der gesamte Wright-Nachlass und sämtliche Taliesin-Materialien befinden sich im Gemeinschaftseigentum des MoMA und der Avery Architectural and Fine Arts Library, wobei die Columbia University einen Großteil der zweidimensionalen Dokumente verwahrt, da sie über die nötige Infrastruktur verfügt, um Forschern und Studenten Einblick in diese Materialien zu gewähren. Die dreidimensionalen Objekte werden in unseren Ausstellungen künftig regelmäßig neben anderen Exponaten aus der Sammlung zu sehen sein, damit sich das Publikum mit Wrights Schaffen im Kontext der modernen Architektur auseinandersetzen kann. Obwohl die Avery Library schon seit über 30 Jahren solche Nachlässe sammelt, werden diese Archive am MoMA eine Ausnahme bleiben. Die Kooperation zwischen beiden Institutionen dürfte in den kommenden Jahrzehnten sogar noch zunehmen, allerdings nicht nur aus räumlichen Gründen; vielmehr stehen heutzutage alle Architekturmuseen vor der Frage, wie sie ihre digitalen Archive, die auf Servern oder anderen Speichermedien immer mehr Platz beanspruchen, erfassen und speichern sollen. Das MoMA hat sich damit bisher vor allem im Designbereich beschäftigt und sucht gemeinsam mit Kollegen an anderen Häusern nach Mitteln und Wegen, auch architektonische Zeichnungen und Pläne auf diese Weise zu erfassen und zu archivieren.
In den mehr als 80 Jahren, die seit der Entscheidung der MoMA-Trustees vergangen sind, einer Abteilung für Architektur eine Chance zu geben, um kleine Wanderausstellungen zu organisieren, ist darin eine bedeutende Sammlung gewachsen, die heute auch die Archive zweier Pioniere der Moderne betreut: Ludwig Mies van der Rohe und Frank Lloyd Wright. Mit

political stances in *9 + 1 Ways of Being Political: 50 Years of Political Stances in Architecture and Urban Design* (2012–13) or at collage in *Cut 'n' Paste: From Architectural Assemblage to Collage City* (2013–14).

During my six-and-a-half years at the helm at MoMA, the collection increased in multiple ways. Not only did we add the first full-scale rooms to the collection, both kitchens—a Frankfurt kitchen (Margarete Schütte-Lihotzky, 1926) and a kitchen from the Marseille Unité d'habitation (Charlotte Perriand and Le Corbusier, 1947)—but we also acquired major sets of drawings and models for single significant projects from historical figures such as Mahmoud Bodo Rasch, Jean Tschumi, Ricardo Porro, Sauerbruch Hutton, Steven Holl, Rem Koolhaas, Paulo Mendes da Rocha, and Weiss / Manfredi. For the first time, in the wake of the museum's highly noted exhibition *Groundswell: Constructing the Contemporary Landscape* (2005), the department has faced the challenge of how to collect works of significant landscape design. The single most significant addition has been the arrival in 2012 of the archives of Frank Lloyd Wright and the implementation of the Taliesin Fellowship, acquired jointly with the Columbia University Libraries. This is not only a transformative acquisition in bringing into the collection several thousand drawings produced over Wright's long career, along with models (many made for his 1940 exhibition at MoMA), building fragments, and material experiments, as well as thousands of photographs and Wright's entire correspondence, it also is the museum's first experiment in the realm of architecture with collaborative acquisition. All of the Wright and Taliesin materials are held jointly by MoMA and the Avery Architectural and Fine Arts Library, the flat material housed for the most part at Columbia University, which has the facilities for making them available to researchers and students. The three-dimensional materials at the museum will regularly draw on the whole collection to integrate Wright into historical and thematic displays on modern architecture. Nonetheless, archives remain an exception at MoMA, even if they have been collected for over three decades by the Avery Library. The collaborative model seems likely to expand in coming years, not only with the challenges of space, but with the challenges that all museums of architecture now share of housing digital archives, equally gluttonous when it comes to space on servers and other forms of "virtual storage." This is a field that MoMA has ventured into with aplomb in the realm of design and continues more and more to study with other colleagues in the realm of architectural design.

Ausstellungen wie *Rising Currents. Projects for New York's Waterfront* (2010), die sich aus gemeinsamen Workshops im MoMA PS1 in Queens, im Internet und in unserem Stammhaus in Manhattan entwickelt haben, baut das Department nicht nur seine Sammlung weiter aus, sondern erprobt auch aktiv neue Wege der Architekturausstellung.

1 Zur Geschichte des Museum of Modern Art vgl. Harriet Schoenholz Bee und Michelle Elligott (Hrsg.), *Art in Our Time. A Chronicle of the Museum of Modern Art*, New York 2004. Zur Familie Rockefeller siehe Suzanne Loebl, *America's Medicis. The Rockefellers and Their Astonishing Cultural Legacy*, New York 2010.

2 Am besten dokumentiert ist die umfangreiche Literatur über diese Ausstellung in Terence Rileys und Stephen Perrellas Buch *The International Style. Exhibition 15 and the Museum of Modern Art*, New York 1992. Siehe auch Barry Bergdoll und Delfim Sardo, *Modern Architects. Uma Introdução / An Introduction*, Lissabon 2011, Begleitheft zu einem Reprint des Originalausstellungskatalogs von 1932.

3 Siehe Nina Stritzler-Levine, »Curating History, Exhibiting Ideas. Henry-Russell Hitchock and Architecture Exhibition Practice at the MoMA«, in: Frank Salmon (Hrsg.), *Summerson and Hitchcock. Centenary Essays on Architectural Historiography (Studies in British Art, 16)*, New Haven 2006, S. 33–68. Siehe auch Paolo Scrivano, *Storia di un'idea di architettura moderna, Henry-Russell Hitchcock e l'International Style*, Mailand 2001.

4 Matilda McQuaid, »Acquiring Architecture. Building a Modern Collection«, in: dies., *Envisioning Architecture. Drawings form the Museum of Modern Art*, New York 2002, S. 22.

5 Siehe Barry Bergdoll, »Introduction«, in: *Home Delivery. Fabricating the Modern Dwelling*, hrsg. von Barry Bergdoll und Peter Christensen, Ausst.-Kat. The Museum of Modern Art, New York 2008, S. 9 ff.; siehe auch Beatriz Colomina, »The Exhibitionary House«, in: Richard Koshalek u. a. (Hrsg.), *At the End of the Century. One Hundred Years of Architecture*, Ausst.-Kat. The Museum of Contemporary Art, Los Angeles 1998.

6 Siehe Peter Reed und William Kaizen (Hrsg.), *The Show to End All Shows. Frank Lloyd Wright and the Museum of Modern Art, 1940 (Studies in Modern Art, 8)* New York 2004.

7 Siehe Terence Riley und Edward Eigen, »Between the Museum and the Marketplace. Selling Good Design«, in: John Szarkowski und John Elderfield (Hrsg.), *The Museum of Modern Art at Mid-Century. At Home and Abroad (Studies in Modern Art, 4)* New York 1995, S. 150–179.

8 Siehe Wallis Miller, »Mies van der Rohe und die Ausstellungen«, in: *Mies in Berlin. Ludwig Mies van der Rohe. Die Berliner Jahre 1907–1938*, hrsg. von Terence Riley und Barry Bergdoll, Ausst.-Kat. The Museum of Modern Art u. a., München u. a. 2001, S. 338–349.

9 Siehe Franz Schulze (Hrsg.), *The Mies van der Rohe Archive*, New York 1987.

10 Barry Bergdoll, »The Synthesis of the Arts and MoMA«, in: *Docomomo Journal*, 42, Sommer 2010, S. 110–113.

11 Barry Bergdoll, »Complexities and Contradictions of Post-Modern Classicism. Notes on the Museum of Modern Art's 1975 Exhibition, The Architecture of the Ecole des Beaux-Arts«, in: Frank Salmon (Hrsg.), *The Persistence of the Classical. Essays on Architecture Presented to David Watkin*, London 2008, S. 202–217.

In the over eighty years since the trustees of MoMA decided to take a chance on a Department of Architecture as a place to organize small traveling exhibitions, a collection of major significance has grown, one which houses the archives of two of the leading figures of modern architecture—Ludwig Mies van der Rohe and Frank Lloyd Wright. With projects developing equally between workshops at MoMA PS1, on the web, and in the galleries, such as *Rising Currents: Projects for New York's Waterfront* (2010), the department continues not only to collect but to think afresh the potentials of the architecture exhibition.

1 For the history of the Museum of Modern Art, see Harriet Schoenholz Bee and Michelle Elligott, eds., *Art in Our Time: A Chronicle of the Museum of Modern Art* (New York, 2004). On the Rockefellers, see Suzanne Loebl, *America's Medicis: The Rockefellers and Their Astonishing Cultural Legacy* (New York, 2010).

2 There is a vast bibliography on this exhibition, best documented in Terence Riley and Stephen Perrella, *The International Style: Exhibition 15 and the Museum of Modern Art* (New York, 1992). See also Barry Bergdoll and Delfim Sardo, *Modern Architects: Uma Introdução / An Introduction* (Lisbon, 2011), brochure accompanying a reprint of the 1932 catalogue for the *Modern Architecture* exhibition.

3 See Nina Stritzler-Levine, "Curating History, Exhibiting Ideas: Henry-Russell Hitchock and Architecture Exhibition Practice at the MoMA," in Frank Salmon, ed., *Summerson and Hitchcock: Centenary Essays on Architectural Historiography.* Studies in British Art vol. 16 (New Haven, 2006), pp. 33–68. See also Paolo Scrivano, *Storia di un'idea di architettura moderna, Henry-Russell Hitchcock e l'International Style* (Milan, 2001).

4 Quoted from *Fortune* magazine (December 1938) by Matilda McQuaid, "Acquiring Architecture: Building a Modern Collection," in idem., *Envisioning Architecture: Drawings form the Museum of Modern Art* (New York, 2002), p. 22.

5 On the houses in the garden, see Barry Bergdoll, "Introduction," in *Home Delivery: Fabricating the Modern Dwelling*, ed. Barry Bergdoll and Peter Christensen, exh. cat. The Museum of Modern Art (New York, 2008), pp. 9–11; see also Beatriz Colomina, "The Exhibitionary House," in Richard Koshalek et al., eds., *At the End of the Century: One Hundred Years of Architecture*, exh. cat. The Museum of Contemporary Art (Los Angeles, 1998).

6 See Peter Reed and William Kaizen, eds., *The Show to End All Shows: Frank Lloyd Wright and the Museum of Modern Art, 1940*, Studies in Modern Art vol. 8 (New York, 2004).

7 See Terence Riley and Edward Eigen, "Between the Museum and the Marketplace: Selling Good Design," in John Szarkowski and John Elderfield, eds., *The Museum of Modern Art at Mid-Century: At Home and Abroad*, Studies in Modern Art vol. 4 (New York, 1995), pp. 150–79.

8 See Wallis Miller, "Mies and Eaxhibitions," in *Mies van der Rohe: Mies in Berlin*, ed. Terence Riley and Barry Bergdoll, exh. cat. The Museum of Modern Art (New York, 2001), pp. 338–49.

9 See Franz Schulze, ed., *The Mies van der Rohe Archive* (New York, 1987).

10 Barry Bergdoll, "The Synthesis of the Arts and MoMA," *Docomomo Journal* 42 (Summer 2010), pp. 110–13.

11 Barry Bergdoll, "Complexities and Contradictions of Post-Modern Classicism: Notes on the Museum of Modern Art's 1975 Exhibition, *The Architecture of the Ecole des Beaux-Arts,*" in Frank Salmon, ed., *The Persistence of the Classical: Essays on Architecture Presented to David Watkin* (London, 2008), pp. 202–17.

DIE ARCHITEKTURSAMMLUNGEN IN FRANKREICH

Die Archive der französischen Architektur – oder vielmehr der Architektur in Frankreich – sind ausgesprochen heterogenen Ursprungs und können nicht nur auf die Archive von Architekten oder anderen gestalterischen Berufsgruppen wie Landschaftsgärtner oder Ingenieure eingeschränkt werden. Sie verfügen mittlerweile über ein ebenso ausgedehntes wie verzweigtes Netzwerk, das nicht nur die Geschichte des Fachs, sondern auch die der Städte, Regionen und Unternehmen widerspiegelt. So lässt sich nur schwer eine umfassende Bestandsaufnahme dieser in den letzten Jahrzehnten permanent im Wandel begriffenen und bisweilen unübersichtlich scheinenden Bestände erbringen. Hier sollen jedoch einige repräsentative Fälle näher betrachtet werden.[1]

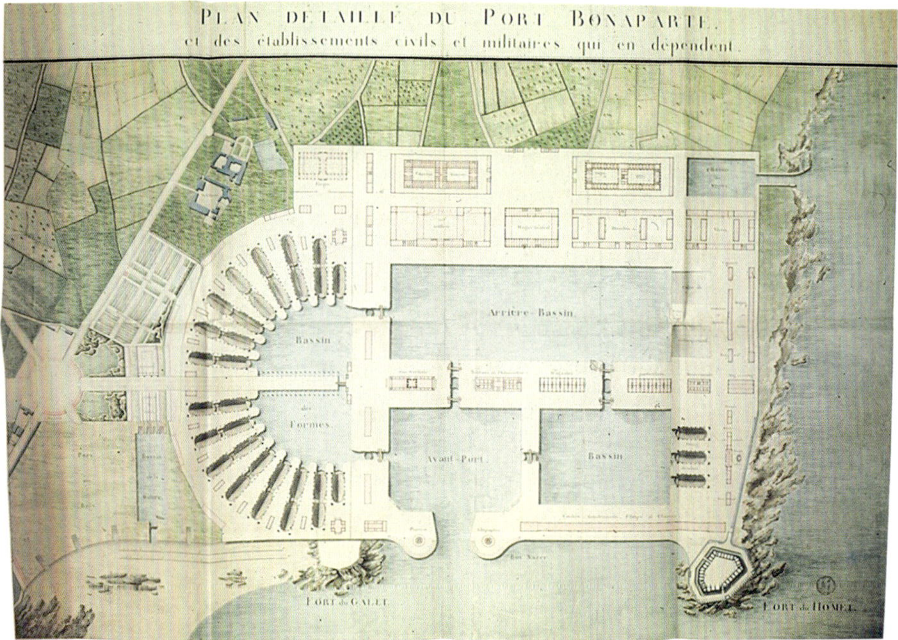

DETAILPLAN DER
PORT-BONAPARTE, ETWA 1800
ARCHIVES NATIONALES, PARIS

DETAILED PLAN OF THE
PORT-BONAPARTE, CA. 1800
ARCHIVES NATIONALES, PARIS

JEAN-LOUIS COHEN

ARCHITECTURE COLLECTIONS IN FRANCE

The archives of French architecture—or rather of architecture in France—have very heterogeneous origins and are not simply limited to the archives of individual architects or of other design and planning professionals, such as landscapers and engineers. Today these archives form a broad and ramified network, which reflects the development of cities, public organizations, and business enterprises as much as the history of the discipline itself. It is difficult to lay out an overall map of such a resource—especially one that has been in constant transformation over the last decades and that can seem so labyrinthine—but it may be useful nonetheless to dwell on a few representative examples.[1]

Since the nineteenth century, the collections that are to be found in public French archives have been assembled by institutions attached to different levels of administration, from municipalities to *départments*, and to the state at the national level. The earliest conservation policies were established at this latter level: for example, in the engineering collections of the Ancien Régime or of the Napoleonic Empire, which, much later, would make the work of Bruno Fortier or Antoine Picon possible.[2] The military have always been most concerned with keeping intact the traces of their history, and the archives of the military engineers and the Service historique de l'armée de terre are indispensable sources not only for the history of conflicts and fortifications but of cities as well.

As far as the twentieth century is concerned, a time when public intervention grew in scope and consequence, the departmental archives are important repositories of drawings and reports related to the three reconstructions that France experienced—the first of these after World War I, the second during the German occupation from 1940 to 1944, and the third starting after World War II.[3] The documents that derive from reports and assessments of war damage or from the collections of chief architects have made it possible to carry out monographic research on the reconstructed cities as well as studies of specific architects or specific issues, such as the beginnings of prefabrication.

Another measure of the significant role of the state in the construction of the large housing projects launched between the early nineteen-fifties and seventies is

Seit dem 19. Jahrhundert werden die öffentlichen Archivbestände Frankreichs von Institutionen zusammengetragen, die zu unterschiedlichen Verwaltungsebenen (Gemeinden, Départements) oder aber direkt zum Staat gehören. Die frühesten Erhaltungsmaßnahmen lassen sich auf nationaler Ebene beobachten, etwa anhand der Bestände von Ingenieuren im Ancien Régime oder während des Ersten Kaiserreichs, wie Bruno Fortier oder Antoine Picon später im Rahmen ihrer Untersuchungen dargelegt haben.[2] Auch das Militär war von jeher an einer sorgfältigen Bewahrung seiner Geschichte interessiert: Die Archives du Génie oder die Bestände des Service historique de l'armée de terre stellen nicht nur für die Geschichte der kriegerischen Auseinandersetzungen oder Befestigungswerke, sondern auch für die der Städte kostbare Quellen dar.

Das 20. Jahrhundert zeichnete sich durch ein immer stärkeres und weiter verzweigtes öffentliches Eingreifen aus. Hier sind es in erster Linie die Archive der Départements, in denen Zeichnungen und Berichte des dreifachen französischen Neubeginns – nach dem Ersten Weltkrieg, während der deutschen Besatzung (1940 bis 1944) und die Zeit nach dem Zweiten Weltkrieg – aufbewahrt werden.[3] Diese Dokumente aus Akten zu Kriegsschäden oder Beständen der zuständigen Architekten haben vor allem monografische Forschungen zu den wiederaufgebauten Städten ermöglicht, aber auch Untersuchungen zu bestimmten Architekten oder spezifischen Neuerungen, beispielsweise zu den Anfängen des Fertigbaus.

Die zwischen den frühen 1950er- und den 1970er-Jahren realisierten großen Wohnsiedlungen sind in den Archives nationales mit einer großen Anzahl an Materialien dokumentiert, da der Staat an diesen Projekten maßgeblich beteiligt war. Diese Bestände sind für die Forschung hilfreich und umfassen sowohl Zeichnungen und Dokumente aus Politik und Verwaltung als auch bemerkenswertes fotografisches Material.[4] Durch die vorhandenen Materialien lässt sich nicht nur der Beginn der industriellen Techniken erschließen, sondern auch die Auftragsbedingungen für neue Stadtviertel und deren Gebäude. In den 1993 in einer ehemaligen Textilfabrik in Roubaix eröffneten Archives nationales du monde du travail befinden sich sowohl Bestände von Bauunternehmen als auch die einzelner Architekten wie Jean und Maria Deroche oder Roland Simounet, dem im Jahr 2000 eine eigene Ausstellung in Villeneuve d'Ascq gewidmet wurde.[5]

Im Zuge der Gründung der Commission nationale des monuments historiques 1837 stand neben der städteplanerischen Modernisierung und Umgestaltung

ROLAND SIMOUNET, WOHNUNGSBAU
IN SAINT-DENIS, STUDIENSKIZZE, 1977
ARCHIVES NATIONALES DU
MONDE DU TRAVAIL, ROUBAIX

ROLAND SIMOUNET,
STUDY FOR A RESIDENTIAL BUILDING
IN SAINT-DENIS, 1977
ARCHIVES NATIONALES
DU MONDE DU TRAVAIL, ROUBAIX

clearly evident in the large amount of relevant material that has been conserved in the collections of the Archives nationales. These collections include not only drawings as well as political or administrative documents, but also a significant amount of photographic material upon which a volume of historical research has been based.[4] This documentation has made it possible to follow the growth of industrial technologies and to retrace the terms and conditions of the commissions for new neighborhoods and their buildings. The Archives nationales du monde du travail, which opened in 1993 in a converted textile mill in Roubaix, contains documents from the building trades as well as some architects' collections, such as those of Jean and Maria Deroche as well as Roland Simounet, who was the subject of an exhibition in 2000 in Villeneuve d'Ascq.[5]

Along with the modernization and transformation of the territories, one of the main registers of public policy was the conservation of historical monuments, following the creation of the Commission nationale des monuments historiques in 1837. The files pertaining to the documentation and restoration of these edifices have been conserved by the Médiathèque de l'architecture et du patrimoine under the Ministère de la culture et de la communication. They make it possible to reconstruct the "biography" of each building over the course of successive campaigns of study and repair work.

auch der Erhalt historischer Denkmäler im Mittelpunkt der öffentlichen Maßnahmen. Die Akten zur Erhebung und Restaurierung dieser Gebäude befinden sich in der dem Ministère de la culture et de la communication unterstellten Médiathèque du Patrimoine. Sie bieten wichtige Einblicke in die Abfolge von Planungs- und Arbeitsphasen und erlauben so die Rekonstruktion der jeweiligen »Gebäudebiografien«. Der bedeutendste Bestand der Médiathèque, der sowohl durch seinen Umfang als auch durch die Qualität der Zeichnungen hervorsticht, stammt von Eugène-Emmanuel Viollet-le-Duc.[6] Die zunächst in den Verwaltungsakten verbliebenen Dokumente wurden 2007 durch eine Sammlung der Familie des Architekten ergänzt, die mit Unterstützung des Bauunternehmens Eiffage erworben werden konnte. Im Besitz der Médiathèque befindet sich zudem die eindrucksvolle Sammlung Anatole de Baudots, einem Schüler Viollet-le-Ducs und Pionier des Stahlbetonbaus.

Auch die Hochschulen für Ingenieurwissenschaften oder Architektur bewahren die Arbeiten ihrer Studenten auf. Das gilt sowohl für die 1747 gegründete École des Ponts et Chaussées als auch ganz besonders für die École des Beaux-Arts, an der von 1819 bis 1968 Architektur unterrichtet wurde. In ihrer Bibliothek befinden sich nicht nur die Wettbewerbszeichnungen für den Prix de Rome, sondern auch viele der bei studienbegleitenden Wettbewerben ausgezeichneten Projekte. Ihre Sammlung wiederum umfasst die vor der Revolution an der École de l'Académie angefertigten Arbeiten. Dieser außergewöhnlich umfangreiche Bestand an großformatigen aquarellierten Zeichnungen bildete die Grundlage für die 1975 im New Yorker Museum of Modern Art gezeigte Ausstellung *The Architecture of the Ecole des Beaux-Arts,*

EUGÈNE-EMMANUEL VIOLLET-LE-DUC, BASILIKA SAINTE-MARIE-MADELEINE, VÉZELAY, ANSICHT DER WESTFASSADE VOR DER RESTAURIERUNG, 1840 MÉDIATHÈQUE DU PATRIMOINE, SAINT-CYR

EUGÈNE-EMMANUEL VIOLLET-LE-DUC, SAINTE-MADELEINE ABBEY, VÉZELAY, ELEVATION OF THE WESTERN FAÇADE BEFORE RESTORATION, 1840 MÉDIATHÈQUE DU PATRIMOINE, SAINT-CYR

The most prestigious collection held by the Médiathèque is Eugène Emmanuel Viollet-le-Duc's, which is remarkable both in its extent and in the quality of its drawings.[6] The documents that had remained in the administrative files were supplemented in 2007 by a collection that had until then remained in the family of the architect and was acquired thanks to the patronage of the Eiffage building company. The Médiathèque also holds the remarkable collection of Anatole de Baudot, Viollet-le-Duc's successor and a pioneer of reinforced concrete.

The institutions dedicated to teaching engineering and architecture usually retained the work of their students. This was true of the École nationale des ponts et chaussées, which was founded in 1747, and was especially true of the École nationale supérieure des beaux-arts, where architecture was taught from 1819 to 1968. Its library held the competition drawings for the Prix de Rome, along with most of the prize-winning projects from the competitions that punctuated the curriculum. Its collection also includes work created at the Académie royale before the revolution. This extraordinary corpus of large-format drawings and watercolors was the primary source for the 1975 exhibition, *The Architecture of the Ecole des Beaux-Arts* at the Museum of Modern Art in New York, whose impact was so memorable.[7] I remember being one of the few students that still frequented the library after 1968, where I would often run into Richard Chafee, one of the curators of the exhibition. Through him I discovered the charm of these projects—and perhaps even of history as such.

As we shall see below, most architects' collections have been placed in public institutions, but some professional associations have played a significant role as well. Some collections remain in their original location; for example, in situations where the contracting authorities retained the bulk of the architect's work related to their buildings. This is the case with Charles Garnier's drawings that are part of the collection of the Bibliothèque-musée de l'opéra in Paris.[8] Since its creation in 1840, the most active professional association has been the Société centrale des architectes français, which in 1953 became the Académie d'architecture. Its collection contains some exceptional material, such as Henri Labrouste's archives, work by the founders of twentieth-century urbanism, such as Léon Jaussely or Henri Prost, as well as the archives of Eugène Beaudouin and Marcel Lods.[9] The Société des architectes diplômés par le gouvernement (SADG), created in 1877, which became the Société française des architectes in 1979, holds the remarkable collections of Henri Sauvage.

die eine breite Rezeption erfuhr.[7] Ich erinnere mich, dass ich – damals einer der wenigen Studenten, die nach 1968 noch in die Bibliothek gingen – dort häufig Richard Chafee traf, einen der Ausstellungskuratoren, der mich für die Projekte (und womöglich auch für Geschichte) begeisterte.

Im Allgemeinen gingen die Bestände einzelner Architekten in öffentliche Einrichtungen über, aber auch Berufsverbände spielten eine wichtige Rolle. Es gibt auch Fälle, in denen die Bauherren Arbeiten ihres Architekten aufbewahrten: So etwa im Falle Charles Garniers, dessen Zeichnungen sich in den Sammlungen des Musée de l'Opéra de Paris befinden.[8] Der wohl tatkräftigste Verband war von seiner Gründung 1840 an die Société centrale des architectes, die 1953 zur Académie d'architecture, die aber keine Beziehung mit der Architekturklasse der Académie des Beaux-Arts hat. Zu ihrem außergewöhnlichen Archivgut zählen der Nachlass Henri Labroustes, die Sammlungen der Anfang des 20. Jahrhunderts maßgeblichen Städteplaner Léon Jaussely oder Henri Prost sowie die Archive Eugène Beaudouins oder Marcel Lods'.[9] Darüber hinaus ist die 1877 gegründete Société des architectes diplômés par le gouvernement (SADG), die seit 1979 Société française des architectes heißt, im Besitz der bedeutenden Sammlung Henri Sauvages.

Einige Historiker wurden mit dem Aufspüren von Architektenarchiven betraut und leiteten diese an Einrichtungen weiter, an denen sie selbst unterrichteten. So übergaben etwa Jean-Baptiste Ache und Henri Poupée dem technisch ausgerichteten Conservatoire national des arts et métiers die Bestände von Architekten wie André Lurçat oder Auguste Perret, zu denen sie selbst Ausstellungen konzipiert hatten – dazu Sammlungen bedeutender Hochschullehrer wie Julien-Azaïs Guadet, wichtiger Architekten wie Charles Le Cœur und sein Sohn François, und nicht zuletzt die insgesamt 150 000 Arbeitsakten des Stahlbetonunternehmens von François Hennebique. Dieser Bestand umfasst Grundrisse, Berechnungsunterlagen und Fotografien der Bauten, die dieses multinationale Unternehmen in zahlreichen Ländern realisiert hatte. Er wird durch Dokumente der Architekten ergänzt, die die von Hennebique ausgeführten Projekte verantworteten und ist damit über seinen Eigenwert hinaus auch für die Untersuchung eines breiten Werkspektrums nützlich.[10]

Unter den in den 1960er-Jahren gegründeten Einrichtungen ragt die Fondation Le Corbusier nicht nur aufgrund der unbestreitbaren Qualität ihrer Bestände und ihres Umfangs, sondern auch durch ihr einzigartiges Konzept heraus. Es handelt sich um eine private Stiftung (in Frankreich sind diese verhältnismäßig selten), die noch zu Lebzeiten des Architekten gegründet und nach seinen

HENRI PROST, DECKENPERSPEKTIVE
DER HAGIA SOPHIA, ISTANBUL, 1905–1907
ARCHIVES D'ARCHITECTURE DU
XXE SIÈCLE / CITÉ DE L'ARCHITECTURE
ET DU PATRIMOINE, PARIS

HENRI PROST, PERSPECTIVE OF
THE CEILING OF THE HAGIA SOPHIA,
ISTANBUL, 1905–07
ARCHIVES D'ARCHITECTURE DU
XXE SIÈCLE / CITÉ DE L'ARCHITECTURE
ET DU PATRIMOINE, PARIS

Some historians have been instrumental in assembling the archives of architects and bringing them to the institutions where they taught. For example, Jean-Baptiste Ache and Henri Poupée collected material on architects such as André Lurçat and Auguste Perret in connection with exhibitions they organized—materials now held at the Conservatoire national des arts et métiers, a place of primarily technical professional training. The Conservatoire also holds the collections of certain central pedagogical figures, such as Julien-Azaïs Guadet, important professionals, such as Charles Le Coeur and his son François, as well as some 150,000 documents from François Hennebique's reinforced concrete construction company. The latter material includes structural concrete plans, calculations, and photographs of completed projects in the scores of countries where this early multinational enterprise worked. It provides parallels and references to documents from the architects who designed the projects

Wünschen entworfen wurde. Sie finanziert sich größtenteils aus den Erlösen der Lizenzgebühren, die die Herstellung der Möbel durch die italienische Firma Cassina erbringt. Die Öffnung des Archivs zu Forschungszwecken hat zu zahlreichen biografischen und thematischen Arbeiten geführt, die durch die seit den 1990er-Jahren erfolgte Digitalisierung der Archive noch weiter vertieft werden konnten. Die Bestände zeichnen sich durch eine bemerkenswerte Vielfalt aus und umfassen – neben dem Herzstück aus insgesamt 32 000 Architekturzeichnungen – 8 000 Skizzen und Kunstzeichnungen, die Notizhefte und Tagebücher Le Corbusiers und nicht zuletzt 1,5 Millionen schriftliche Dokumente, sowohl Korrespondenzen als auch für die Mitarbeiter verfasste Notizen, mit deren Hilfe sich sämtliche Werk- und Lebensphasen erschließen lassen. Unabhängig von den oft subjektiven Deutungen der Forscher wurden diese Sammlungen systematisch in digitaler Form oder als Buchpublikationen veröffentlicht, darunter etwa die Korrespondenz Le Corbusiers.[11]

MARCEL LODS (ASSOCIATION
BEAUDOUIN ET LODS), MODELL
FÜR EINE NEUE AUSSTELLUNGSHALLE,
LA DÉFENSE, 1933/34
ARCHIVES D'ARCHITECTURE DU
XXE SIÈCLE / CITÉ DE L'ARCHITECTURE
ET DU PATRIMOINE, PARIS

MARCEL LODS (ASSOCIATION
BEAUDOUIN ET LODS), MODEL OF A
PROJECT FOR A NEW EXHIBITION
HALL, LA DÉFENSE, 1933–34
ARCHIVES D'ARCHITECTURE DU
XXE SIÈCLE / CITÉ DE L'ARCHITECTURE
ET DU PATRIMOINE, PARIS

that Hennebique became involved in. This material is thus both of value in itself and relevant to the study of a vast range of works.[10]

Among the institutions founded in the nineteen-sixties, the Fondation Le Corbusier stands out not only because of the unquestionable quality and volume of its collections, but also for its unique status. It is a private foundation—rather unusual in France—which was set up during the architect's lifetime and according to his wishes, and is primarily funded through royalties derived from the sale of furniture commercialized by the Italian manufacturer Cassina. Access to this foundation has enabled a significant number of biographical or thematic studies, which were further facilitated in the early nineteen-nineties by the numerical cataloguing of the archival material. The collections are very diverse in nature, with a central core of 32,000 architectural drawings, along with 8,000 sketches and artistic drawings, notebooks, agendas, and, most notably, some 1.5 million written documents, from letters to little notes to colleagues, which shed light on every episode of Le Corbusier's life and work. Aside from the interpretations of researchers, who use this material in their own way, these collections have been systematically published in numerical form or in printed volumes, such as that on Le Corbusier's correspondence.[11] While the Fondation Le Corbusier was setting up and making its contents accessible, new institutional actors appeared on the scene: art museums of broad scope, the most important being the Musée du Louvre. In 1890 it had attempted to establish a gallery of architectural drawings, but had soon given up on the project. Few of these museums held collections of architectural work comparable to the holdings of the Musée des beaux-arts de Lyon, where a part of Tony Garnier's archive had been deposited, most notably the watercolors of his project for *Cité industrielle* (1916), along with many of his pencil drawings. This collection made several significant exhibitions possible, most markedly at the Centre Pompidou, which will be addressed below.[12]

From the outset, the Musée d'Orsay, which opened in 1987, included architecture in its presentation of the "long" nineteenth century, which extended to World War I. The permanent installation of the museum highlighted Charles Garnier's Opera (Opéra Garnier) as the *Gesamtkunstwerk* of Georges-Eugène Haussmann's Paris. In addition, it assembled a remarkable collection of archival material, especially the documents of Gustave Eiffel's company along with the archives of Victor Ruprich-Robert (whose theories on ornament were fundamental to Louis Sullivan), the collection of Marcel Guilleminault (who had been director of Henry Van de Velde's Parisian atelier), and archival

LE CORBUSIER, BLICK AUF DIE PONT NEUF
UND DIE ÎLE DE LA CITÉ, ZEICHNUNG, 1917
FONDATION LE CORBUSIER, PARIS

LE CORBUSIER, VIEW OF THE PONT NEUF
AND THE ÎLE DE LA CITÉ, DRAWING, 1917
FONDATION LE CORBUSIER, PARIS

Während die Fondation Le Corbusier ihre Archive langsam öffnete, traten neue institutionelle Akteure auf den Plan: die Kunstmuseen. Das bedeutendste unter ihnen, das Musée du Louvre, hatte bereits in den 1890er-Jahren eine Galerie mit Architekturzeichnungen einrichten wollen, aber rasch wieder Abstand davon genommen. Nur wenige Museen besaßen Architektursammlungen, etwa das Musée des Beaux-Arts in Lyon, dem ein Teil der Archive Tony Garniers übergeben worden war, insbesondere die Aquarelle zu seinem Projekt »Cité industrielle« (1916) und zahlreiche Bleistiftzeichnungen. Diesem Bestand waren prägende Ausstellungen zu verdanken, insbesondere im Centre Pompidou.[12]

Das 1987 eröffnete Musée d'Orsay bezog von Anfang an die Architektur in seine Darstellung eines »langen«, bis zum Ersten Weltkrieg reichenden 19. Jahrhunderts ein und präsentierte unter anderem die Oper Charles Garniers als Gesamtkunstwerk des haussmannschen Paris in seiner Dauerausstellung. Darüber hinaus verfügt das Museum über außergewöhnliche Bestände: in erster Linie über die Archive des von Gustav Eiffel geleiteten Unternehmens, die Archive Victor Ruprich-Roberts, dessen Theorien zur Ornamentik für Louis Sullivan maßgeblich waren, die Sammlung von Marcel Guilleminault, dem Leiter des Pariser Ateliers von Henry van de Velde, sowie Archive von Firmen, die gemeinsam mit den Architekten dekorative Inneneinrichtungen entwickelten. Außerdem übernahm das Musée d'Orsay eine Sammlung aus insgesamt 70 Zeichnungen, die der Louvre für sein geplantes Kabinett zusammengetragen hatte, und investierte in sammlungsergänzende Ankäufe, darunter 2 000 Zeichnungen Hector Guimards (Ankauf 1995) sowie 40 Zeichnungen der Otto-Wagner-Schüler Otto Schönthal, Emil Hoppe und Marcel Kammerer (Ankauf 1997).

Das 1977 eröffnete Centre Georges Pompidou umfasste ursprünglich ein vor allem den zeitgenössischen Arbeiten gewidmetes Centre de création industrielle. Dessen Ausstellungen setzten jedoch rasch historische Schwerpunkte: Schon bald wurden weniger komplette Archivbestände, sondern vielmehr Zeichnungen gesammelt, und das Centre de création industrielle ging 1992 im neu gegründeten Musée national d'art moderne auf.[13] Es gab allerdings auch Ausnahmen: So gingen etwa Pol Abrahams Archive, ein Teil der Bestände Georges Candilis' sowie ein Teil der Archive Jean Prouvés (ein anderer Teil verblieb in den Archives départementales de Meurthe-et-Moselle in Nancy) in den Museumsbestand ein. Darüber hinaus wurden weitere Modelle und Zeichnungen erworben, unter anderem Arbeiten ver-

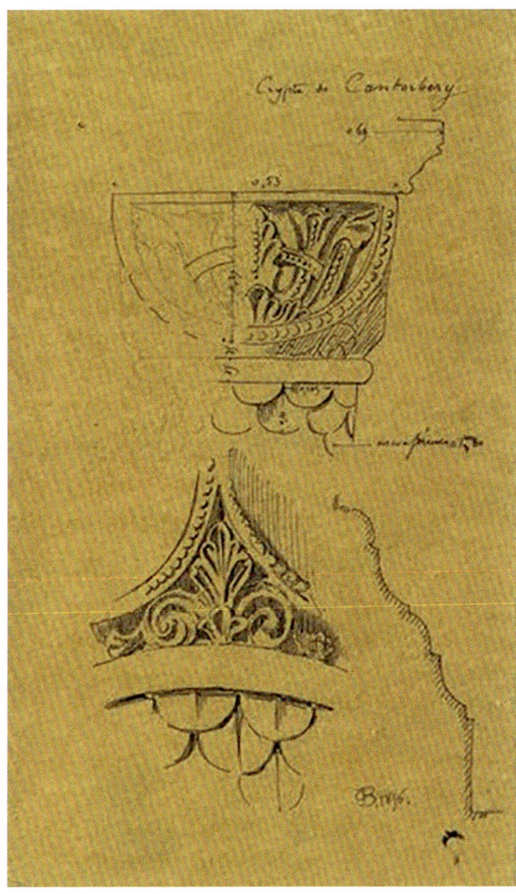

VICTOR RUPRICH-ROBERT, DETAILANSICHT EINES KAPITELS IN DER KRYPTA DER KATHEDRALE VON CANTERBURY, 1856 MUSÉE D'ORSAY, PARIS

VICTOR RUPRICH-ROBERT, DETAILED VIEW OF A CAPITAL FROM THE CRYPT OF THE CANTERBURY CATHEDRAL, 1856 MUSÉE D'ORSAY, PARIS

material from companies that produced decorative interiors in collaboration with architects. The Musée d'Orsay also inherited a group of some seventy drawings that had been assembled by the Louvre in its abandoned project for an architectural cabinet. The museum used its own resources to acquire material to diversify its collection, including the two thousand drawings of Hector Guimard (acquired in 1995) and some forty drawings by the students of Otto Wagner—Otto Schönthal, Emil Hoppe, and Marcel Kammerer (acquired in 1997). The Centre Georges Pompidou, which opened in 1977, originally included the Centre de création industrielle, which was meant to be devoted primarily to contemporary work, but whose exhibitions soon took a historical turn and led to the creation of a collection of drawings rather than a complete archive. These are now located in the Musée national d'art moderne, which absorbed the Centre de création industrielle in 1992.[13] Some exceptions to the Pompidou's turn away from archival collecting have nonetheless occurred; for example, its incorporation of Pol Abraham's archives, some of Georges Candilis's collection, and part of Jean Prouvé's archive, which is shared with the Archives départementales de Meurthe-et-Moselle in Nancy. Other groups of models and drawings have been acquired: works, for example, by the different partners of the Atelier d'urbanisme et d'architecture

FRANÇOIS HENNEBIQUE, BETONSTRUKTUR
DES NATURHISTORISCHEN MUSEUM,
GENUA
ARCHIVES D'ARCHITECTURE DU
XXE SIÈCLE / CITÉ DE L'ARCHITECTURE
ET DU PATRIMOINE, PARIS

FRANÇOIS HENNEBIQUE, CONCRETE
STRUCTURE OF THE MUSEUM OF
NATURAL HISTORY, GENOA, 1905
ARCHIVES D'ARCHITECTURE DU
XXE SIÈCLE / CITÉ DE L'ARCHITECTURE
ET DU PATRIMOINE, PARIS

schiedener Partner des Atelier d'Urbanisme et d'Architecture, aber auch von zahlreichen italienischen Designbüros aus der Nachkriegszeit bis in die 1980er-Jahre, die 2012 in der Ausstellung *La Tendenza* gezeigt wurden.[14] Die Bibliothèque Kandinsky im Centre Pompidou besitzt Bestände von Kunstkritikern oder Verlegern wie Christian Zervos – für die Erforschung der europäischen Architektur der 1930er-Jahre unentbehrlich – sowie Fotografien von Pierre Joly und Véra Cardot, die die französische Architektur von den 1950er- bis zu den 1980er-Jahren dokumentieren. Eine andere bedeutende Bibliothek, die Bibliothèque nationale de France, erwarb die Bestände von Frantz und Francis Jourdain, zwei wichtigen Vertreter des Jugendstils und der Moderne, für ihre Grafische Sammlung, nachdem sie sich erfolgreich gegen das Getty Research Institute durchsetzen konnte.

Anders als in Deutschland oder der Schweiz, wo die Architekturhochschulen für die Sammlung und Aufbewahrung der Archive maßgeblich sind, scheinen die französischen Hochschulen dieser Frage keine Bedeutung beizumessen.

and by a number of Italian design offices from the postwar period to the nineteen-eighties, which were presented in the 2012 exhibition at the Centre Pompidou, *La Tendenza*.[14] The Bibliothèque Kandinsky, held by the Centre Pompidou, contains material from critics and publishers such as Christian Zervos, which are indispensable to the understanding of European architecture from the nineteen-thirties, along with photographs by Pierre Joly and Véra Cardot, which document French architecture from the nineteen-fifties to the eighties. Another important library, the Bibliothèque nationale de France, acquired the collection of Frantz and Francis Jourdain, fundamental figures of Art Nouveau and modernity, which it now holds in the cabinet of prints after prohibiting its sale to the Getty Research Institute.

Unlike countries such as Germany or Switzerland, where architecture schools are important places for the collection and conservation of archives, French schools of architecture seem essentially uninterested in this issue. While the Centre Pompidou and the Musée d'Orsay were developing their programs, a network of local and regional organizations was also developing through associations independent of both the administration and professions. These groups were collecting material on architects important to various French cities.[15] Such was the case, for example, with the Archives d'architecture de la Côte Basque (which were subsequently integrated into the Centre d'archives d'architecture et de paysage en Aquitaine in Bordeaux), the Archives modernes d'architecture Lorraine in Nancy (now part of the municipal archives of the city), the Association des archives d'architecture du Nord, the Archives modernes d'architecture de Bretagne, or the Centre d'architecture en Savoie. The departmental archives played a similar role elsewhere; for instance, the Archives départementales des Bouches-du-Rhône, which now house the archives of Gaston Castel, the important Marseilles architect from the first half of the twentieth century.[16]

The situation changed significantly with the opening of the Institut français d'architecture (IFA) in 1981. A center for archives of twentieth-century architecture, the Archives d'architecture du XXe siècle, was created within the IFA, which has been located since 1989 in the facilities of the former Hôpital Marie-Lannelongue.[17] With the support and agreement of the Archives nationales, the center collects, restores, conserves, and displays material from the archives of architects, urbanists, engineers, and professional associations. Its guiding principle is not to collect "beautiful drawings" taken out of context—a sort of skimming off the cream of the

Während das Centre Pompidou und das Musée d'Orsay ihre Programmschwerpunkte entwickelten, bildete sich ein Netzwerk aus lokalen oder regionalen Organisationen, die wichtige Architektenbestände der französischen Städte sammelten:[15] beispielsweise die Archives de la Côte Basque, die inzwischen im Centre d'archives d'architecture et de paysage en Aquitaine de Bordeaux aufgegangen sind, die Archives modernes de l'architecture Lorraine in Nancy, die mittlerweile den Archives municipales de la ville angehören, die Association des archives d'architecture du Nord, die Association des Archives modernes d'architecture de Bretagne oder das Centre d'architecture en Savoie. Die Archive der Départements spielten eine vergleichbare Rolle, so etwa im Département Bouches-du-Rhône, wo sich die Bestände des Architekten Gaston Castel befinden, der in der ersten Hälfte des 20. Jahrhunderts in Marseille bedeutend war.[16]

Mit der Gründung des Institut français d'architecture (IFA) 1981 erfuhr diese Lage eine bedeutende Veränderung. Innerhalb des IFA bildete sich das Centre d'archives d'architecture du XXe siècle heraus, das sich seit 1989 im ehemaligen Hôpital Marie-Lannelongue in Paris befindet.[17] Eine Vereinbarung mit den Archives de France unterstützt die Arbeit des IFA, das Archivbestände von Architekten, Städteplanern oder Berufsverbänden sammelt, ordnet, klimatisiert, konserviert und angemessen präsentiert. Es hat sich weder der Sammlung von aus ihrem Ursprungskontext gelösten »schönen Zeichnungen« – eine Art »Rosinenpickerei« in den Archiven –, noch einer ideologisch bestimmten Auswahl verschrieben. Vielmehr möchte es komplette Bestände zusammentragen, um die historische Erforschung und die öffentliche Präsentation derjenigen Dokumente zu ermöglichen, die über die Entstehung und Konstruktionsphasen von Gebäuden Aufschluss geben.

In den verhältnismäßig großzügigen Räumlichkeiten des Centre vom IFA befinden sich die zuvor in der SADG aufbewahrte Sammlung Sauvage, die Bestände des Conservatoire des arts et métiers (von Perret bis Hennebique) sowie Teile der auch im Centre Pompidou untergebrachten Sammlung Candilis. Aufgrund eines Abkommens mit der Académie d'architecture aus dem Jahr 2000 ist das Centre für die Konservierung und Kommunikation ihrer Bestände zuständig.[18] Dank dieses Archivguts sowie der unabhängig erworbenen Sammlungen ist das Centre zur bedeutendsten Konservierungsinstanz Frankreichs geworden. Insgesamt 380 Sammlungen mit 600 Modellen und Hunderttausenden Zeichnungen machen es zu einer der umfangreichsten Einrichtung Europas. Dazu zählen die Archive von Ingenieuren wie Bernard

PIERRE JOLY UND VÉRA CARDOT,
JEAN PROUVÉ IN SEINEM
HAUS IN NANCY, UNDATIERT
CENTRE POMPIDOU, MUSÉE NATIONAL
D'ART MODERNE, BIBLIOTHÈQUE KANDINSKY

PIERRE JOLY AND VÉRA CARDOT,
JEAN PROUVÉ AT HIS HOME
IN NANCY, NO DATE
CENTRE POMPIDOU, MUSÉE NATIONAL
D'ART MODERNE, BIBLIOTHÈQUE KANDINSKY

archives—nor to make selections based on some doctrinal orientations, but rather to assemble the most complete collection possible, so as to enable historical research and public presentations of the ensemble of documents pertaining to the design, development, and construction of buildings.

With its relatively large facility, the IFA now houses the Sauvage collection, which was previously held by the SADG, the archives of the Conservatoire national des arts et métiers, from Perret to Hennebique, and part of the Candilis collection, shared with the Centre Pompidou. Most importantly, by virtue of an agreement established with the Académie d'Architecture in 2000, it is responsible for

Laffaille, die Archive des Atelier de Montrouge sowie die Bestände maßgeblicher französischer Architektenpersönlichkeiten nach 1945 wie Émile Aillaud, Jean Bossu, Jean Dubuisson, Guillaume Gillet, Claude Parent, Pierre Vago oder Bernard Zehrfuss. Die genauen Bestände sind mit ausgewähltem Bildmaterial auf der Webseite ArchiWebture online zugänglich.[19] Mit seinem Bulletin *Colonnes* pflegt das Centre Verbindungen zu anderen französischen Archiven. Als Teil der 2007 in Paris eröffneten Cité de l'architecture et du patrimoine kann es deren Räume für Wechselausstellungen nutzen und der Galerie für moderne und zeitgenössische Architektur des angegliederten Museums seinerseits Arbeiten zur Verfügung stellen. Nicht zuletzt beschäftigen sich die Mitarbeiter des Centre mit den Möglichkeiten und Herausforderungen der digitalen Archivierung.

Schließlich konnte dank der finanziellen Unterstützung der Region Centre und des von der französischen Regierung gegründeten und in Orléans ansässigen FRAC Centre (Fonds régional pour l'art contemporain) seit 1992 eine bemerkenswerte Sammlung zeitgenössischer Kunst und Architektur aufgebaut werden. Die häufig in Wanderausstellungen gezeigte Sammlung verfügt seit 2013 über einen festen Ausstellungsort, der von Dominique Jakob und Brendan MacFarlane erbaut wurde. 800 Modelle und 15 000 Zeichnungen dokumentieren das Werk von insgesamt 160 Architekten, die eher mit bemerkenswerten Einzelstücken als mit kompletten Archivbeständen vertreten sind. Das Spektrum reicht von der Architekturskulptur der 1950er-Jahre bis hin zu »radikalen« Gruppen wie Archigram, Superstudio, Haus-Rucker-Co oder Architecture Principe. Forschungen zu räumlichen Strukturen und Kunststoffschalen sind ebenso präsent wie Projekte, die ab den 1980er-Jahren unter die schwer greifbare Strömung des Dekonstruktivismus fielen.[20]

Die Maßnahmen dieser verschiedenen Einrichtungen unterscheiden sich in ihrer Schwerpunktsetzung – beispielsweise bevorzugt das FRAC Centre bestimmte Teile der jüngeren Architekturgeschichte –, nach ihrer Kapazität vollständige Bestände aufzunehmen oder aber ausschließlich Zeichnungen, nach ihrem regionalen oder nationalen geografischen Standort und nach ihrer jeweiligen internationalen Ausrichtung, die in Orléans, am Centre Pompidou und – mit einer leichten Einschränkung – am Musée d'Orsay dominiert. Sie leisten innerhalb des universitären Rahmens einen Beitrag zur historischen Forschung und bilden die Grundlage für Ausstellungen und Veröffentlichungen, die sich sowohl an ein hochspezialisiertes als auch an ein breites Publikum wenden können. Sammlungen, die sich mit der Architektur

the conservation and communication of these collections.[18] Along with these ensembles and other materials that it has collected on its own, IFA's center has become one of the most important sites of conservation in France and one of the richest in Europe, with 380 collections that include some 600 models and thousands of drawings. The collection includes archives of engineers, such as Bernard Laffaille, those of the Atelier de Montrouge, as well as fundamental figures of French architecture after 1945, such as Émile Aillaud, Jean Bossu, Jean Dubuisson, Guillaume Gillet, Claude Parent, Pierre Vago, or Bernard Zehrfuss. Detailed inventories of the archives and a selection of images are accessible online on the ArchiWebture site.[19] Through its bulletin *Colonnes*, the IFA's center maintains relations with other centers in France. As part of the Cité de l'architecture et du patrimoine, which opened in Paris in 2007, center has access to galleries for temporary exhibitions and contributes to the ongoing development of the gallery of modern and contemporary architecture inside the complex of the Cité. Teams from the center have been involved in addressing the new challenges of creating and maintaining archives in the digital age.

Finally, the FRAC Centre, the Fonds régional d'art contemporain, based in Orléans and set up with the financial support of France's Centre region and of the state, has been able to devote considerable resources to creating a remarkable collection of contemporary art and architecture. While the collection is mostly presented through travelling exhibitions, it also has a permanent presentation space built by Dominique Jakob and Brendan MacFarlane in 2013. The FRAC's collection of 800 models and 15,000 drawings from some 160 architects consists more of remarkable pieces than of archival ensembles. These range from the architecture-sculptures of the nineteen-fifties to radical groups such as Archigram, Superstudio, Haus-Rucker-Co, or Architecture Principe. Research on spatial structures and plastic shell forms are well represented, as are projects from the nineteen-eighties that claim to adhere to the rather slippery and indefinite movement of deconstructivism.[20]

The policies followed by these various organizations address different issues and diverge in their approach. Some, like the FRAC Centre, focus on certain features of recent architecture. Others vary in their capacities, housing complete collections or drawings only, and differ in their regional or national context or in the international scope of their chosen fields. Interest in international developments is greatest in Orléans, at the Centre Pompidou, and to a somewhat lesser extent at the Musée d'Orsay. These institutions help support historical research in a university setting, and they provide a platform for

JAKOB + MACFARLANE,
LES TURBULENCES, MODELL
FÜR DAS FRAC CENTRE, ORLÉANS, 2006
FRAC CENTRE, ORLÉANS

JAKOB + MACFARLANE,
LES TURBULENCES, MODEL
FOR THE FRAC CENTRE, ORLÉANS, 2006
FRAC CENTRE, ORLÉANS

vor dem späten 20. Jahrhundert beschäftigen, sind in ihren Erwerbsbemühungen, seien es Ankäufe oder Schenkungen, oft aus räumlichen Gründen eingeschränkt, zumal manche Bestände einen riesigen Umfang erreichen. Einerseits erleichtert das digitale Zeitalter – zugegebenermaßen nur mithilfe weitreichender Investitionen – den Überblick über die Bestände. Andererseits stellen sich in seiner Folge heikle methodologische und juristische Probleme in Bezug auf die Sammlung von Materialien, anhand derer sich die zeitgenössische Arbeit nachvollziehen lässt: Die Kehrseite der rettenden Technik sind ethische und sogar praktische Probleme bei der Konservierung des architektonischen Gedächtnisses.

1 Für einen Gesamtüberblick vor etwa 20 Jahren siehe David Peyceré u. a., *Archives d'architectes: état des fonds, XIXe-XXe siècles*, Paris 1996.

2 Alain Demangeon und Bruno Fortier, *Les vaisseaux et les villes; l'arsenal de Cherbourg*, Brüssel 1978; Antoine Picon, *Architectes et ingénieurs au siècle des lumières*, Marseille 1988.

3 Jean-Daniel Pariset (Hrsg.), *Reconstructions et modernisation, la France après les ruines 1918…1945…*, Ausst.-Kat. Musée de l'histoire de France, Paris 1991.

4 Ministère de l'équipement, du logement, des transports et du tourisme (Hrsg.), *Archives du Ministère de l'équipement, du logement, des transports et du tourisme et des anciens ministères de la construction et des travaux publics*, Paris 1997.

5 Richard Klein (Hrsg.), *Roland Simounet à l'œuvre: architecture, 1951–1996*, Ausst.-Kat. Musée d'art moderne Lille métropole, Paris 2000.

6 Der Bestand bildete die Grundlage für die Ausstellung anlässlich des 100. Geburtstags des Architekten: Bruno Foucart (Hrsg.), *Viollet-le-Duc*, Ausst.-Kat. Galeries nationales du Grand Palais, Paris 1980.

7 Arthur Drexler (Hrsg.), *The Architecture of the Ecole des Beaux-Arts*, Ausst.-Kat. The Museum of Modern Art, New York 1975.

8 Bruno Girveau (Hrsg.), *Charles Garnier. Un architecte pour un empire*, Ausst.-Kat. École nationale supérieure des beaux-arts, Paris 2010.

9 Paul Henri Dufournet, *Catalogue des collections de l'Académie d'architecture*, Paris 1988.

10 Gwenaël Delhumeau, *L'Invention du béton armé. Hennebique, 1890–1914*, Paris 1999.

11 Fondation Le Corbusier, *Le Corbusier Plans*, 16 DVDs, Paris 2005; Le Corbusier, *Lettres à ses maîtres*, Bd. 1, 2 und 3, Paris 2002, 2003 und 2014; Le Corbusier, *Correspondance. Lettres à la famille*, Bde. 1 und 2, Gollion 2011 und 2013.

12 Alain Guiheux u. a. (Hrsg.), *Tony Garnier. L'œuvre complète*, Ausst.-Kat. Centre de création industrielle, Centre Pompidou, Paris 1989.

13 Alain Guiheux (Hrsg.), *Collection d'architecture du Centre Pompidou*, Paris.

14 Frédéric Migayrou (Hrsg.), *La Tendenza. Italian Architectures, 1965–1985*, Ausst.-Kat. Centre Pompidou, Paris 2012.

15 »Associations d'archives d'architectes. Collectes d'archives en France. Archives orales, archives informatiques«, in: *Colonnes*, 22, Dezember 2004.

16 Isabelle Chiavassa u. a. (Hrsg.), *Gaston Castel, architecte marseillais*, Ausst.-Kat. Musées de Marseille, Aix-en-Provence, Marseille, 1988.

17 Maurice Culot (Hrsg.), *Institut français d'architecture; archives d'architecture du XXe siècle*, Liège 1991.

18 David Peyceré, »Le Centre d'archives d'architecture du XXe siècle«, in: *Sociétés et Représentations*, 30, 2010, S. 181–193.

19 ArchiWebture, online unter http://archiwebture.citechaillot.fr (Stand: 23.1.2014)

20 Marie-Ange Brayer (Hrsg.), *Architectures expérimentales, 1950–2012. Collection du FRAC Centre*, Ausst.-Kat. FRAC Centre u. a., Orléans 2003.

exhibitions and publications for audiences ranging from the most specialized to the public at large. Collections devoted to architecture prior to the twentieth century are limited in their efforts at acquisition, either through purchase or through donation, by their own spatial limitations, as certain office archives can attain a staggering size. At the same time, the digital age, which facilitates searches of the archives—although these require significant initial investments—has raised a host of knotty methodological and legal problems regarding the collection of materials that document contemporary production. On the one hand, the new techniques are a salvation, but, on the other, they also call into question the ethics and the very practice of conserving the memory of architecture.

1   For a general survey of the French archives twenty years ago, see Sonia Gaubert et al., *Archives d'architectes: état des fonds, XIXe-XXe siècles* (Paris, 1996).

2   Alain Demangeon and Bruno Fortier, *Les vaisseaux et les villes: l'arsenal de Cherbourg* (Brussels, 1978); Antoine Picon, *Architectes et ingénieurs au siècle des lumières* (Marseilles, 1988).

3   Jean-Daniel Pariset, ed., *Reconstructions et modernisation, la France après les ruines, 1918 . . . 1945 . . .*, exh. cat. Musée de l'histoire de France (Paris, 1991).

4   Ministère de l'équipement, du logement, des transports et du tourisme, eds., *Archives du Ministère de l'équipement, du logement, des transports et du tourisme et des anciens ministères de la construction et des travaux publics*, Mission des archives nationales (Paris, 1997).

5   Richard Klein, ed., *Roland Simounet à l'œuvre: architecture, 1951–1996*, exh. cat. Musée d'art moderne de Lille métropole (Paris, 2000).

6   The collection made it possible to organize an exhibition celebrating the one-hundredth anniversary of the birth of the architect. See Bruno Foucart, ed., *Viollet-le-Duc*, exh. cat. Galeries nationales du Grand Palais (Paris, 1980).

7   Arthur Drexler, ed., *The Architecture of the Ecole des Beaux-Arts*, exh. cat. Museum of Modern Art (New York, 1975).

8   Bruno Girveau, ed., *Charles Garnier: un architecte pour un empire*, exh. cat. École nationale supérieure des beaux-arts (Paris, 2010).

9   Paul Henri Dufournet, *Catalogue des collections de l'Académie d'architecture* (Paris, 1988).

10 Gwenaël Delhumeau, *L'Invention du béton armé: Hennebique, 1890–1914* (Paris, 1999).

11 Fondation Le Corbusier, ed., *Le Corbusier Plans*, collection of 16 DVDs (Paris, 2005); Le Corbusier, *Lettres à ses maîtres*, vols. 1, 2, 3 (Paris, 2002, 2003, 2014); Le Corbusier, *Correspondence*, ed. Fondation Le Corbusier et al., vols. 1, 2 (Gollion, 2011, 2013).

12 Alain Guiheux et al., eds., *Tony Garnier: l'œuvre complète*, exh. cat. Centre de création industrielle, Centre Pompidou (Paris, 1989).

13 Alain Guiheux, ed., *Collection d'architecture du Centre Georges Pompidou* (Paris, 1998).

14 Frédéric Migayrou, ed., *La Tendenza: Italian Architectures, 1965–1985*, exh. cat. Centre Pompidou (Paris, 2012).

15 "Associations d'archives d'architectes: Collectes d'archives en France; Archives orales, archives informatiques," *Colonnes* 22 (December 2004).

16 Isabelle Chiavassa et al., eds., , *Gaston Castel: architecte marseillais*, exh. cat. Musée d'histoire de Marseille Aix-en-Provence (Marseilles, 1988).

17 Maurice Culot, ed., *Archives d'architecture du XXe siècle, Institut français d'architecture* (Liège, 1991).

18 David Peyceré, "Le Centre d'archives d'architecture du XXe siècle," *Sociétés et Représentations* 30 (December 2010), pp. 181–93.

19 ArchiWebture, http://archiwebture.citechaillot.fr (accessed January 23, 2014).

20 Marie-Ange Brayer, ed., *Architectures expérimentales, 1950–2012: collection du FRAC Centre*, exh. cat. FRAC Centre et al. (Orléans, 2003).

ÖFFENTLICHES LEBEN ALS SAMMLUNGSSCHWERPUNKT DES V&A

Das Vereinigte Königreich verfügt über kein ausschließlich der Architektur gewidmetes Museum. Es gibt zwar zahlreiche Institutionen, die die Leistungen der Disziplin vermitteln, allerdings keine, die sowohl einen Überblick über historische als auch zeitgenössische Entwicklungen des Faches verschafft. Diese Situation geht mit gewissen Nachteilen einher. Die Londoner Architekturszene ist sehr vielfältig und zerfällt in mehrere Strömungen. Deshalb hat man nur selten den Eindruck, dass es zwischen diesen Gruppen eine Zusammengehörigkeit gibt. Wer zum Beispiel die Ausstellungen der Architectural Association School of Architecture besucht, wird dort nicht nur auf ein vollkommen anderes Architekturverständnis stoßen als etwa in der Royal Academy of Arts, sondern sogar ein völlig anderes Publikum antreffen. Gewiss: Es gibt in der Stadt einige Orte, an denen Architekturausstellungen zu sehen sind (etwa die Barbican Art Gallery, das Design Museum, die Tate Modern, das British Museum, das Royal Institute of British Architects [RIBA], die Architecture Foundation und so weiter), doch von allen öffentlichen Kultureinrichtungen hat sich einzig das Victoria and Albert Museum (V&A) dem Ziel der systematischen Sammlung von architekturbezogenem Material verschrieben.

Das V&A zeigt nicht nur die einzige architekturgeschichtliche Dauerausstellung in England, es beherbergt auch die Nationalsammlung architektonischer Zeichnungen. Überdies ist es die einzige nationale Kultureinrichtung, die sich der architektonischen Entwurfs- und Bauplanung schon von jeher kuratorisch annimmt; seit der Gründung meines eigenen kuratorischen Aufgabenbereichs ist auch die Gegenwartsarchitektur in unserem Haus ein wichtiges Forschungsgebiet. Zurzeit umfasst unsere Sammlung rund 100 000 Baupläne. Dazu kommen noch eine Million Bauzeichnungen aus den Beständen des Royal Institute of British Architects.

Seit das RIBA 2004 seine Bestände nach South Kensington überführt hat, sind beide Sammlungen im Prints and Drawings Study Room des V&A untergebracht. Sie ergänzen sich zwar, haben aber dennoch ihre Eigenständigkeit bewahrt: So werden etwa beide von eigenen kuratorischen Teams betreut

COLLECTING CONTEMPORARY PUBLIC LIFE AT THE V&A

The UK has no museum dedicated to architecture, and while there are many institutions that exhibit and advocate for the discipline, there is no one place to experience an account of its history combined with an impression of contemporary architectural production. This has certain disadvantages. Architectural discourse in London is rich and diverse, but very encamped; there is rarely a sense of the city's architectural factions coming together on common ground. You would experience a very particular take on architecture (in terms of its practice and its audience) if you spent time visiting exhibitions at the Architectural Association School of Architecture, as opposed to the Royal Academy of Arts, for instance. The list of spaces for architectural exhibitions in the city is long (the Barbican, the Design Museum, Tate Modern, the British Museum, the Royal Institute of British Architects (RIBA), the Architecture Foundation, and more), but it is only the Victoria and Albert Museum (V&A), of the public institutions, that has an explicit commitment to the systematic collection of architectural material.

The V&A houses the only permanent gallery of the history of architecture in the country and the national collection of architectural drawings. It is the only national institution that has always held the design and making of buildings as a core part of its curatorial mission, and now, with the creation of my own curatorial section, architecture is a field of contemporary study for the museum once again. We currently hold around 100,000 architectural drawings in the collection, forcefully complemented by one million drawings from the Royal Institute of British Architects' collection.

Both the RIBA and V&A collections have been housed in the Prints and Drawings Study Room at the V&A since 2004, when the RIBA moved its holdings to South Kensington. The collections are complementary but distinct. They have separate curatorial teams and separate storage, and while it is the V&A's that is the designated national collection, there is an agreement that the two do not compete for acquisitions. The study rooms allow easy public access to both architecture collections, alongside the V&A's huge holdings of other works on paper.[1]

WRIGHT & WRIGHT
ARCHITECTS,
RIBA-STUDIENSAAL
IM VICTORIA
AND ALBERT MUSEUM
WRIGHT & WRIGHT
ARCHITECTS,
RIBA STUDY ROOM
AT THE VICTORIA
AND ALBERT MUSEUM

und sind auch in unterschiedlichen Archiven untergebracht. Und obwohl das V&A offiziell den Status einer Nationalsammlung hat, ist vereinbart, dass beide Institute bei Erwerbungen nicht als Konkurrenten auftreten. In beiden Archiven kann sich der Besucher Blätter zur Ansicht vorlegen lassen, was auch für die übrigen riesigen grafischen Bestände des V&A gilt.[1]

Noch interessanter ist vielleicht, dass das Museum eine Vielzahl weiterer architektonischer Artefakte in seinen Beständen beherbergt: in den asiatischen Sammlungen beispielsweise dekorative skulpturale Arbeiten und Schmuckelemente; dazu kommen noch zwei große Säle mit Abgüssen (die sogenannten Cast Courts), in denen auch Eins-zu-eins-Abgüsse der Trajanssäule und des Pórtico de la Gloria aus Santiago di Compostela zu sehen sind; dazu noch ein Raum mit verschiedenen Inneneinrichtungen (darunter auch Frank Lloyd Wrights Ausstattung von Edgar J. Kaufmanns Büro). Architektur ist in allen Facetten im gesamten V&A zu finden. Wir besitzen (und zeigen) selbst das Telegramm, das Joseph Paxton an seine Frau geschickt hat, als er 1850 mit der Planung des Londoner Kristallpalast beauftragt wurde.

Sogar das Museumsgebäude selbst ist als architektonisches Ausstellungsstück konzipiert. Henry Cole, der den Bau zwischen 1856 und 1873 als Gründungsdirektor überwachte, begrüßte es sogar, dass der Komplex nicht aus einem Guss war. Auf diesen Umstand hat Christopher Marsden, Chefarchivar des V&A

ABGUSS DER TRAJANSSÄULE
IN DEN CAST COURTS

CAST OF TRAJAN'S COLUMN
IN THE CAST COURTS

ABGUSS DER TRAJANSSÄULE
IN DEN CAST COURTS

CAST OF TRAJAN'S COLUMN
IN THE CAST COURTS

Perhaps most interestingly, the museum also holds a diversity of other architectural artifacts in its collections, from decorative sculptural works and building fragments in the Asian collections, to the spectacular artifacts of the Cast Courts (originally known as the Architectural Courts, and including one-to-one casts of Trajan's Column and the Pórtico de la Gloria in Santiago de Compostela), as well as room sets and interiors (including Frank Lloyd Wright's Kaufmann Office interior among others). The practice and art of architecture are everywhere at the V&A. We even have (on display) the telegraph that Joseph Paxton sent to his wife the day he won the job of designing the Crystal Palace in Hyde Park in 1850.

Even the museum building itself is explicitly conceived as an architectural exhibit. When the museum's founder Henry Cole was building it between 1856 and 1873, he made the piecemeal development of the site into a virtue. Christopher Marsden, the V&A's senior archivist, writes: "[Cole] saw that each stage of the building could provide opportunities for experimentation

DAUERAUSSTELLUNG
DER ARCHITEKTURSAMMLUNG,
VICTORIA AND ALBERT
MUSEUM, LONDON
PERMANENT EXHIBITION OF
THE ARCHITECTURE GALLERY,
VICTORIA AND ALBERT
MUSEUM, LONDON

erst unlängst in einem Aufsatz wieder hingewiesen: »[Cole] hatte begriffen«, schreibt er dort, »dass jede Planungs- und Entstehungsphase des Museums die Möglichkeit bot, neue Baustoffe und planerische Optionen auszuprobieren und sich beispielsweise immer wieder neu mit der Frage zu befassen, wie man ein großes öffentliches Gebäude am effizientesten beheizen, beleuchten und belüften kann.«[2] Tatsächlich lag dieser schrittweisen Erweiterung des Hauses sogar ein pädagogischer Gedanke zugrunde: Denn das Museum sollte sowohl Fachleuten als auch dem breiten Publikum auch einen Eindruck davon vermitteln, wie die dort gezeigten Exponate selbst entstanden waren. Die Gipsnachbildungen antiker und mittelalterlicher Gebäude, die in den beiden erwähnten Sälen zu sehen sind, sollten ihrerseits als Vorlagen für weitere Kopien und als Anregungen für neue Entwürfe dienen. Inzwischen haben sie diese Funktion natürlich längst eingebüßt. Daher könnte man die beiden Cast Courts heute als baugeschichtlichen »Elefantenfriedhof« bezeichnen.

Das V&A verfügt über keine explizit als solche deklarierte Architekturabteilung, die Zuständigkeit für die Sammlung zeitgenössischer Architektur liegt vielmehr in verschiedenen Händen, und streng genommen hat das Haus die Gegenwartsarchitektur in den letzten Jahren sogar vernachlässigt. Dazu passt auch, dass das Museum keine einzige digitalisierte Architekturzeichnung besitzt. Außerdem gibt es kaum Bauzeichnungen aus dem späten 20. Jahrhundert, und unsere Sammlung zeitgenössischer Bauentwürfe und -pläne ist sogar noch lückenhafter.

Ich selbst bin erst seit Januar 2013 als Chefkurator der neuen Abteilung Contemporary Architecture, Design and Digital am V&A tätig und befasse mich seither mit dem Aufbau einer neuen, zeitgenössischen Sammlung. Die neue Abteilung zeugt von dem Bestreben des Museums, sich intensiver mit Fragen des zeitgenössischen Designs zu befassen, sie kann aber auch als Eingeständnis dafür gelten, dass die mehr oder weniger seit den 1850er-Jahren etablierten Strukturen nicht mehr dazu geeignet sind, eine Sammlung heutiger, bisher nicht gesammelter Designobjekte aufzubauen.

Ich selbst bin als Quereinsteiger an das V&A gekommen, vorher hatte ich noch nie fest an einem Museum gearbeitet, sondern war vor allem als Kritiker und Journalist, mitunter auch als Kurator tätig gewesen. Noch kurz vor der Aufnahme meiner neuen Funktion schrieb ich jede Woche eine Kolumne für den *London Evening Standard*. Dabei war es mir wichtig, die – von manchen Kritikern für völlig ahnungslos gehaltenen – Leser mit Belehrungen darüber zu verschonen, was es mit der Arbeit des Architekten eigentlich

DAUERAUSSTELLUNG
DER ARCHITEKTURSAMMLUNG,
VICTORIA AND ALBERT
MUSEUM, LONDON

PERMANENT EXHIBITION OF
THE ARCHITECTURE GALLERY,
VICTORIA AND ALBERT
MUSEUM, LONDON

auf sich hat. Vielmehr wies ich immer wieder darauf hin, dass es vor allem auf das gesellschaftliche Engagement ankommt, dass also jeder Bürger die Möglichkeit hat, sich aktiv einzubringen. Ich glaube nämlich, dass sich die Menschen, die in einer Stadt leben und arbeiten, dort im Allgemeinen besser auskennen als sogenannte Experten. Mir ging es also vor allem darum, dieses intuitive Verständnis zu würdigen und seine Bedeutung für architektonische und städtebauliche Fragen deutlich zu machen. Dabei lag es mir natürlich völlig fern, den Beitrag der Architekten und Stadtplaner zur Entwicklung der Stadt in Abrede zu stellen, ganz im Gegenteil. Eine Zeitung wie der *London Evening Standard,* die jeden Tag von einer Million Menschen gelesen wird, ist natürlich ein wundervolles Forum, um über die ganze Vielfalt und den gesellschaftlichen und kulturellen Reichtum der britischen Hauptstadt zu sprechen. Die Leser des Blattes kennen sich in der Stadt aus und sind stolz darauf, Londoner zu sein. Die meisten von ihnen lassen sich nun einmal am ehesten mit einer Mischung aus Historie, Anekdote, Reportage und Kritik gewinnen. Das heißt, meine Leser haben von mir sicher nicht erwartet, dass ich ihnen vorgaukele, sämtliche Probleme ließen sich mit ein paar architektonischen Attraktionen aus der Welt schaffen. Aus dieser Erkenntnis ergaben sich für mich interessante Schlussfolgerungen. Am erfolgreichsten waren nämlich jene Artikel, die nicht nur das Bauen als solches thematisieren, sondern die sich vielmehr ausdrücklich mit dem öffentlichen Raum beschäftigen.

In einem Artikel über ein zur Bebauung freigegebenes großes Grundstück an der Themse im Londoner Südosten habe ich beispielsweise 2011 die Frage aufgeworfen, wieso man einen derart geschichtsträchtigen Ort einfach wie ein unbeschriebenes Blatt behandelt (schließlich befand sich in Convoys Wharf bereits im 16. Jahrhundert eine von Heinrich VIII. gegründete Marinewerft).[3] Wieso musste ungeachtet des ausgeprägten Bewusstseins der Anwohner für die historische Bedeutung des Ortes und des durchaus vorhandenen Geschichtsbewusstseins zahlreicher Londoner Architekten auch hier wieder mit allen Tricks der übliche investorenfreundliche Bebauungsplan durchgedrückt werden? Ich habe diese Frage unbeantwortet gelassen und lediglich versucht, die widerstreitenden Interessengruppen beim Namen zu nennen, also die engagierten Bürger im Londoner Südosten, die mit dem Bebauungsplan befassten Institutionen, ferner die Politik und den Finanzsektor sowie die ausländischen Investoren. Zum Schluss habe ich noch auf die historische Komponente hingewiesen, die bei jeder Londoner Baustelle dazugehört. Der Artikel wurde sogar in einer

in materials, in design and in such practical questions as how large modern public buildings could be heated, lighted, and ventilated."[2] This came with a pedagogical intent; practitioners and the broader public should learn about the process of design and making through what they see in the museum. The plaster copies of classical and medieval buildings in the Cast Courts were intended to be copied and used as source material for new designs. It would be difficult to argue for their use as such today. The Cast Courts are a spectacular elephant's graveyard of architectural education.

The V&A has no architecture department as such and has never had one. This means that responsibility for collecting contemporary architecture has been fragmented, and in recent years the museum has neglected contemporary architectural practice. As of today, the museum holds not a single architectural drawing in digital form. Our late twentieth-century selection of architectural drawings is not strong, and our contemporary holdings even patchier.

My own engagement with the question of how to build a contemporary collection for the V&A began in January 2013, when I joined the museum as senior curator and head of a new curatorial section of the collections department called Contemporary Architecture, Design and Digital. The section signals the museum's ambition to renew its approach to contemporary design, but it is also a tacit admission that the structures of the museum, more or less intact since the eighteen-fifties, are not suited to building a collection of new forms of design practice.

I arrived at the V&A from outside the museum world, having worked as a critic and journalist, as well as on occasional curatorial projects. Most recently, I had been writing a weekly column in the *London Evening Standard*. One of my main concerns there had been to move away from a model of criticism that aimed to substantiate the value of architects' work in the face of an uncomprehending world. I was more interested in developing a sense among readers that the important part of any story was the civic realm, a territory that everyone has a stake in. I believe this realm is one that is always understood better by the citizens that live in it than by a professional caste. The aim of my writing was to dignify people's intuitive understanding of their city, and to ensure that the works of architecture and urban design I wrote about were posed in dialogue with those intuitions, for good or ill.

This is not to diminish the contribution of architects and urban designers to the development of the city, quite the opposite. But a newspaper like the *London Evening Standard*, read daily by a million people, is a place where it is possible

Sitzung des Londoner Stadtrats (London Assembly) erwähnt und auch in einer Diskussion zwischen dem Abgeordneten des Wahlkreises Deptford und Gegnern des Projektes. Er hatte jedoch keinen anklagenden Charakter, sondern plädierte lediglich für ein weit gefasstes Verständnis von Architektur, in dem sich das Großstadtleben in seiner ganzen Vielfalt abbildet.

Im Jahr 2012 habe ich dann mit David Chipperfield zusammengearbeitet und das Team der Architekturbiennale in Venedig geleitet. Unser Titel *Common Ground* hatte eine doppelte Bedeutung. Zunächst einmal wollte David mit diesem Motto das Gemeinsame zwischen allen Architekten betonen und die Aufsplitterung in unterschiedliche Gruppen überwinden. Ferner handelte es sich auch um einen Appell an die Teilnehmer, sich über ihre gemeinsamen Sorgen und Probleme auszutauschen. Zweitens sollte *Common Ground* auf den allen Bürgern gehörenden Boden der Stadt verweisen. Schließlich ist es dieser Boden, auf dem der Architekt Gebäude errichtet, den er strukturiert, auf dem er Zeichen setzt, obwohl er durchaus nicht der Einzige ist, der zum Gelingen solcher Projekte beiträgt.

Nach meinem Eindruck waren die Installationen auf der Biennale umso erfolgreicher, je besser sie dem zweiten Aspekt des Biennale-Mottos gerecht wurden. Wir haben mit unserem Konzept ganz bewusst versucht, die Realität des Großstadtlebens in seiner ganzen Vielfalt abzubilden, auch wenn dies vielleicht nicht in allen Räumen gleich gut gelungen ist. So sollte etwa das mit dem Goldenen Löwen ausgezeichnete Projekt »Gran Horizonte« von Urban-Think Tank und Justin McGuirk (eine Café-Bar mit einer Ausstellung über den Torre David, ein halbfertiges, von 750 Familien »besetztes« Hochhaus in Caracas) nicht nur einen Eindruck einer urbanen Situation vermitteln, sondern überdies einen ungewöhnlichen Ort vorstellen.[4]

Diese biografischen Details sind hier deshalb wichtig, weil ich seit der Übernahme meiner neuen Funktion am V&A nicht mehr nur für die Architektur zuständig bin, sondern noch weitere Gestaltungsbereiche betreue. Das Museum erwartet von unserer Abteilung, dass wir in den Bereichen Architektur und Städtebau, Produktdesign (womit nicht nur das Möbeldesign gemeint ist) und digitales Design ein hohes wissenschaftliches Niveau erreichen. Dabei ist es unsere Aufgabe, uns vor allem mit »Gestaltung und Gesellschaft« zu befassen, ein Kriterium, das bewusst sehr vage und allgemein gehalten ist. Das neue Projekt verdankt seine Entstehung einigen größeren Veränderungen hier im Haus, darunter auch dem Amtsantritt des neuen Direktors Martin Roth im September 2011.

to speak about the full richness of London. The readership is knowledgeable about and proud of their association with the city. Readers would engage most of all with a combination of history, anecdote, reportage, and criticism—they were not interested in me reducing a problem to parameters that can be solved by a building alone. This had interesting consequences. The articles with the most impact were those that broadened the discourse away from just buildings and toward what the public realm might mean in a given place.

For instance, my article in 2011 about a large piece of undeveloped riverside in South East London tried to open up the question of why a site with half a millennium of history (Convoys Wharf had been the site of Henry VIII's dockyard in the sixteenth century) was being treated as a blank canvas.[3] Why is it that despite passionate local understanding of the historical significance of the site, plus a city full of architects whose work is interested in such history, the standard tricks of large-scale commercial residential master planning are rolled out? I proposed no particular answers to this, but tried to present the competing forces: passionate local advocacy, the pragmatic development of a master plan, politicians, finance, overseas land ownership, and the palimpsest of history always present in any London site. The article was quoted in a London Assembly meeting and used in a debate between the Member of Parliament for Deptford and objectors. But it was not a campaigning article, more an appeal for an expanded definition of architecture that embraces the gravidity of urban situations and how they change.

In 2012 I worked with David Chipperfield as head of his team for the Venice Architecture Biennale. Our theme and title, *Common Ground,* was intended to have a twofold connotation. First, David wanted to propose a Biennale that recognized the commonalities between architects, going beyond factionalism to try to ask participants to describe their common concerns and predicaments. Second, the titular *Common Ground* was conceived as addressing the common ground of the city, a ground that architects build on, frame, and contribute to, but are not solely responsible for creating.

How all this played out at the Biennale was revealing, and the success of installations, in my view, was dependent more on their engagement with the latter definition of the Biennale title than with the former. Our exhibition brief was a deliberate attempt to engage something like the reality of urban situations in all their richness, and while this was not visible in every room, the Golden Lion-winning project, *Gran Horizonte* by Urban-Think Tank and Justin McGuirk (a bar and cafe with an exhibition on the topic of the Torre

Aus den genannten Gründen war es meine erste Aufgabe, eine neue Sammlungsstrategie zu entwickeln, die allen drei Bereichen gerecht wird, eine Strategie, die das zeitgenössische Sammeln mit rascher Reaktion ermöglicht. Natürlich hätten wir das Gewicht der umfangreichen Bestände auch als Belastung empfinden können, als Verpflichtung, die historischen Traditionslinien möglichst nahtlos fortzuschreiben und noch vorhandene Lücken in der bestehenden Sammlung zu schließen. Doch ich möchte, dass sich die neue Sammlung nach außen, an die Welt richtet und sich nicht nur auf unsere eigenen Besitzstände konzentriert. Mittlerweile verfolgen viele Abteilungen des Museums diese Strategie und verabschieden sich von der für das 19. Jahrhundert typischen Tradition, lediglich erlesene Objekte zu sammeln. Stattdessen möchten auch sie die Objekte im Rahmen ihres jeweiligen Kontexts präsentieren. So waren etwa die 1998 fertiggestellten British Galleries die erste Abteilung des Museums, die Objekte aus allen Sammlungen des Hauses zeigten, um eine Chronologie der Designkultur sichtbar zu machen. Das Rapid Response Collecting, also das Sammeln, das eine schnelle Reaktion auf aktuelle Strömungen ermöglicht, ergänzt diese Vorgehensweise. Kulturelle Institutionen wie das V&A haben von jeher viel Zeit, Geld und Geduld investiert, um herauszufinden, welche Objekte wirklich bedeutsam sind. So ist eine Hierarchie der Erwerbungen entstanden, die dem Haus jetzt bisweilen zu schaffen macht. In der Geschichte des V&A war die Kennerschaft stets das wichtigste Kriterium, und die einzelnen Sammlungen waren (und sind es teilweise bis heute) vor allem an Unikaten (oder Fast-Unikaten) und an handwerklich erzeugten Produkten interessiert. Natürlich gibt es an unserem Museum immer noch Abteilungen, die sich vor allem mit bestimmten Werkstoffen und / oder Techniken befassen (Metallarbeiten, Schmuck, Porträtminiaturen, Schnupftabaksdosen und so weiter). Dennoch haben sich die British Galleries dafür entschieden, künftig nicht mehr nur auf die Karte »Expertise« zu setzen, sondern ihre Exponate lieber breit zu kontextualisieren.
Natürlich bleibt noch viel zu tun. Auf der Höhe der Zeit werden die Sammlungen des V&A nämlich nur so lange bleiben, wie es uns gelingt, auch die neuen Entwicklungen in den Bereichen Architektur, Design und Herstellung angemessen zu dokumentieren. Um dies zu gewährleisten und künftigen Forschergenerationen einen realistischen Eindruck von den heute üblichen Gestaltungs- und Herstellungsverfahren zu vermitteln, beschreiten wir jetzt einen neuen Weg und sammeln fortan auch fabrikneue Objekte.

David, a slum in a half-finished office building in central Caracas), clearly attempted to make an exhibition that was both a setting and a proposition about an extraordinary place.[4]

This biographical detail is important because my joining the V&A broadened my field of engagement beyond architecture, and gave me the responsibility for two further fields of design. The brief from the museum for our new curatorial section was to develop specific expertise in these three fields of contemporary collecting and exhibiting: architecture and urbanism, product design (which we loosely define as design that is not furniture), and digital design. The intellectual background to this was articulated by the museum as an interest in "design and society," a parameter that was left deliberately vague and undefined. This new effort was provoked by a number of changes in the museum, including the arrival of a new director, Martin Roth, in September 2011.

My first engagement with these topics was to propose a new collecting strategy that spanned all three of our fields, one that tried to find a way that contemporary collecting could be done with timeliness and urgency. The weight of a great collection could be seen as a constraint, in the sense that we all feel a responsibility to continue historical trajectories of collecting and filling holes in what currently exists. I wanted our collecting to be addressed outward, toward the world, rather than to be focused on what's in our stores. This continued a trajectory that can be seen in many parts of the museum, away from a nineteenth-century tradition of collecting based on taste and connoisseurship and toward considering objects as part of their contexts. The British Galleries, for instance, completed in 1998, were the first (of several since) to bring all the collections of the museum together to tell a chronological story of design culture.

Rapid Response Collecting contributes to this trajectory. Cultural institutions like the V&A have spent a lot of time, money, and patience on establishing which objects are valuable. In doing so, they have created a hierarchy in which they are invested. In the history of the V&A, connoisseurship was a priority, and there was (and in some collections still is) an emphasis on the unique (or nearly unique) and handmade. We still have galleries dedicated to particular materials or techniques (metalwork, jewelry, portrait miniatures, snuff boxes, etc.), but the British Galleries began a trajectory from deep and narrow expertise to a more synthetic approach.

There is still further to go. In the long term, there is a risk that our collections will cease to have relevance to the contemporary moment, if they cannot reflect the reality of design and production in the interconnected, globalized

Diese neue Strategie zielt darauf ab, sowohl dem Publikum als auch der Forschung ein genaueres Bild von der materiellen Kultur des frühen 21. Jahrhunderts zu vermitteln und zugleich die Zukunft unseres Instituts zu sichern. Sie erlaubt uns ferner, den Besucher unmittelbar an der Entstehung der Sammlung teilhaben zu lassen. Natürlich ist nichts von alledem gegen die spezialisierten Sammlungen gerichtet, die nicht zuletzt den Ruhm des Museums begründet haben. Wir möchten das bestehende Konzept vielmehr erweitern.

Die erste Erwerbung, die wir unter diesem neuen Vorzeichen getätigt haben, war der von Cody Wilson von Defense Distributed entworfene *Liberator,* eine von einem 3-D-Drucker hergestellte Schusswaffe. Bei diesem umstrittenen Erzeugnis neuester Design- und Herstellungsverfahren handelt es sich jedoch nicht etwa um die Arbeit eines professionellen Designers und ebenso wenig um ein Objekt des Kunstgewerbes. Für mich war die Waffe vielmehr eine Art Warnschild, ein Symbol für die Hybris jenes Techno-Optimismus, der in der Welt des digitalen und des Industriedesigns so verbreitet ist. Das Objekt ist zugleich ein Stück Industriedesign und Sinnbild einer radikalen Wende in der Designgeschichte.

Die Erwerbung der Waffe fand in den Medien ein großes Echo, was zugleich auf einen anderen für unsere Ankaufsstrategie mitentscheidenden Gesichtspunkt verwies. Denn die Bedeutung der Waffe liegt vor allem darin, dass sie ein Designobjekt ist, welches das Verhältnis zwischen den Menschen in der Gesellschaft grundlegend verändert. Denn in der Tat werfen gerade die interessantesten und einflussreichsten Produkte des zeitgenössischen Designs und der Gegenwartsarchitektur immer wieder die Frage nach unserem Zusammenleben und danach auf, was sie für das öffentliche Leben bedeuten – begünstigen sie eher Freiheit oder Zwang? Weitere geplante Erwerbungen sind unter anderem zwei Paar Jeans der Modekette Primark aus der 2013 eingestürzten Fabrik in Bangladesch (in der 1 100 Arbeiter den Tod fanden), ein Neonschild, das lange Zeit über dem Eingang einer berühmten Lesben-Bar in Soho hing (die jedoch wegen der explodierenden Mieten schließen musste), ein Paar künstliche Wimpern (von Pop-Diva Katy Perry und hergestellt von indonesischen Arbeitern, die am Tag nicht einmal einen Dollar Lohn erhalten), schließlich noch mehrere Paare »nudefarbener« Christian-Louboutin-Schuhe (die es wegen der zahlreichen nichtkaukasischen neuen Kundschaft in fünf Hauttönen gibt).

Kaum eines dieser Objekte hat einen unmittelbaren Bezug zur Alltagspraxis des Architekten; allerdings könnte man das Neonschild der Lesben-Bar ex negativo durchaus als Symbol der Gentrifizierung interpretieren. Dass unsere

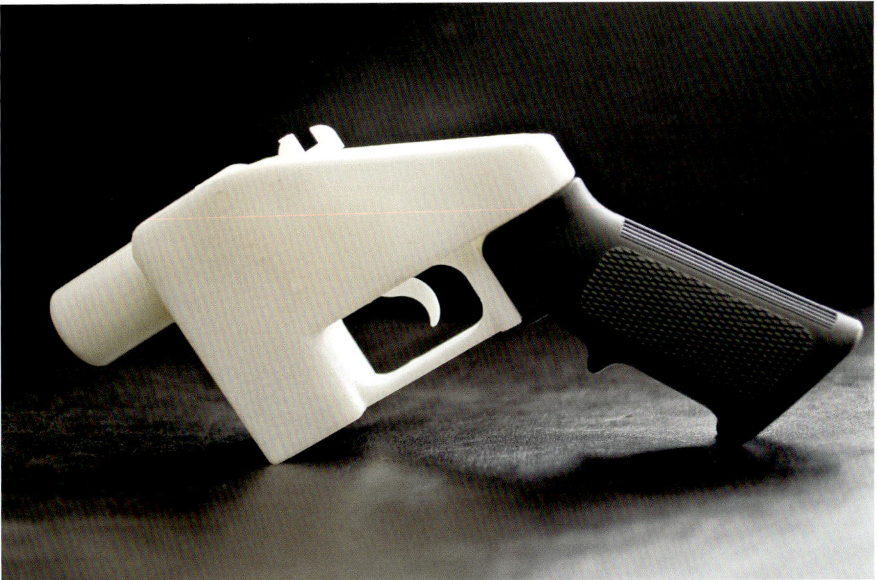

CODY WILSON / DEFENSE DISTRIBUTED,
THE LIBERATOR, 2013

CODY WILSON / DEFENSE DISTRIBUTED,
THE LIBERATOR, 2013

economy. To address this, and to ensure the collections reveal the reality of contemporary design and manufacturing for future researchers, we proposed a new approach: to collect objects in timely response to global events.

This is a new logic for collecting at the museum that will allow us to paint a more accurate picture of the material culture of the twenty-first century and prepare our institution for the future. It also allows the museum to reveal its logic to the public and engage visitors directly with the process of collecting. None of this is intended to prevent any of the specialized collecting in which the museum excels; we aim to add something new.

Our first acquisition using this logic was the Liberator, a 3D-printed gun designed by Cody Wilson of Defense Distributed. This highly controversial use of contemporary design and manufacturing technologies was not produced by a professional designer, and it is certainly not a piece of decorative art. For me, the gun was a signpost, a moment of nemesis for the techno-optimism that is so common in digital and industrial design. The object was a compelling piece of industrial design, but also a turning point in design history.

The acquisition of the gun had significant media impact, and the external interest in it crystallized another important intellectual motivation for our

Abteilung bislang nur so wenige Architekturexponate vorzuweisen hat, ist natürlich auch dem geringen Umfang unserer Sammlung für Gegenwartsarchitektur geschuldet. Dafür gibt es aber auch noch eine andere Erklärung: Wir wollten uns in unserer Sammlung nämlich nicht nur auf die Bereiche Architektur, Produkt- und digitales Design als Fachdisziplinen beschränken, sondern diesen Einzelsparten unter dem inoffiziellen Titel »Abteilung für öffentliches Leben« sozusagen ein gemeinsames Dach geben. Deshalb konnten wir uns natürlich nicht darauf beschränken, lediglich Baupläne zusammentragen. Denn die Arbeit des Architekten hängt nun einmal besonders eng mit den drängendsten Fragen des Großstadtlebens zusammen: also mit der Gentrifizierung, mit Differenzen, Überwachung und Sicherheit, mit den verschiedenen Formen des politischen Protests, mit demokratischer Teilhabe und so weiter. Deshalb möchten wir die drei Disziplinen in den Gesamtkontext »öffentliches Leben« stellen, um deutlich zu machen, wie sie die gesellschaftliche Realität beeinflussen. Doch natürlich sind wir nicht so naiv zu glauben, dass einer der drei Bereiche auf alles eine Antwort wüsste.

Im November 2013 ist der Architekt und Dozent Rory Hyde als Kurator für Architektur und Städtebau zu unserem Team gestoßen. Ich arbeite gerade gemeinsam mit ihm daran, eine detaillierte Strategie für die Architektur am V&A zu entwickeln. Dabei müssen wir uns einerseits Klarheit über unsere Ankaufsstrategie verschaffen, andererseits dürfen wir jedoch keinesfalls den öffentlichen Raum vernachlässigen, der ja unser eigentliches Hauptanliegen ist. Die Frage, vor der wir stehen, lautet also: Wie können wir den Charakter der Stadt am besten einfangen – ohne einfach nur Beispiele mehr oder weniger gelungener Architektur zusammenzutragen? Wie soll das V&A Entwürfe und Baupläne sammeln, die ja meist gar nicht mehr auf Papier ausgeführt sind? Wie lässt sich unser breit angelegtes Konzept des öffentlichen Raumes mit dem (völlig verständlichen) Wunsch des

PRIMARK-JEANS AUS DER EINGESTÜRZTEN FABRIK IN BANGLADESCH

PRIMARK JEANS MADE IN THE COLLAPSED RANA PLAZA FACTORY IN BANGLADESH

collecting. The significance of the gun was that it was a work of design that changes the relationship we have with others in society. All of the most interesting and impactive works of contemporary design (and of course of architecture) bear most strongly on questions of how we live together today, and how the public realm is articulated, made free, or constrained. Other objects we are working on acquiring in this vein include two pairs of Primark jeans made in the Rana Plaza factory in Bangladesh (which collapsed in April 2013, killing over 1,100 workers), a neon sign from the most famous lesbian bar in Soho (which is closing due to escalating rents), a pair of false eyelashes (endorsed by the pop star Katy Perry, and made by workers in Indonesia who earn less than a dollar a day to make them), as well as several pairs of Christian Louboutin "nude" shoes (in five skin tones to suit the major new non-Caucasian markets for high fashion).

Few of these objects are directly addressed in architectural practice, although the bar sign is, for us, an artifact that shows the normative cultural influence of gentrification. This lack of architectural authorship is today partly explained by the fact that our contemporary architectural collecting is still just beginning. The broader point is that instead of our curatorial section being limited to considering architecture, product design, and digital design as separate areas of expertise with distinct parameters conforming to professional fields, we have brought them together under the rubric of what we like to call a "department of public life." We could not look at this topic by limiting ourselves to material produced by architects. The majority of architects' work rarely addresses the topics that seem most urgent in the city: gentrification, inequality, surveillance and security, protest, democratic participation, and so on. The combination of our three fields gives us an opportunity to look at how design and architecture define and reflect our lives in society without pretending one professional field has the answers.

In November 2013, architect, curator, and academic Rory Hyde joined our team as curator of architecture and urbanism. His and my work to create a detailed strategy for architecture at the V&A is just beginning. We face a number of primary challenges in collecting the work we are interested in, while maintaining our focus on the public realm. How do we collect the city, not just the work of architects? How does the V&A collect the output of design practices no longer limited to drawings on paper? How can we reconcile a commitment to a broad definition of the public realm with the desire of the institution (and the understandable cultural pressure)

Museums (und kulturell interessierter Kreise) vereinbaren, dass in den Sammlungen nach Möglichkeit nur künstlerische Spitzenleistungen dokumentiert werden? Forscher, die künftig einmal die Studiensäle des V&A besuchen, werden natürlich erwarten, dort Arbeiten bedeutender Gestalter und Architekten anzutreffen, selbst wenn deren Leistungen aus unserer kuratorischen Sicht nur wenig zur Entwicklung des urbanen Raums im 21. Jahrhundert beigetragen haben. Hier eine allgemein akzeptable Balance zu finden, wird eine wichtige Aufgabe sein. Das Rapid Response Collecting ist nicht die einzige Sammlungsmethode, die wir verfolgen: Wir werden gleichzeitig eine eher konventionelle Strategie verfolgen und unsere Sammlungen als kohärente Geschichte präsentieren, in dem sich unser Interesse am öffentlichen Raum und an der Stadt widerspiegelt. Dabei hoffe ich, dass sich aus der Wechselwirkung zwischen digitalen Infrastrukturen und Objekten, architektonischen und städtebaulichen Prämissen und dem Entwurfsprozess selbst wichtige Aufschlüsse ergeben. So wird unsere neue Sammlung künftigen Forschern ebenso vielfältige wie erstaunliche Einblicke bieten, Forschern, die den urbanen Raum nicht mehr nur als das Produkt eines bestimmten Berufsstandes betrachten. Natürlich werden die Architekten und Stadtplaner die Entwicklung des öffentlichen Raumes auch in Zukunft maßgeblich beeinflussen. Noch wichtiger sind aber womöglich die sozialen Medien, die neuen digitalen Möglichkeiten, das neue Design der Überwachungs- und Sicherheitsinfrastruktur und diverse andere mehr oder weniger unspektakuläre Faktoren, die uns sehr viel über das Leben im öffentlichen Raum sagen.

Wir Mitarbeiter des V&A müssen uns täglich am Beispiel unserer ebenso ambitionierten wie engagierten Vorgänger messen lassen: Architekturkuratoren, die bereit waren, nach Rom zu reisen und dort lebensgroße Gipsabgüsse ganzer Gebäude zu machen, um britischen Studenten und Museumsbesuchern einen Eindruck von der Baukunst vergangener Zeiten zu vermitteln. Eine Sammlung zu schaffen, in der sich die Vielfalt und Komplexität des heutigen Großstadtlebens abbilden, ist in meinen Augen eine ebenso anspruchsvolle Aufgabe. Wenn es uns gelingt, die Wechselwirkungen zwischen Gesellschaft und Design in all seinen Facetten sichtbar zu machen, können auch wir zum Ruhm dieses bedeutenden Museums beitragen.

1 Nähere Auskünfte über die Lese- und Unterrichtsräume des V&A- und des RIBA-Archivs online unter www.vam.ac.uk/content/articles/v/study-and-teaching-rooms (Stand: 13.2.2014).

2 Christopher Marsden, »Une espèce de monument socialiste modern‹. Architecture for the South Kensington Museum«, in: Julius Bryant (Hrsg.), *Art and Design for All. The Victoria and Albert Museum*, London 2011.

3 Kieran Long, »Battle of Convoys Wharf«, in: *London Evening Standard*, 26.10.2011, online unter www.standard.co.uk/arts/architecture/battle-of-convoys-wharf-6361469.html (Stand: 13.2.2014).

4 Justin McGuirk, »Gran Horizonte. Torre David«, in: David Chipperfield u. a. (Hrsg.), *Common Ground. A Critical Reader. Venice Biennale of Architecture 2012*, Venedig 2012.

to accommodate within the collections the highest artistic achievements of the field? The future researcher coming to the V&A's study rooms will expect to find works by significant authors, even if we think history might judge their work to be marginal to how cities developed in the twenty-first century. Striking this balance will be crucial.

Rapid Response Collecting is not the only method of collecting for us. We will accumulate works of architecture in a more conventional way and try to develop a coherent narrative in our collections that reflect our interest in publicness and the city. But my hope is that the real values will come from the interrelationship of digital infrastructures, objects, design process, and architectural and urban propositions. Together, our new collection will provide a richer, unpredictable resource for future researchers that will reflect a world where no single profession defines urban change. Public life today is still framed by urbanism and architecture. But perhaps more often it is social media, new digital devices, the industrial design of surveillance and security infrastructure, or countless other tiny contributions to the public realm that tell us most about public life.

At the V&A we are faced daily with the ambition of our forebearers, architectural curators who were ready to go to Rome and make full-scale plaster casts of buildings in order that students, and the public, might better learn about them. I believe that trying to assemble a collection that reflects the richness and complexity of contemporary urban situations is as demanding an ambition; bringing together these different scales and fields of design gives us an opportunity to try.

1 For more information on the V&A and RIBA Study and Teaching Rooms, see http://www.vam.ac.uk/content/articles/v/study-and-teaching-rooms (accessed January 27, 2014).

2 Christopher Marsden, "'Une espèce de monument socialiste moderne': Architecture for the South Kensington Museum," in *Art and Design for All: The Victoria and Albert Museum*, ed. Julius Bryant, (London, 2011).

3 Kieran Long, "Battle of Convoys Wharf," *London Evening Standard*, October 26, 2011, http://www.standard.co.uk/arts/architecture/battle-of-convoys-wharf-6361469.html (accessed January 27, 2014).

4 Justin McGuirk, "Gran Horizonte: Torre David," in *Common Ground: A Critical Reader. Venice Biennal of Architecture*, ed. David Chipperfield et al., (Venice, 2012).

DIE SAMMLUNG DES MAXXI ARCHITETTURA

SIMONE BADER IM GESPRÄCH MIT MARGHERITA GUCCIONE UND PIPPO CIORRA

Das im November 2009 eingeweihte Museo nazionale delle arti del XXI secolo, kurz MAXXI, hat seit März 2010 für Besucher geöffnet. Das von der Architektin Zaha Hadid entworfene Gebäude fügt sich trotz seiner futuristisch anmutenden Beton-, Glas- und Stahlformen respektvoll in den nördlich des historischen Zentrums gelegenen römischen Stadtteil Flaminio ein, dessen Erscheinungsbild vor allem durch Kasernen und Mietshäuser aus dem 19. Jahrhundert geprägt ist. Diese Einrichtung ist auf nationaler Ebene die erste ihrer Art, die zugleich als Schauplatz kultureller Aktivitäten, aber auch als Laboratorium und Forschungszentrum fungiert. Ihre Entstehung verdankt sie der finanziellen Unterstützung des Ministero dei beni e delle attività culturali e del turismo (Ministerium für Kultur und Tourismus). In den riesigen Ausstellungsräumen des Hauses sind zwei Museen untergebracht, das MAXXI Arte und das MAXXI Architettura. Beide verfügen über beeindruckende Sammlungen, wozu zahlreiche bedeutende Werke aus dem 20. und dem 21. Jahrhundert gehören. Obwohl die Architekturabteilung noch jung ist, verzeichnet sie nach Auskunft ihrer Direktorin Margherita Guccione bereits 50 000 Zeichnungen und 25 000 Fotografien sowie zahlreiche Modelle, Briefe und sonstige Dokumente in ihren Beständen. Das Archivmaterial des Hauses stammt von international renommierten italienischen Architekten wie Aldo Rossi, Carlo Scarpa, Pier Luigi Nervi, Paolo Soleri, Vittorio de Feo und Giancarlo de Carlo. Aus diesem Fundus kann Pippo Ciorra, Chefkurator der Architekturabteilung, schöpfen. Er organisiert jedes Jahr eine Themenausstellung, die den Besuchern einen Eindruck von den Leistungen der historischen Baukunst und der Gegenwartsarchitektur vermittelt. Auf diese Weise sind das Museum und die Sammlung eng miteinander verbunden.

THE MAXXI ARCHITETTURA COLLECTION

SIMONE BADER IN CONVERSATION WITH MARGHERITA GUCCIONE AND PIPPO CIORRA

The Museo nazionale delle arti del XXI secolo, in short MAXXI, was opened in November 2009 and has been in operation since March 2010. Despite its futuristic-looking forms of concrete, glass, and steel, the building, designed by the architect Zaha Hadid, fits respectfully into the Roman city quarter of Flaminio outside the historical center, where mainly barracks and residential complexes of the late nineteenth century characterize its surroundings. This first-of-its-kind national institute, which serves as a space for cultural activities as well as a laboratory and research center, has been made possible through the financial support of the Ministero dei beni e delle attività culturali e del turismo (Ministry for Cultural Heritage and Tourism). Two museums are based in the monumental museum showrooms: MAXXI Arte and MAXXI Architettura. Both of them have notable collections, including works from the twentieth and twenty-first centuries. Although it opened only a few years ago, the architecture department already owns a significant collection of about 50,000 drawings, 25,000 photographs, numerous models, letters, and documents, according to its proud director, Margherita Guccione. The archival material comes from internationally renowned Italian architects, such as Aldo Rossi, Carlo Scarpa, Pier Luigi Nervi, Paolo Soleri, Vittorio de Feo, and Giancarlo de Carlo. Using this basis, Pippo Ciorra, senior curator for the architecture department, organizes annual thematic exhibitions that present the culture of past and present architecture. Thus, the collection and the museum are closely aligned.

SIMONE BADER: Margherita, how did you acquire these bequests?
MARGHERITA GUCCIONE: The bequests of designers' private collections has turned out to be an important starting point for the establishment

AUSSTELLUNGSANSICHT YAP MAXXI,
FONDAZIONE MAXXI, 2012

INSTALLATION VIEW, YAP MAXXI,
FONDAZIONE MAXXI, 2012

material that I would like to
mention is known as
Ecofloor. This material is a
synthetic grass that will be
used to form a part of the
external installation, which
can be totally recycled and
ensures the safe use of the in
stallation, especially by
children.
For this project we used a
technique of spatial modelling
based on the succession of
two-dimensional layers.
This technique, which we
defined "Spatial Layering"

structures and permit the
creation of areas of shade and
at the same time accumulate
photovoltaic energy for the
lighting system by using
special panels.
We specifically decided to
make the lighting system as
simple as possible and thus
we designed simple LED
spotlights that self-charge
during the day from solar
energy and turn on at night.
The LED spots have a small
photovoltaic cell and a
micro-battery that lasts a few

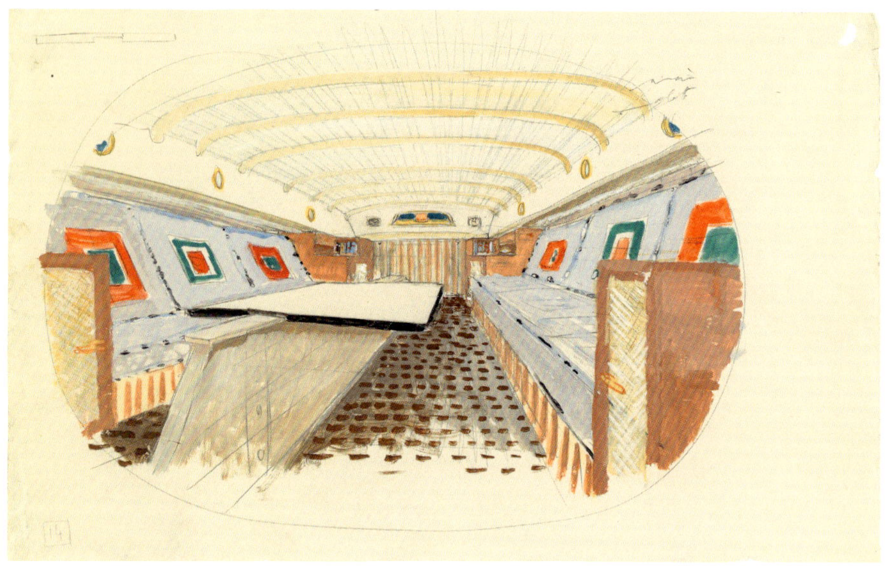

CARLO SCARPA, YACHT ASTA,
ENTWURFSZEICHNUNG, 1935

CARLO SCARPA, YACHT ASTA,
DRAWING, 1935

SIMONE BADER: Margherita, wie sind Sie in den Besitz dieser Nachlässe gelangt?

MARGHERITA GUCCIONE: Den Grundstein der Sammlung des MAXXI Architettura, die das Schaffen international bekannter Architekten und Ingenieure dokumentiert, bilden vor allem die Nächlässe der Architekten selbst. Im Jahr 2001 hat das Ministero dei beni e delle attività culturali e del turismo für das MAXXI zunächst Carlo Scarpas und Enrico del Debbios Nachlass angekauft sowie Aldo Rossis Privatarchiv und Pier Luigi Nervis Büroarchiv. Seither hat das Museum zahlreiche weitere Archive entweder als Schenkung (Vittorio de Feo, Sergio Musmeci, Paolo Soleri, Michele Valori, Giulio Gra und Francesco Montuori) oder als auf 10 Jahre befristete Leihgaben (Costantino Dardi, Giancarlo de Carlo, Carlo Aymonino, Mario Fiorentino, Lucio Pasarelli, Maurizio Sacripanti, Piero Sartogo und Italo Rota) erhalten. In einer Sammlungssektion sind aber auch Entwurfszeichnungen, Modelle, Skizzen, Videos und Dokumente zu sehen, die sich lediglich auf einzelne Projekte oder Planvorgaben beziehen und im Gegensatz zu einem vollwertigen Archiv keine organische Einheit bilden (Superstudio, die *Roma-Interrotta*-Ausstellung, Massimiliano Fuksas, Yona Friedman, Aimaro Isola, Alberto Campo Baeza, Toyo Ito, Ian+, Franco Purini und Laura Thermes).

of the collections of MAXXI Architettura, oriented toward the personal archives of twentieth and twenty-first century architects and engineers of international renown. The first direct acquisitions, carried out by the Ministero dei beni e delle attività culturali e del turismo in 2001 for the MAXXI, were the complete archives of Carlo Scarpa and Enrico del Debbio, Aldo Rossi's personal archive, and Pier Luigi Nervi's professional archive. Over the years, many other professional archives were donated (Vittorio de Feo, Sergio Musmeci, Paolo Soleri, Michele Valori, Giulio Gra, and Francesco Montuori) or entered into the museum collection as ten-year loan agreements (Costantino Dardi, Giancarlo de Carlo, Carlo Aymonino, Mario Fiorentino, Lucio Pasarelli, Maurizio Sacripanti, Piero Sartogo, and Italo Rota). There is also a section of the collection that gathers together drawings, models, sketches, videos, and documents relating to a project or a single theme; these include groups of items that do not make up the kind of organic whole of a complete archive or substantial portion of an archive (Superstudio, the Roma Interrotta exhibition, Massimiliano Fuksas, Yona Friedman, Aimaro Isola, Alberto Campo Baeza, Toyo Ito, Ian+, Franco Purini, and Laura Thermes). Products of activities such as exhibitions, workshops, and commissions promoted by MAXXI Architettura compose the assets of the museum: the collection of architecture photography, the video documentaries on architecture, the materials of architecture competitions sponsored by the ministry, such as the international competition held for the design of the MAXXI Museum (Adam Caruso, Francesco Cellini, Michele de Lucchi, Eduardo Souto de Moura, Vittorio Gregotti, Zaha Hadid, Steven Holl, Toyo Ito, Rem Koolhaas, Pierluigi Nicolin, Jean Nouvel, Mosè Ricci, Kazuyo Sejima, and Cino Zucchi).

SB: What are the criteria for future collections? Is there a collection strategy?
MG: The research activity of the museum seeks to analyze those examples and experiences that are particularly significant and definitive of the architecture of the twentieth and twenty-first centuries. In this sense, the museum aims to document diverse processes: from creative production (the designs), to realization (construction, techniques, and materials); from its use to its insertion into the physical (the site, the city, the landscape) and cultural context. Specifically, in MAXXI Architettura, the Centro Archivi di Architettura (Archive Center) operates within a reference time frame that goes from the twentieth century to today, studying and maintaining various architecture

Ferner besitzt das MAXXI Architettura Arbeiten, die im Kontext von den vom Museum selbst ausgeschriebenen Workshops und den Wettbewerben entstanden sind, etwa Architekturfotografien, Videodokumentationen über bedeutende architektonische Leistungen und die Entwürfe der Architekten, die sich an der internationalen Ausschreibung des MAXXI-Projekts beteiligt haben (Adam Caruso, Francesco Cellini, Michele de Lucchi, Eduardo Souto de Moura, Vittorio Gregotti, Zaha Hadid, Steven Holl, Toyo Ito, Rem Koolhaas, Pierluigi Nicolin, Jean Nouvel, Mosè Ricci, Kazuyo Sejima und Cino Zucchi).

SB: Und wie sieht Ihre künftige Sammlungsstrategie aus?
MG: Die Forschungsarbeit unseres Museums zielt darauf ab, die für das 20. und das 21. Jahrhundert besonders bedeutsamen architektonischen Entwicklungen zu erkunden. So gesehen handelt es sich hier um ein mehrgleisiges Vorgehen. Unser Interesse gilt nicht nur dem kreativen Aspekt des Bauens (also der Entwurfsplanung), sondern auch der technischen Umsetzung des Entwurfs (und den entsprechenden konstruktiven Verfahren und den Werkstoffen). Darüber hinaus möchten wir dokumentieren, wie ein solcher baulicher Eingriff einen natürlichen und / oder geschichtlich-kulturellen Umraum (etwa ein Stadtgefüge oder eine Landschaft) verändert. Dabei deckt vor allem das Centro archivi di architettura den Zeitraum des 20. und des frühen 21. Jahrhunderts komplett ab und verwahrt und erforscht neben den eigenen Dokumenten auch diverse Architektursammlungen. Die Spezialsammlungen verwahren überdies auch jene Artefakte, die im Rahmen unserer eigenen Aktivitäten entstanden sind, etwa architektonisch relevante Installationen und standortspezifische Objekte.

SB: Wie hat man sich den Nachlass eines Architekten vorzustellen? Gehören auch der Schriftverkehr mit den Baufirmen oder nur das gestalterische Werk dazu?
MG: Das Archiv des typischen Architekten oder Bauingenieurs des 20. oder 21. Jahrhunderts weist materiell und inhaltlich bestimmte Merkmale auf und erfordert deshalb unsererseits große Sorgfalt. Ein solcher Nachlass besteht unter anderem aus Dokumenten, die über die einzelnen Planungs- und Bauphasen der von dem jeweiligen Architekten geplanten Bauwerke Aufschluss geben. Dazu gehören: Entwurfs- und Ausführungspläne, Skizzen, technische Zeichnungen, ferner schriftliche Aufzeichnungen und Modelle, Fotografien, behördliche Schreiben, aber auch Dokumente aus der Buchhaltung und Teile des Schriftverkehrs. Das können detaillierte Entwurfszeichnungen sein, die auf

collections as well as its own collection of documents. The special collections gather together the products of the activities of the museum itself, such as installations and site-specific objects with particular architectural significance.

S B : What characterizes the bequests of architects? Do they include correspondence with construction companies, or is the bequest limited to creative work only?
M G : The archives of twentieth-century and twenty-first-century architects and engineers have special characteristics, both physically and in terms of content, that make them at once fragile and interesting. The acquisitions and bequests of architects include documents that record the architectural "production" of the particular building's design phase over various stages: plans, graphics, sketches, technical drawings, written notes and models, photographs, administrative and book-keeping documents, and correspondence. They range from graphic elaborations on delicate or erasable mediums to true works of art, such as temperas, engravings, oil paintings, prototypes, models, and glass work. Some media and techniques lack durability, making them susceptible, in a few cases and even only after a few years, to irreversible damage sustained after one handling. In the Italian tradition of preserving the unity of the architectural archive, MAXXI manages complete archival complexes of many architects and engineers. The Pier Luigi Nervi

PIER LUIGI NERVI, *CATTEDRALE SAN FRANCISCO*, ENTWURFSZEICHNUNG, UNDATIERT

PIER LUIGI NERVI, *CATTEDRALE SAN FRANCISCO*, DRAWING, NO DATE

hochempfindlichen Medien gespeichert sind, aber auch wahre Kunstwerke, etwa Temperaarbeiten, druckgrafische Reproduktionen, Ölbilder, Prototypen, Modelle und Glasarbeiten: Medien und Techniken, die so empfindlich sind, dass sie in einzelen Fällen nicht einmal die erste Präsentation unbeschadet überstehen und nach wenigen Jahren bereits unwiederbringlich verloren sind. Da es in Italien Tradition ist, die Einheit solcher Nachlässe zu erhalten, verwahrt das MAXXI ganze Archivkomplexe mit vollständigem Nachlass zahlreicher Architekten und Ingenieure. So sind etwa im Pier-Luigi-Nervi-Archiv sämtliche Aktivitäten der Baufirma Nervi e Bartoli in Italien und im Ausland dokumentiert. Wir verwahren in unserem Archivzentrum hier am MAXXI derzeit über 50 000 Entwurfszeichnungen, 25 000 Fotografien, 134 Modelle, 98 Videos sowie über 1 000 Artefakte, Skulpturen, Installationen, standortspezifische Prototypen, Collagen und Modelle in Originalgröße.

SB: Wer arbeitet mit diesen Dokumenten? Wie viele Forscher greifen pro Jahr auf die Bestände zurück?
MG: Wir haben hier bis zu 1 000 Gäste pro Jahr. Zudem können Forscher, die hier wissenschaftlich arbeiten wollen, den Lesesaal des Archivzentrums kostenlos aufsuchen; das gilt auch für interessierte Fachleute und Laien. Dabei haben wir natürlich auch an Architektur- und Ingenieuersstudenten gedacht, die hauptsächlich unsere digitalen Speichermedien nutzen. Gleichzeitig versuchen wir sie dazu zu bringen, sich auch mit dem Originalmaterial selbst zu befassen. Über unsere Webseite können Forscher auf die Datenbank der Architekturarchive zurückgreifen, sich also bereits vor einem Besuch in unserem Lesesaal eine Vorstellung von unserem Angebot machen.
Besonders interessant finde ich die Rolle der AAA Italia (Associazione nazionale Archivi Architettura contemporanea), des Verbandes der italienischen Archive für zeitgenössische Architektur, der jedes Jahr hier am MAXXI eine Tagung organisiert, auf der sich die Leiter der italienischen Archive über Fragen der optimalen Betreuung und Erhaltung ihrer Bestände austauschen. Das MAXXI finanziert aber auch Studien- und Forschungsgruppen, die an den diversen Archiven ihrerseits Ausstellungen oder Konferenzen organisieren oder Publikationen vorbereiten. So haben wir beispielsweise einen Katalog über die Fotosammlung des MAXXI herausgebracht und arbeiten gerade an einem Katalog über die Architektursammlung des MAXXI, der in den nächsten Monaten erscheinen soll.

archive documents the entire activity of the building firm Nervi e Bartoli in Italy and abroad. The Archive Center at MAXXI Architettura currently preserves more than 50,000 design drawings, 25,000 photographs, 134 models, 98 videos, over 1,000 artifacts, sculptures, installations, site-specific prototypes, collages, and mock-ups.

SB: Who uses these documents? How many researchers come per year?
MG: The range of visitors is very wide and can reach nearly 1,000 people per year. In particular, research in the Archive Center study room is free of charge and open to qualified scholars conducting academic studies, but it also welcomes professionals, experts, research groups, and amateurs. Special attention is given to architecture and engineering students, who usually approach the digital repositories, but in many cases we try to entice them with the opportunity of consulting original material. The website with the architecture archive database offers the possibility of drawing in potential researchers—it is our first point of contact before their visit to the study room.
I think that the role of AAA Italia (Associazione nazionale Archivi Architettura contemporanea, the National Association of Contemporary Architecture Archives) is particularly interesting: it works and studies issues relevant to architecture archives, and every year it organizes a meeting of the heads of the Italian archives at MAXXI to focus on management and preservation strategies. On some specific archives, MAXXI Architettura organizes and curates study groups and research projects for exhibitions, conferences, and publications. We published a catalogue of the MAXXI Architettura photography collection, and are now working on a catalogue of the MAXXI Architettura collection that will be published in the next few months.

SB: What are the most important functions that the collection fulfills?
MG: With the Archive Center, the MAXXI Architettura intends to facilitate the creation of a network and enhance what may be considered a large, national "gold mine," rich in designers' public and private collections. It works as an experimental laboratory that carries out cultural promotion to foster historical research. The systematic study of the extremely abundant Italian experience of recent centuries, as well as contemporary examples, establishes strategies, standards, and instruments for the conservation, restoration, and accessibility of documentary sources. It also intends to work toward creating diversified modes of "navigation," such as analytical inventories

SB: Worin sehen Sie die Hauptaufgaben der Sammlung?

MG: Das Archivzentrum des MAXXI Architettura plant ein auf Kooperation angelegtes Netzwerk zu etablieren, gewissermaßen einen großen nationalen Fundus, in dem private und öffentliche Sammlungen vertreten sind. Wir verstehen uns als ein Labor, das sich der Erforschung der historischen Bestände widmet. Wir sehen unsere Aufgabe darin, sowohl das ungemein reiche italienische Kulturerbe der vergangenen Jahrhunderte als auch das derzeitige künstlerische Schaffen in diesem Land zu studieren. Zugleich sind wir darum bemüht, neue Konservierungs- und Restaurierungsverfahren zu entwickeln und den Zugriff auf diese Dokumente zu erleichtern. Zudem möchten wir die Inventarisierung unserer wichtigsten Bestände verbessern, die Entwicklung der Architektur und des Städtebaus seit dem 20. Jahrhundert in neue Datenbanken dokumentieren und Ausstellungskonzepte entwickeln, die in der breiten Öffentlichkeit ein Interesse an der Architektur wecken.

SB: Wie würden Sie Ihre Sammlung im Kontext anderer italienischer Sammlungen einordnen?

MG: Das MAXXI Architettura ist das erste nationale Architekturmuseum Italiens und betreut die Nachlässe einiger der bedeutendsten Architekten des Landes. Das Museum besitzt zahlreiche Arbeiten der großen Baumeister des 20. Jahrhunderts und genießt national wie international als baugeschichtliches Dokumentationszentrum einen bedeutenden Ruf. Dabei verfolgen wir jedoch kein ausschließlich zentralistisches Konzept, vielmehr möchte das Archivzentrum des MAXXI Architettura, das dem Nationalmuseum zugeordnet ist, gemeinsam mit diesem neue konservatorische Wege beschreiten und jene Dokumente für die Nachwelt bewahren, die als kollektives Erbe und kostbarer Nationalbesitz gelten. Um den Zugriff auf die Bestände zu erleichtern, müssen wir die baugeschichtlichen und städtebaulichen Dokumente vor allem des 20. Jahrhunderts jedoch zunächst einmal digitalisieren und für das Internet verfügbar machen. Und genau darauf zielen alle Anstrengungen des Archivzentrums des MAXXI Architettura ab, das auch neue Formen der Organisation und Inventarisierung und der digitalen Reproduktion erkunden und die Ergebnisse dieser Bemühungen in seinen Ausstellungen und Publikationen dokumentieren möchte.

Diese Aktivitäten haben nicht nur eine kunsthistorische, sondern auch eine ethische Dimension, da sie einen Eindruck von der historischen, künstlerischen und ökologischen Bedeutung der Architektur des 20. Jahrhunderts vermitteln und zudem Auskunft darüber geben, wie sich diese Dokumente am sichersten bewahren lassen.

of major collections, the creation and management of data banks, and the architectural and urban legacy from the twentieth century to the present, as well as the realization of exhibitions that can better familiarize the general public with architecture.

SB: Could you please describe how this collection has been integrated into the context of other collections in Italy?

MG: MAXXI Architettura is the first national architecture museum in Italy, and in its collection there are examples of some of the most important architects throughout the country. The museum owns a vast amount of works by major figures of the twentieth century, and it is rapidly becoming a significant national and international testimony to our time—building and preserving what will constitute the heritage of twenty-first-century architecture.

Subverting the "patriarchal" idea of the singular institution, the Archive Center at MAXXI Architettura is part of a national museum. It is intended to coordinate the activity of beneficially sharing and spreading instruments for the conservation and use of its holdings, which should be viewed as a collective resource and national treasure.

For sharing, accessibility, and distribution to function optimally, it is fundamental to create a data bank as well as digitized documents that are representative of their sources and the architectural and urban legacy from the nineteen-hundreds to now. That is the direction of all the efforts made by the MAXXI Architettura Archive Center, which, alongside the activities of the museum, highlights the potential of reorganization, inventory, and digital reproductions, also realized through exhibitions and publications.

Finally, an ethical mission over a cultural one, this set of goals can have a substantial impact on the promotion of knowledge and awareness of the historical, artistic, and environmental value of the works of twentieth-century architecture, as well as the correct practice of their conservation.

SB: In an interview, Pippo, you mentioned that the museum and the exhibitions you are curating serve to build up the collection. What kind of relationship result from this combination? And what kind of profile does it create?

PIPPO CIORRA: As a member of the large team responsible for the collections and exhibitions at MAXXI, my role is clear. My task is to curate exhibitions on contemporary architecture and to complement them with projects—workshops, seminars, discussions, lectures—aiming to bridge the

SB: Pippo, Sie haben in einem Interview einmal gesagt, dass das Museum und die Ausstellungen, die Sie dort kuratieren, dazu dienen, die Sammlung aufzubauen. Wie hat man sich diese Interaktion in der Praxis vorzustellen? Und welches Profil ergibt sich daraus?

PIPPO CIORRA: Unter den zahlreichen Mitarbeitern, die sich hier am MAXXI um die Sammlungen und Ausstellungen kümmern, betreue ich ein relativ klar umrissenes Aufgabenfeld. Meine Arbeit besteht darin, Ausstellungen zur zeitgenössischen Architektur zu organisieren – dazu gehören auch Workshops, Seminare, Symposien und Vortragsreihen. Auf diese Weise hoffen wir, die Kluft zwischen dem interessierten Publikum und den Architekten und Künstlern zu verringern, deren Schaffen wir hier am Museum dokumentieren. Dieser Ansatz verfolgt zwei Ideen, die sich in der Praxis deutlich bemerkbar machen: Zum einen geht es darum, das Material, das die Architekten uns für bestimmte Ausstellungen überlassen – ob es ganz neu oder schon älter ist –, in die bereits bestehende Sammlung zu integrieren und zum anderen die museumseigene Sammlung in den Ausstellungen selbst angemessen zur Geltung zu bringen. Wir stehen also im Wesentlichen vor der Aufgabe, die Vergangenheit mit der Zukunft – und nicht bloß mit der Gegenwart – zu verbinden, bisweilen sogar in ein und derselben Ausstellung historische Materialien aus unseren Architektur-, aber auch Kunst- und Fotosammlungen, Leihgaben und von Gastautoren verfasste Beiträge mit Objekten zu kombinieren, die eigens für die betreffende Schau produziert worden sind. Die Ausstellungen *Re-cycle. Strategies for Architecture, City and Planet* (2011/12) und *Energy. Oil and Post-Oil Architecture and Grids* (2013) stehen beispielhaft für diese Vorgehensweise. In beiden Ausstellungen waren (einige Erwerbungen mit sich bringend) Arbeiten der beteiligten Architekten, (später in unsere Sammlung übernommene) »anlassspezifische« Materialien sowie Zeichnungen, Videos und Modelle aus den MAXXI-Archiven (Rossi, Nervi, Musmeci et cetera) und Arbeiten aus unserer Kunstsammlung zu sehen, darunter auch Nina Fishers und Maroan El Sanis Video *Sayonara Hashima*. Diesen Ansatz verfolgen wir inzwischen seit 4 Jahren und hoffen, dem neuen Trend zum Mehr-Sparten-Museum auf diese Weise Rechnung zu tragen. Wir versuchen also, genreübergreifende Ausstellungen zu produzieren, in denen es zwischen Kunst, Architektur, Fotografie, Film und anderen künstlerischen Genres keine strikten Grenzen mehr gibt.

gap between the public and the designers and artists involved in the museum programs. This approach entails two important aspects: expanding the collection through the material submitted by architects for specific exhibitions (either existing or newly produced), and introducing the museum collections in the exhibitions themselves. Basically this involves an intention to make connections between the past and the future (not only the present), bringing together, even in the same exhibition, historical materials from our collections (architecture as well as art and photography), loans, contributions from the archives by invited authors, and material specifically produced for the show. *Re-cycle: Strategies for Architecture, City and Planet* (2011–12) and *Energy: Oil and Post-Oil Architecture and Grids* (2013) are clear examples of this approach. The shows presented works from the contributing architects' careers (which generally meant some acquisitions), "exhibition-specific" material, which became part of the collection, as well as drawings, videos, models from the MAXXI archives (Rossi, Nervi, Musmeci, etc.), and items from the art collection, such as the video by Nina Fisher and Maroan El Sani on Sayonara Hashima. This is an approach we've been developing over the last four years to create a strong foundation based on the emerging trend towards multi-departmental museums, i.e., displaying fluid, multidisciplinary collections with no "borders" between art, architecture, photography, film, and other areas.

SB: Exhibiting is certainly one significant pillar of the collection. Teaching and research are further important aspects. However, you also promote the idea of supporting cultural innovation as much as you emphasize certain topics. What precisely do you mean by this, and how do you proceed?
PC: Good question. When you become a curator of architecture at an institution like MAXXI, which ideally serves both a local audience as well as a virtual and global one, you basically have the entire geography and history of architecture in front of you. Especially now, when there's no leading tendency (or there are too many), and there's a lot of discussion about the role of architecture. This can be daunting, and you can easily get lost in a maze of formats and ideas. In order to react to this, we take a two-part approach that focuses on topics that, on the one hand, can be interesting both for the artistically and architecturally educated audience and for passionate "non-specialized" citizen those who do not have an affinity for drawing and models but deal on a daily basis with issues like recycling or energy, who have children who went abroad on the Erasmus program and decided not to come back, who try to understand

AUSSTELLUNGSANSICHT *ENERGY.
OIL AND POST-OIL ARCHITECTURE
AND GRIDS*, FONDAZIONE MAXXI, 2013
MIT SOU FUJIMOTO ARCHITECTS,
ENERGY FOREST, 2013

INSTALLATION VIEW, *ENERGY:
OIL AND POST-OIL ARCHITECTURE
AND GRIDS*, FONDAZIONE MAXXI, 2013
WITH SOU FUJIMOTO ARCHITECTS,
ENERGY FOREST, 2013

SB: Die Ausstellungen sind gewiss ein wichtiges Standbein Ihrer Sammlung. Genauso wichtig sind auch Forschung und Lehre. Außerdem unterstützen Sie kulturelle Innovationen, setzen aber auch Themenschwerpunkte. Was genau hat es damit auf sich und wie gehen Sie dabei vor?

PC: Wer an einer Institution wie dem MAXXI als Architekturkurator anfängt, einem Haus, das nicht nur für die Museumsbesucher gedacht ist, sondern im Netz weltweit präsent ist, hat es im Grunde mit der gesamten Geografie und Geschichte der Architektur zu tun. Das gilt umso mehr, da es heutzutage keinen bestimmten Trend mehr gibt (sondern viel zu viele) und die Rolle der Architektur vielfach hinterfragt wird. Das kann manchmal ganz schön verwirrend sein und dazu führen, dass man vor lauter Formaten und Ideen den Überblick verliert. Wir verfolgen daher einen zweigleisigen Ansatz und möchten sowohl Themen für das künstlerisch und architektonisch gebildete Publikum als auch für fachfremde Besucher anbieten. Also für diejenigen, die sich nicht für Modelle und Zeichnungen begeistern, sich aber beispielsweise mit Recycling und Energiefragen beschäftigen, deren Kinder mit einem Erasmus-Stipendium ins Ausland gehen und dann nicht mehr zurückkommen, oder für Menschen, die einfach daran interessiert sind, was in ihrer eigenen, aber natürlich auch in anderen Städten aktuell passiert. Diese Umstände bedeuten für unsere Arbeit, dass wir uns im Architekturdiskurs mit den Problemen auseinandersetzen müssen, mit denen es die heutige Gesellschaft zu tun hat, und das halte ich für ganz entscheidend. Das heißt, wir müssen uns hier mit der »Architektur der Zukunft« befassen, ohne die Leistungen der Vergangenheit deswegen zu vernachlässigen. Wir werden immer wieder monografische Ausstellungen zeigen, besonders zu den großen Architekten des 20. Jahrhunderts (Luigi Moretti, Le Corbusier in Italien, Nervi und andere). Was die Gegenwart betrifft, möchten wir in der Forschung jedoch lieber zweigleisig fahren mit Themen, mit denen sich die Architekten von heute auseinandersetzen und die im Kontext neuer Ideen, neuer Arbeitsgemeinschaften, neuer Formen und neuer Arbeitsweisen stehen und dabei einen starken Akzent auf ein geografisches Spektrum setzen.

SB: Wie gehen Sie bei der Digitalisierung Ihrer Dokumente und Medien vor? Und was bedeutet die Digitalisierung für Sie als Kurator?

PC: Hier am MAXXI ist gleich ein ganzes Team für die Betreuung der Archive zuständig. In Abstimmung mit der Direktion haben diese Fachleute sich für eine Digitalisierung der »zwei Geschwindigkeiten« entschieden. Sobald ein neues Archiv (oder ein Teil eines solchen) hier eintrifft, wählen unsere Fachleute die »wichtigsten« Dokumente und Objekte aus und bereiten sie digital auf. Der Rest wird im

INSTALLATIONSANSICHT *YAP MAXXI,*
FONDAZIONE MAXXI, 2011
MIT STARTT, *WHATAMI,* 2011

INSTALLATION VIEW, *YAP MAXXI,*
FONDAZIONE MAXXI, 2011
WITH STARTT, *WHATAMI,* 2011

what's happening in their own and others' cities. On the other hand, within the architecture discourse we consider the aim of our work—which I consider vital—expanding our discipline and challenging designers to get inspired by the set of problems that contemporary space is facing nowadays. To me, this is a way to address "the architecture of the future" while involving our cultural past as much as possible. We do not reject the idea of monographic exhibitions, especially when they display work of the masters of the twentieth century (Luigi Moretti, Le Corbusier in Italy, Nervi, etc.). For the contemporary scene, however, we prefer to work using a process of double mapping, which merges a map of the contemporary issues architects are expected to address with a map of new ideas, new teams, new forms, and new ways of working—while placing a strong accent on the geographic width of our investigation.

SB: How do you go about the digitization of your documents and media? And what does that mean for you as a curator?
PC: MAXXI has a specific team who takes care of the archives. Together with the director they developed a "two-speed" strategy for digitization. As

INSTALLATIONSANSICHT YAP MAXXI,
FONDAZIONE MAXXI, 2011
MIT STARTT, WHATAMI, 2011

INSTALLATION VIEW, YAP MAXXI,
FONDAZIONE MAXXI, 2011
WITH STARTT, WHATAMI, 2011

Verlauf eines längerwierigen Verfahrens ebenfalls digitalisiert. Die meisten unserer »herausragenden« Archive (Rossi, Scarpa, Musmeci) sind allerdings schon digitalisiert. In der Ausstellung *Modelli / Models. MAXXI Architettura Collection* (2012) haben wir bereits physische Objekte mit digitalem Material kombiniert, was uns gleichzeitig gewisse neuartige didaktische Möglichkeiten eröffnet. Das ist auch aus den beiden folgenden Gründen sehr wichtig: Die Wissenschaftler, die zum Forschen hierher kommen, können jetzt im Lesesaal leichter auf unsere digitalisierten Bestände zugreifen. Und, wenn wir das Werk eines zeitgenössischen Architekten in einer kleinen Ausstellung oder Installation würdigen, kann sich ein Forscher dank der digitalen Unterstützung viel leichter eine Vorstellung von dem kunsthistorischen oder auch dem technischen Kontext der betreffenden Exponate verschaffen.

SB: Welchen Stellenwert haben heutzutage Kooperationsprojekte für die operative Arbeit des Museums, beispielsweise mit dem New Yorker Museum of Modern Art und dessen Young Architects Program (YAP)?
PC: Das Museum ist ein lebendiges öffentliches Forum, das den Leuten hier aus der Umgebung und allen Bürgern und Besuchern der Stadt zur Verfügung steht, die sich an seiner Piazza, seiner Architektur und den sonstigen Angeboten erfreuen möchten, auch wenn sie gar keine Ausstellung besuchen. Das YAP ist ein extrem wichtiges Hilfsmittel, die architektonische Situation hervorzuheben und sie näher zu beleuchten. Wir alle wissen um die immense Bedeutung des öffentlichen Raumes und sind der Meinung, dass die Demonstrationen auf dem Taksimplatz in Istanbul 2013 auch für die Architektur äußerst bedeutend waren. Die Bebauung des Gezi-Parks war schließlich der Auslöser. Wir möchten diese Vorfälle daher auch nutzen, um das Museum so weit wie möglich zu öffnen und um das Thema weiter zu erforschen. Außerdem, und das ist für eine Institution wie unser Haus vielleicht sogar noch wichtiger, hat das YAP einigen bis dahin völlig unbekannten und noch sehr jungen italienischen Architekten die Chance eröffnet, »innovative« Installationen zu realisieren und mit Institutionen und Kollegen aus anderen Teilnehmerländern in Kontakt zu treten. Ich war sehr stolz, als ich vor ein paar Tagen die von dem römischen Team stARTT, Gewinner des YAP MAXXI 2011, entworfenen Mohnblüten auf der Shenzhen Bi-City Biennale of Urbanism / Architecture sah und erlebte, wie die Designer ihre Arbeit in China vorstellen konnten. In einer so »trägen« Architekturszene, wie sie heute in Italien vorherrscht, müssen die Impulse von unten kommen, aus der jungen Generation und von jungen Institutionen, denen der Status quo ganz egal ist.

soon as a new archive (or section of an archive) comes in, the team selects the "most important" items, which are immediately digitized. The rest goes through a progressive process that takes longer to be completed. It is obvious, though, that most of the "outstanding" archives we hold (Rossi, Scarpa, Musmeci) have already been fully digitized. The exhibition *Modelli / Models: MAXXI Architettura Collection* (2012) allowed us to put together physical objects with digital material and to display a more effective didactic frame for some of the work. This is also very important for two additional reasons: First, scholars who come to the museum for research can easily digitally access most of our historical materials in our study room. Second, when doing small shows or installations by contemporary architects, researchers can use the digital support to contextualize the single or limited work within a wider professional, cultural, and historical framework.

SB: Concerning your cooperation with the Museum of Modern Art in New York and the associated Young Architects Program (YAP)—what significance do such temporary programs have for the work of the museum?
PC: The museum is an active public space, open to people from the neighborhood and the rest of the city, who decide to take advantage of its open piazza, architecture, and facilities, even when they are not attending an exhibition. YAP is an extremely effective tool for emphasizing this and turning it into research on architecture. We know how important the issue of public space in the city is today—we all think the most relevant architecture events of 2013 were the Gezi Park demonstrations in Taksim Square, Istanbul— and again we want to use it both to "open the museum" as much as possible and to transform the topic into a device for fueling research on architecture. Besides that, and this is even more important for an institution like ours, YAP has also allowed previously unknown and very young Italian architects to be given the chance to build "innovative" installations, putting them into contact with institutions and colleagues from other participant countries. I was particularly proud when, a few days ago, I saw the red poppies designed by the Rome-based team stARTT, winner of YAP MAXXI 2011, displayed at the Shenzhen Bi-City Biennale of Urbanism / Architecture in 2011, and the authors lecturing on their work in China. In such a "lazy" architectural scene as Italy, the waves have to come from the bottom up, from younger generations and young institutions that have no interest in maintaining the status quo.

EINIGE GRUNDFRAGEN ZUM SAMMELN VON ARCHITEKTENNACHLÄSSEN

Im Jahr 2007 beauftragte der Architekt Frank Gehry einen Gutachter, den Wert seines privaten Nachlassarchivs in Los Angeles zu schätzen: insgesamt 2 800 Quadratmeter an Architekturmodellen, dazu eine Diathek, ein digitales Archiv und ungefähr 5 000 Zeichnungen auf Papier.[1] Anschließend bot er das Archiv, das angeblich mehrere Millionen Dollar wert ist, diversen Institutionen an – vor allem mit Stiftungsgeldern reich ausgestatteten Museen –, die den Schatz nach Auflösung des Büros verwahren, die Objekte und Akten wissenschaftlich betreuen und der Öffentlichkeit präsentieren sollten. Während sich Gehry zu dem Vorgang öffentlich nicht geäußert hat, ließ sein Kollege Peter Eisenman verlauten, dass er sein Privatarchiv an das Canadian Centre for Architecture (CCA) veräußert habe, da er sich außerstande sehe, es »einfach zu verschenken«, eine Feststellung, die impliziert, dass ihm nach eigenem Dafürhalten der finanzielle Gegenwert des Archivs höchstpersönlich zusteht.[2]

Gehry und Eisenman betrachten ihren Nachlass also nicht etwa als Ressource, sondern vielmehr als Ware, und ihr Beispiel hat seither Schule gemacht. Barry Bergdoll zufolge markiert das Verhalten der beiden Männer einen tief greifenden Umbruch in der Beziehung zu den Institutionen, die bislang für die Pflege der Nachlässe bedeutender Architekten zuständig waren – also Museen oder Bibliotheken. Bergdoll berichtet: »Früher waren die Architekten sogar dankbar, wenn jemand bereit war, ihre Arbeit zu archivieren, und überließen solchen Einrichtungen ihre Pläne und Modelle sogar bereitwillig als Schenkung. Heute dagegen betrachten sie ihre Entwürfe als eine Art Profitcenter. Das heißt, sie sind darauf aus, einen möglichst hohen Preis zu erzielen, etwa so, als ob sie Picassos Nachlass im Angebot hätten.«[3]

Dass Bauentwürfe und -zeichnungen auf dem Kunstmarkt schon immer einen deutlich geringeren Preis erzielt haben als Kunstwerke, ist in der Literatur gut dokumentiert.[4] Aber selbst wenn wir hier nicht darüber urteilen möchten, ob ein Gemälde Pablo Picassos mehr wert ist als eine Entwurfsskizze von Andrea Palladio, kann uns ein solcher Vergleich trotzdem über

SOME CONCEPTUAL PROBLEMS IN THE COLLECTION OF ARCHITECTS' ARCHIVES

PETER CHRISTENSEN

In 2007 the architect Frank Gehry hired a consultant to appraise the archival holdings of his Los Angeles office, consisting of 30,000 square feet of architectural models, a slide library, a digital archive, and roughly 5,000 drawings on paper.[1] Assessed at a multimillion-dollar figure, the collection was pitched to a spate of institutions, mostly museums with large endowments, in an effort to find the trove a home to outlive the office, presumably one where the objects and files could be researched and displayed. While Gehry did not publicly comment on the effort, his colleague Peter Eisenman did, noting that his own motivation to systematically parcel his archive to the Canadian Centre for Architecture (CCA) was the result of not being in a position "to give it away," or, in other words, that he felt entitled to what he thought was the archive's financial value.[2]

The trend signaled by the Gehry and Eisenman archives—the architect's valuation of his or her own archive as a commodity rather than a resource—is a paradigmatic one. As Barry Bergdoll has noted, it marks a "seismic shift" in architectural culture and its relationship to the institutions—namely museums and libraries—that typically serve as the custodians of architectural history. "It used to be," Bergdoll remarks, that "architects would be so grateful that there was someone interested in dedicating space to their work, and they would donate it. Now architects view their designs as a kind of profit center. Architects are getting valuations of them as though they were selling the studio of Picasso."[3]

The long history of the divergent valuation of documents of architectural process and works of art is well accounted for.[4] While a distinction between the relative value of a painting by Pablo Picasso and a sketch by Andrea Palladio is not the object of this reflection, it is the departure point from which to explore a number of themes that form the backdrop of the contemporary matter of the architect's archive and where, precisely, they should end up amid the competitive interests of museums, private collectors, scholarly research, and private acquisitiveness. The seismic shift, as it were, sits on the

FRANK GEHRYS ATELIER
IN SANTA MONICA,
KALIFORNIEN, 2006

218

FRANK GEHRY'S STUDIO
IN SANTA MONICA,
CALIFORNIA, 2006

einige wichtige Punkte Aufschluss geben. Denn tatsächlich konkurrieren die Archive der großen Museen inzwischen bereits mit diversen Forschungseinrichtungen und Privatsammlern um die Nachlässe bedeutender Architekten. Um zu verstehen, worum es hier eigentlich geht, müssen wir uns daher zuerst einmal Klarheit über Begriffe wie Urheberschaft, Ruhm, Kanonisierung und Museologie verschaffen, Konzepte, die sehr eng miteinander verbunden und allesamt von dem kulturellen Umbruch betroffen sind, um den es hier geht. Dieses Essay wird sich mit diesem Umbruch näher befassen und versuchen, die Probleme darzulegen, vor die sich ein monografisches Archiv heute gestellt sieht – vor allem wenn es das Werk eines noch lebenden Architekten betreut, für den beträchtliche materielle Interessen im Spiel sind.

KONTEXT

Wenn wir die neue Situation vor dem Hintergrund der historischen Entwicklung betrachten, tritt der Paradigmenwechsel umso deutlicher zutage. So haben etwa Renaissancearchitekten wie Michelangelo üblicherweise auf Pergament gezeichnet und am Ende alle Blätter, die ein bestimmtes Projekt betrafen – egal, ob der Meister selbst oder seine Gehilfen sie ausgeführt hatten –, aufgerollt und trocken verwahrt.[5] Diese Pergamentrollen waren das ausschließliche Eigentum des Architekten und wurden zusammen mit seinem sonstigen Nachlass an Angehörige oder enge Freunde und Kollegen vererbt. Im Frankreich der Aufklärung schuf der absolutistische Staat dann das Modell eines bürokratisch und hierarchisch geordneten, professionell geführten Archivs. Die als Bâtiments du Roi bezeichnete Königliche Baubehörde war der Dachverband aller Architekten, und ihre Bauzeichnungen und Modelle waren faktisch Eigentum des Staates, der diese Arbeiten genau wie alle anderen amtlichen Dokumente katalogisierte.[6] Durch die rasanten Entwicklungen des Publikationswesens seit dem späten 18. Jahrhundert erreichten die Entwurfszeichnungen der führenden Architekten plötzlich ein breites Publikum. Der Offsetdruck und die Lithografie sorgten aber nicht nur für eine weite Verbreitung solcher Zeichnungen, sie führten auch zu einer zuvor unbekannten Wertschätzung des Originals. Denn die beliebige Reproduzierbarkeit verursacht einen Bedeutungsverlust des Kunstwerks, auf den schon Walter Benjamin hingewiesen hat.[7] So bewirkten die neuen Vervielfältigungsmöglichkeiten, dass nun auch architektonische Originalentwürfe und -modelle sehr wertvoll erschienen.

ALEXANDRE CABANEL, *MICHELANGELO
IN SEINEM ATELIER*, 1859
MUSÉE GOUPIL, BORDEAUX

ALEXANDRE CABANEL, *MICHELANGELO IN
HIS STUDIO VISITED BY POPE JULIUS II*, 1859
MUSÉE GOUPIL, BORDEAUX

fault lines of a cluster of related contemporary concerns including authorship, fame, canonization, and museology, phenomena which are as interrelated as they are complicit in the cultural shift. This essay will articulate the problems born of their tectonic ruptures in order to suggest more critical and conceptual ways of dealing with monographic archives, particularly of living architects where the issues are the most existentially fraught.

CONTEXT

Framing these contemporary developments in history situates this paradigm shift in the relevant context and indicates the gradual nature of the tectonic shifts. In the Renaissance, architects such as Michelangelo typically sketched and drew on vellum and would roll several related sheets together, whether executed by the master designer or assistants, before storing them somewhere dry.[5] These boxes and storage units were the exclusive property of the architect and their bequeathal was typically part of the architect's greater estate passed on to loved ones or otherwise trusted friends or colleagues. In Enlightenment-era France, a bureaucratic and hierarchical model for the

Allerdings war es im 20. Jahrhundert üblich, die Leistungen eines Architekten erst postum endgültig zu bewerten. Erst die Nachwelt, also die Fachmagazine, Forscher, Ausstellungsmacher und Architekten der nachfolgenden Generationen, entschied durch ihr Urteil über den Wert einer Lebensleistung und damit auch des betreffenden Nachlasses. Vor allem in Nordamerika erwarben Universitäts- und Privatmuseen, etwa das CCA in Montreal oder das Museum of Modern Art (MoMA) in New York umfangreiche Architekturarchive: Richard Neutras Nachlass ging an die University of California, Los Angeles, die Syracuse University übernahm Marcel Breuer, die University of Pennsylvania Louis Kahn, die Harvard Graduate School of Design Josep Lluís Sert und Edward Larrabee Barnes, die Yale University Eero Saarinen, die J. Paul Getty Foundation Pierre Koenig und so fort. Das MoMA wiederum erwarb 1969 das Mies van der Rohe Archive, während das CCA anfing, Archivbestände von noch lebenden Architekten zu sammeln, die aber nicht mehr aktiv praktizierten, beispielsweise James Stirling, Aldo Rossi, Cedric Price und John Hejduk, um nur die Prominentesten zu nennen. Dazu kamen noch etliche neue Stiftungen, die die Nachlässe wichtiger Architekten verwahrten, etwa die 1968 in Paris gegründete Fondation Le Corbusier, das 1990 in São Paulo eröffnete Instituto Lina Bo Bardi oder die 1996 in Basel gegründete Barragán Foundation, die unter anderem Luis Barragáns Nachlass betreut. Ferner baute Heinrich Klotz als Gründungsdirektor ab 1979 das bahnbrechende Deutsche Architekturmuseum in Frankfurt am Main auf, das sowohl die deutsche wie die internationale Entwicklung dokumentiert. Seither sind in immer rascherer Folge weitere Einrichtungen dieser Art entstanden.

URHEBERSCHAFT

Dass der Nachlass des Architekten heute nicht mehr bloß als kostbarer privater Besitz gilt, sondern als Ware auf dem Kulturmarkt gehandelt wird, ist in der Tat ein gewaltiger Umbruch. Deshalb entbrennt seit einiger Zeit immer wieder Streit darüber, wem das Urheberrecht an architektonischen Entwurfs- und Bauzeichnungen eigentlich obliegt. Denn das poststrukturalistische Denken hat den Begriff der Urheberschaft völlig neu definiert. Diese neue Sicht hat sich zunächst in der Literaturwissenschaft durchgesetzt. »Einem Text einen ›Autor‹ beigeben heißt«, Roland Barthes zufolge, »diesen Text einrasten lassen, ihn mit einem letzten Signifikat versehen, das Schreiben

professional archive evolved and was made consonant with methods of absolutist governance. The Bâtiments du Roi (Royal Building Administration) was the umbrella organization for all architects, and the drawings and models they created were de facto property of the state, which in turn catalogued these works as they would all other official government records.[6] With the explosion of the publishing industry in the later eighteenth and nineteenth centuries, architectural representations gained mass media outlets. What offset printing and lithographic technology did to ubiquitize architectural drawing, it also did to enhance the perceived value of the original work. The endlessly reproduced images of the modern era, in Walter Benjamin's view, evoked a sense of melancholia that only served to reinforce the perceiver of architecture as one part of modernity's greater ethos of alienation.[7] Consequently, the original drawing, model, or other form of architectural representation took on, quite literally, more value *because* of its propensity for dissemination in modern times.

Yet still, in the twentieth century the valuation of the architectural process and its artifacts was typically something engaged after the fact, when clearer ways of gauging the "worth" of these objects could be tabulated. This tacitly put the ultimate worth of an archive in the hands of a generation or two of collective public appraisals: first magazines, then scholarship and exhibitions, and ultimately subsequent generations of architects and their lists of who they cited as sources of inspiration. Particularly in North America, university and private museums, such as the CCA in Montreal and the Museum of Modern Art (MoMA) in New York, began to accession massive architectural archives in settings distinct from the common repositories of libraries: Richard Neutra to the University of California, Los Angeles, Marcel Breuer to Syracuse University, Louis Kahn to the University of Pennsylvania, Josep Lluís Sert and Edward Larrabee Barnes to the Harvard Graduate School of Design, Eero Saarinen to Yale University, Pierre Koenig to the J. Paul Getty Foundation, and so on. MoMA accessioned the Mies van der Rohe archive in 1969, while the CCA began collecting parts of the archives of architects who had only recently stopped practicing but were still alive: James Stirling, Aldo Rossi, Cedric Price, and John Hejduk, among the most prominent. Either through endowments, trusts, or other legacy projects, a number of new freestanding institutions were formed to autonomously maintain and care for the records of important architects: the Fondation Le Corbusier, established in Paris in 1968 and housing the works of Le Corbusier, the Instituto Lina

GORDON MATTA-CLARK,
CONICAL INTERSECT, 1975

GORDON MATTA-CLARK,
CONICAL INTERSECT, 1975

abriegeln.«[8] Diese Argumentation setzt voraus, dass der Autor / Urheber zwar autografisch Wörter erzeugt, dass aber in Wahrheit erst der Leser den Text allografisch generiert.[9] Nach diesem Verständnis ist ein Text also kein ein für alle Mal fertiges, kompaktes Gebilde, sondern ein Gewebe aus zahllosen möglichen Lesarten mitsamt den zugehörigen Subtexten und subjektiven Deutungen.[10] Roland Barthes hat also den Vorrang des Autors / Urhebers zugunsten des Lesers / Rezipienten aufgelöst.

Diese grundlegend neue, dezidiert relativistische Deutung des Urheberstatus ist auch für das Konzept des Architekturarchivs von weit größerer Bedeutung, als es zunächst scheinen mag. Denn das grundlegende Maß eines solchen Archivs ist schließlich die Urheberschaft. Das betrifft nicht nur die Katalogisierung, sondern vor allem die Forschung. Das Archiv ist daher mitursächlich für jenen Kult der Urheberschaft, den Barthes gerade überwinden wollte. Doch was würde aus der für das Archiv geradezu konstitutiven Urheberschaft werden, wenn diese erst durch die Nutzer im Lesesaal oder die Besucher der betreffenden Ausstellung konkret Gestalt annimmt? Ein provozierendes Beispiel einer solchen Transformation ist das Werk des amerikanischen Architekten und Konzeptkünstlers Gordon Matta-Clark, der durch seine massiven Interventionen

Bo Bardi established in São Paulo in 1990 and housing the works of Lina Bo Bardi, the Barragán Foundation founded established in Basel, Switzerland in 1996 and housing the works of Luis Barragán, among others. Heinrich Klotz established a pioneering museum model dedicated exclusively to architecture in Frankfurt in 1979, balancing national interests with international themes. This pattern continues into the present with increasing frequency.

AUTHORSHIP

The slow transformation of the architect's archive from a thing of personal property to a commodity for the cultural market is not only a seismic shift, but also one with important reverberations. The most notable one is a growing tension between artifacts of architectural process and the question of who their authors, in fact, are. The ways in which the identity of the author and the nature of authority in creative fields changed is a dramatic result of the post-structuralist turn. The changes first came into question in the study of literature. "To give a text an author," Roland Barthes argued, "is to impose a limit on that text."[8] This hypothesis suggested that the author produced words autographically, but that actual authorship was transmitted through the allographic perception of the reader.[9] That placed a primacy on the reading of multiple layers, subtexts, and subjectivities, rather than a solitary, individual experience.[10] The meaning of the concept, in turn, shifted authority from that of the author to that of the reader.

This 180-degree turn in the conception of authorship, and the relativism that it suggests, has more meaning to the question of architectural archives than it may at first appear. First and foremost, a fundamental metric of the archive itself is authorship. It is probably the first field in the cataloging process and, to be sure, the first in the research process. The archive, barring any alternative means of organization, is complicit in the cult of authorship Barthes sought to undo. What might authorship, as it is inherently produced by the archive, do if it was to shift *its* agency to the viewer when made public, either on display or in the research room? One provocative example of such a transfiguration is the work of Gordon Matta-Clark, who renewed the capacity of authorship in his interventions with numerous existing structures, all the while documenting the process. Barthes draws a highly memorable material analogue that might be useful in answering this question: he likens the literary text to a "tissue" of quotations.

in bereits vorhandene Bauwerke nicht nur die Frage der Urheberschaft thematisierte, sondern diesen Vorgang auch noch filmisch dokumentierte. Um zu verdeutlichen, worum es bei dieser Frage geht, vergleicht Barthes den literarischen Text mit einem »Geflecht von Zitaten«. Und ein solches Geflecht bilden auch die zahllosen Lesarten und Komponenten dessen, was den Nachlass eines Architekten ausmacht. Die Entwurfsskizzen gehen in die Baupläne ein, die Pläne wiederum befruchten die Modelle, die Modelle das Ausstellungskonzept und die eine Ausstellung die nächste und so weiter. Die einsame Entwurfszeichnung an der Galeriewand oder das Modell in der Vitrine blendet nicht nur die zahlreichen Mitwirkenden hinter den Kulissen aus, sondern auch den auktorialen Zusammenhang dieser Zeichnung oder dieses Modells mit anderen Teilen des Archivs. Beide banalisieren also den »Geflecht«-Charakter des Archivs zugunsten ihrer eigenen Bedeutung und lassen den konstitutiven Anteil des Betrachters klein erscheinen.

Der heute weit verbreitete Verdruss über das Phänomen des »Stararchitekten« hängt in hohem Maße mit der Frage der Urheberschaft zusammen. Im Gegensatz zu vielen anderen Kunstbereichen impliziert die Baukunst schon von jeher ein hohes Maß an Kooperation. Umso mehr erscheint der durch die Galeriesituation traditionell sogar noch untermauerte Geniestatus des Architekten heutzutage wie ein peinlicher Anachronismus. Die Illusion des unfehlbaren Genies erweist sich zusehends als völlig unhaltbar, und sogar die Auflistung der für Entwurf und Planung eines Gebäudes verantwortlichen Architekten folgt inzwischen nicht mehr den früher üblichen Statusvorgaben. Deshalb stellt sich die Frage, wie das Archiv, ohne die Geschichte seiner Erwerbungen komplett umzuschreiben, dem Faktum der multiplen Urheberschaft und seinem eigenen Geflecht-Status angemessen Ausdruck verleihen kann?

RUHM

Immer neu befeuert werden der hartnäckige Personenkult und der Status des Archivs im Bereich des Bauens durch das Motiv des Ruhms. Das Archiv bestätigt und untermauert diesen Ruhm und gewährleistet dessen Dauer. Mark Jarzombek hat das Geheimnis des Ruhms, der mit dem Status des Stararchitekten einhergeht, einmal so erklärt: »Die Moralisten brandmarken den Ruhm als unangemessene Verherrlichung des Individuums. Die Linken sehen in ihm die Verdinglichung eines Produkts der kapitalistischen Maschinerie: das Ergebnis

The proverbial "tissue"—making manifest the infinite and interdependent nature of text—is not unlike the interwoven and interdependent components of an architect's archive. The architect's sketches inform his or her drawings, and his or her drawings inform his or her models, and his or her models inform the presentation strategy, and one presentation informs another, and so on. The solitary drawing on the gallery wall or the model in the vitrine has a penchant to suppress not only hints of the multiple makers behind it, but also its greater authorial relationship to other parts of the archive. In this way, it is a practice that tends to downplay the "tissue" qualities of an archive in favor of the solitary, subjective reading, which bestows authorship on the perceiver.

A contemporary malaise with the "starchitect" phenomenon is certainly a palpable cultural turn related to this question of authorship. Unlike many art practices, architecture has been a discipline that has been fundamentally collaborative since time immemorial. The presence of the architect-genius in the cultural imagination, reinforced oddly enough by the subjectivity of the gallery experience, seems increasingly like an awkward holdover from an earlier era. The notion of the infallible genius is continually being debunked and the attributions in "project credits" are becoming notably less hierarchical. How can the archive, short of rewriting the history of its own acquisitions, recognize, promote, and underscore multi-authorship and the tissue-like nature of archives as entities with interwoven parts?

FAME

Fueling the persistent cult of authorship in architectural culture in general, and the archive in particular, is the quiet yet mighty subtext of fame. The archive both reaffirms and preserves fame and consequently is a key, if unwitting, actor in its perpetuation. Mark Jarzombek has explained the conundrum of fame that emerges from this matter of authorship and its relationship to architecture and its production as such:

Moralists protest that fame is a false glorification of the individual; leftists argue that it is the reified product of a capitalist machinery, the result of "an autonomous ego organization," to use a phrase from Jürgen Habermas; psychoanalysts hold that personal hunger for fame derives from feelings of inadequacy; and cultural critics see in fame nothing more than the reflection of a debased popular taste. And yet fame's irrepressible force is not without its own philosophical import.[11]

›einer autonomen Ich-Organisation‹, wie Jürgen Habermas den Vorgang nennt. Die Psychoanalyse wiederum führt die Ruhmsucht auf ein Inferioritätsgefühl zurück. Und aus kulturkritischer Sicht ist der Ruhm nichts weiter als der Widerhall eines verkommenen Massengeschmacks. Und dennoch hat die unbändige Macht des Ruhms ganz eigene philosophische Implikationen.«[11]
Jarzombek weist ferner darauf hin, dass der Ruhm des Architekten erst seit der Renaissance eine Rolle spielt und seither durch die Massenmedien (vor allem die gedruckte Presse) verbreitet worden ist. Allerdings hängt die Bedeutung des Ruhms in diesem Zusammenhang angeblich auch mit dem tief sitzenden psychologischen Bedürfnis zusammen, die Architektur auch in der Zeit so zu verewigen, wie sie sich (angeblich) im Raum verewigen lässt. Dieses Konzept hat die Entwicklung der Architektur seither begleitet. Während jedoch für die Renaissance die zeitliche Dauer des Ruhms im Vordergrund stand, ist er für die heutigen Massenmedien eher ein Augenblicksphänomen. Obwohl es natürlich auch im 21. Jahrhundert noch berühmte Architekten und Bauwerke gibt, dürfte es heute wesentlich schwieriger sein vorherzusagen, welche Lebenszeit dem Ruhm eines Bauwerks oder einer Person beschieden sein wird. Jarzombek weist darauf hin, dass der Ruhm die Reputation eines Bauwerks oder eines Architekten sowohl in schwindelnde Höhen katapultieren als auch zerstören kann: denn ein Gebäude, aber auch der Architekt sind den Launen der Öffentlichkeit (und den Kunden) ausgesetzt und ernten mal Bewunderung, mal Spott. Bis vor Kurzem wurde nur wenigen Architekten die Ehre eines eigenen Archivs zuteil – und das meist auch erst nach dem Tod. So hatte ein solches Archiv nicht zuletzt die Funktion, das Werk des betreffenden Architekten gegen das Sinken der Publikumsgunst abzusichern, da der institutionelle Charakter einer solchen Einrichtung einen beträchtlichen Schutz bot. Seit die Entwürfe und Modelle bedeutender Architekten jedoch in klimatisierten Depots verwahrt und von Archivaren, Bibliothekaren oder Kuratoren betreut werden, würde es sich der Herausgeber eines Hochglanzmagazins gewiss zweimal überlegen, bevor er sich über ein solchermaßen für die Nachwelt verwahrtes »Oeuvre complète« abwertend äußert. Was nicht heißen soll, dass eine solche Einrichtung jede Kritik im Keim erstickt, aber wenigstens bleibt sie von den schnell wechselnden Moden der Massenkultur weitgehend unberührt und bietet dem Ruhm somit eine dauerhafte Plattform.
Inzwischen haben wir es jedoch mit einer Generation von Architekten zu tun, die (wenn zuweilen auch heimlich) nach Mitteln und Wegen suchen, sich bereits zu Lebzeiten mit einem Archiv zu verewigen. Das heißt, sie möchten

Jarzombek contends that fame as a factor in the profession of architecture originates in the Renaissance, at which point it became a product not only of the proliferation of mass media (namely the printing press) but also of a deeper psychological desire to freeze architecture in time, the same way it could (ostensibly) be frozen in space. This is its conceptual import to the development of architectural culture since. If this notion of fame had a largely temporal aspect for the Renaissance, it has only shrunken in inverse proportion to the proliferation of mass media, which ostensibly confers fame in the first place. While famous architects and famous buildings naturally still exist in the twenty-first century, it would seem to have become significantly more difficult to gauge how long and why fame may be bestowed upon a building or on a person. As Jarzombek notes, fame is as capable of building up a building and an architect's reputation as it is tearing it down: buildings as well as architects are prey to the vicissitudes of a public's (and a clientele's) alternate adoration and rejection.

Until only recently, architects' archives have rarely been collected en masse, and, when archived, were typically only well after the architect had passed away. In this context, the archive had the capacity to buffer the architect's works from the modern and violent oscillations of fame, shielding them by the layers of protection institutions provide. With drawings and models stowed away in climate-controlled repositories and with the care and oversight of the archivist, librarian, or curator, it is difficult to conjure the name of an architect whose *oeuvre complète* has been both archived and called into question for its merits as it would be in the editorials of glossy magazines. This is not to suggest that the institution has the omniscient ability to squash historical criticality, but it does reflect the institution's inscrutable capacity to circumvent the fashion of mass culture and make fame a lasting proposition on one scale or another.

The emergence of a generation of architects who seek out (even if clandestinely) ways to be archived and memorialized prior to their death call the conventional capacities of the institution to reify and insure architectural careers and buffer them from the downside of fame into question. The main line of conflict would appear to be the desire to be archived versus the desire to remain an active practitioner. This simultaneity can be interpreted as the desire to mortgage current fame and convert its currency into a fame of perpetuity that may yet further accelerate the career, a cyclical and self-perpetuating amplification of one's public profile. Can this really be done—converting current fame into perpetual

sich mit Hilfe eines Archivs von vornherein nicht nur gegen Kritik an ihrer Arbeit, sondern gegen jegliche Minderung ihres Ruhms immunisieren. Dabei ist jedoch offenkundig, dass das Verlangen nach archivalischer Unsterblichkeit nicht so ohne Weiteres mit dem Wunsch nach weiterer Berufsausübung in Einklang zu bringen ist. Dieses zweigleisige Modell lässt sich wohl als Versuch interpretieren, dem aktuellen Ruhm bereits jene Ewigkeitskomponente beizumischen, die dann wiederum der aktuellen Karriere Flügel verleiht. Das heißt, wir haben es hier mit dem Versuch zu tun, die eigene öffentliche Bedeutung mithilfe eines Mechanismus der permanenten Selbstverstärkung dauerhaft zu etablieren. Aber lässt sich der Ruhm einer Person auf diese Weise tatsächlich gegen die Wirkungen der Zeit immunisieren? Wohl kaum. Denn die weltliche Unsterblichkeit, die der Ruhm nach Auffassung der Renaissance gewährt, ist nicht nur mit dem Charakter der heutigen Massenmedien schwer zu vereinbaren, sondern auch mit dem Wunsch eines solchen Architekten, weiterhin eine aktive Rolle zu spielen. Nüchterner ausgedrückt: Ein Berufsleben, das noch nicht zu Ende ist, lässt sich nicht in jener Detailliertheit und Vollständigkeit dokumentieren, wie es ein Archiv normalerweise kann. Womit wir beim Thema Kanonisierung angelangt wären.

KANONISIERUNG

Die Kanonisierung und der Ruhm unterscheiden sich durch ihr Verhältnis zur Kultur und zur Zeit. Seit den 1970er-Jahren herrscht in den Kulturwissenschaften weitgehend Einigkeit darüber, dass die Kanonisierung vor allem den Zweck erfüllt, die Bevölkerungsmehrheit – also Frauen, ethnische Minderheiten, ökonomisch Benachteiligte und andere weniger privilegierte Gruppen – aus dem Kreis der kreativen Leistungsträger auszuschließen. Dabei steht der Prozess der Kanonisierung, der nicht selten sogar von einer Archivbürokratie initiiert wird, repräsentativ für all jene im Bereich der Baukultur vorhandenen Probleme, die es den einen erleichtern, kreativ tätig zu sein, während sie es den anderen erschweren. Gülsüm Baydar hat darauf hingewiesen, dass die Architektur automatisch der sogenannten Hochkultur zugerechnet wird und sich daher an jenen Werten orientiert, die eine männliche Elite westlich-heroischer Denkart in den vergangenen 200 Jahren auf breiter Front durchgesetzt hat.[12] Baydar wirft deshalb die provozierende Frage auf, was wohl geschehen würde, wenn man eine solch direkte Beziehung

fame? Skepticism is healthy, primarily because the "freezing" effect of fame we know from the Renaissance is one at odds both with the nature of contemporary mass media and the architect's desire to maintain a dynamism of his or her own volition. On a more prosaic level, there is the fact that a career in motion is also a career that is not finished and thus not tidy and complete to the extent towards which an archive typically strives. Enter the canon.

CANONIZATION

Canonization is distinct from the production of fame, primarily by way of its relationship to culture and the function of time. Since the nineteen-seventies, canons across humanistic fields in general have come to be understood as complicit in the sustained disenfranchisement of the majority of the human population—women, minorities, the economically disadvantaged, and other marginalized figures—from the due recognition of creative achievement. The process of canonization, very often undertaken by the same institutions that archive, is, however, merely an extension of greater systemic problems of architectural culture, which make creative production easier for some and more difficult for others in the first place. As Gülsüm Baydar has pointed out, architecture is automatically assumed to be a cultural product and thus derives its valuative metrics from entrenched cultural systems, which have for the last two centuries been those defined by elite men in a heroic West.[12] Baydar asks the provocative question about what it would mean to resist the assumption that culture and architecture have an unmediated, one-to-one relationship. What would, in other words, a museum look like if it were not a place of culture? This would mean not only problematizing the way in which a canon is formed; but it would also necessitate shedding a new light on those architects and buildings that have to date been canonized, be it by being archived, written about, or exhibited.

It requires the synthesis of a new analytic prism which could recalibrate how (and if) canons are formulated in the first place—from the school syllabus to the gallery. Of course, this project has been well under way for some time but it has often led to a situation endemic to post-structuralist projects: where the proverbial baby (durable bodies of knowledge and systems of valuation) has been thrown out with the proverbial bathwater (the uncritical parade of monographs and exhibitions). It is clear that in 2014 we remain without paradigmatic models of what a canon should actually be and how it should be made.

zwischen Architektur und Hochkultur einfach bestreiten würde. Mit anderen Worten: Wie hätte man sich ein Museum vorzustellen, das nicht zugleich automatisch als Ort der Kultur gelten würde? Diese Frage problematisiert nicht nur die Art und Weise, wie ein Kanon entsteht, sie wirft auch ein neues Licht auf jene Architekten, die bereits einen kanonischen Status erlangt haben, sei es, weil ihre Entwürfe sich schon in einem Archiv befinden oder aber weil ihr Schaffen bereits in Publikationen oder Ausstellungen gewürdigt worden ist.

Wir brauchen deshalb einen neuen analytischen Mechanismus, der es uns erlaubt zu bestimmen, ob und in welcher Form wir solch normativer Leistungen bedürfen, sei es im Schulunterricht oder im Museum. Und tatsächlich gibt es schon seit Längerem derartige Forschungsprojekte, die – wie viele poststrukturalistische Projekte – die Tendenz haben, das sprichwörtliche Kind (angeblich zeitresistente Wissens- und Bewertungssysteme) mit dem Bade (immer neuer Monografien und Ausstellungen) auszuschütten. Wobei bereits jetzt klar ist, dass wir auch im Jahr 2014 keine prinzipiell gültigen Erkenntnisse darüber erlangen werden, wie ein Kanon konkret auszusehen hat und wie man ihn überhaupt definieren könnte.

Und was hat es mit dem Archiv selbst auf sich? Auch wenn es so scheinen mag, als ob die vollständige monografische Archivierung der Entwurfspläne berühmter Architekten die Dominanz der erwähnten hegemonialen Kanonisierungen auch für die Zukunft festschreibt, ist dies in Wahrheit nur bedingt der Fall. So könnten die Archive bei der Auseinandersetzung mit dem Thema etwa zu dem Ergebnis kommen, dass die vollständige Dokumentation des Schaffens noch lebender Architekten überhaupt nicht erforderlich ist. Alternativ könnten sie sich darauf konzentrieren, einer bestimmten theoretischen oder technischen Richtung innerhalb der Baugeschichte einen kanonischen Rang zu verschaffen: beispielsweise der internationalen Nachkriegsavantgarde-Sammlung des FRAC Centre (Fonds régional pour l'art contemporain) in Orléans oder der beeindruckenden postmodernen Sammlung des CCA. So ließen sich Ausstellungs- und Forschungsaktivitäten unterstützen, die nicht nur eine größere Anzahl von Architekten einbeziehen, sondern überdies der akademischen Szene und dem allgemeinen Publikum ein größeres Gewicht geben. Die Institutionen sollten sich aber der Gefahren einer thematischen beziehungsweise einer monografischen Kanonisierung bewusst bleiben, wobei die eher narrative, inkludierende Vorgehensweise gewiss die wünschenswertere ist.

ALDO ROSSI,
TEATRO DEL MONDO,
ENTWURFS-
ZEICHNUNG, 1979/80
ALDO ROSSI FONDS,
CANADIAN CENTRE
FOR ARCHITECTURE,
MONTREAL

ALDO ROSSI,
TEATRO DEL
MONDO,
DRAWING, 1979–80
ALDO ROSSI FONDS,
CANADIAN CENTRE
FOR ARCHITECTURE,
MONTREAL

What of the archive? As much as the complete and monographic archiving of an architect's work may appear to perpetuate the hegemonic systems of canonization called into question here, this is only conditionally true. Archives may, for example, rethink canonization in such a way that complete archives of living architects may not be necessary as a definitive record of their work. Rather, they may concentrate on the canonization of a theoretical or technological movement within architectural history—such as the international postwar avant-garde collection at the FRAC Centre (Fonds régional d'art contemporain) in Orléans or the strong postmodernism holdings of the Canadian Center for Architecture, which can in turn support exhibition and research agendas that include both a greater diversity of architects as well as more of the scholarly and general public. The institution need remain aware of the perils of canonization—even if thematic as opposed to monographic—but the possibilities inevitably remain more open to narrative adaptation and inclusiveness. The example of the architect Richard Meier offers some indication as to what could be done with the balance of the archive that remains uncollected (several individual works being contained in several different institutions), provided one has the resources. In 2013, Meier installed the models and other documentation of his over-forty-year-old practice in a publicly accessible, self-operated museum in Jersey City, New Jersey.[13] Other architects use the Internet to either partially or fully document their in-house archives online at much less of a cost. Although both forms of self-display are unconventional when considered over a longer span of history, they do demonstrate a resolute desire to take matters into one's own hands and self-direct the processes of canonization and posterity.

Der Architekt Richard Meier ist ein Beispiel dafür, wie man mit einem Privatarchiv umgehen kann, für das es keinen Kaufinteressenten gibt, vorausgesetzt, man kann es sich leisten. Im Jahr 2013 hat Meier nämlich die Modelle und Pläne, die er in seinem mehr als 40 Jahre währenden Berufsleben angesammelt hatte, einem von ihm selbst betriebenen, öffentlich zugänglichen Museum in Jersey City, New Jersey, übergeben.[13] Andere Architekten stellen ihre eigenen Archive – selbstverständlich viel kostengünstiger – entweder teilweise oder vollständig ins Internet. Obwohl beide Vorgehensweisen historisch neu sind, bekundet sich in ihnen das klare Bedürfnis, die Dinge selbst in die Hand zu nehmen und den Prozess der Kanonisierung und Präsentation der eigenen Lebensleistung zu steuern.

MUSEOLOGIE

Wie Richard Meiers Beispiel zeigt, nimmt die Präsentation des Gesamtwerks eines Architekten viel Platz in Anspruch, den die meisten Institute weder zur Verfügung stellen können noch wollen. Aber selbst wenn bestimmte Teile eines Archivs öffentlich gezeigt werden – wie es etwa bei Louis Sullivan am Art Institute of Chicago oder bei Ludwig Mies van der Rohe im MoMA der Fall ist –, der größte Teil einer solchen Sammlung bleibt trotzdem einzig der Forschung vorbehalten. Wer jedoch versucht, ein solches Archiv zwischen Publikums- und Forschungsinteresse angemessen aufzuteilen, sieht sich sogleich vor einige museologische Dilemmata gestellt, etwa vor eine Statusfrage. Denn bei einem Gemälde gilt die Endfassung üblicherweise als logischer Schlusspunkt diverser Vorstudien in unterschiedlichen Medien, die (nach gängiger Auffassung) keinen gesteigerten Eigenwert besitzen. Dagegen ist die Präsentation von Archivmaterial, das ja ursprünglich nicht für Ausstellungszwecke gedacht war, Bestandteil eines zirkulären und iterativen Vorgangs. Denn dort gilt es einerseits zwischen den ausgewählten Materialien oder der Abfolge ihrer Präsentation und jenem anderen Prozess zu unterscheiden, in dem sie sich nicht etwa teleologisch, sondern in einem gestischen Verfahren wechselseitig unterstützen.
Da dies unvermeidlich geschieht, sobald ein Archiv öffentlich gezeigt wird, sind von Anfang an gewisse Kompromisse erforderlich. Soll man nach Exponaten Ausschau halten, die als halbwegs repräsentativ für die gesamte Sammlung gelten können, sofern das überhaupt möglich ist? Oder soll man sich für das künstlerisch eindrucksvollste Objekt entscheiden? Oder stellt man ein bestimmtes Projekt in den Vordergrund? Noch viel komplizierter würde sich dies alles bei

MUSEOLOGY

As the Meier example alludes to, the display of the entire oeuvre of an architect requires an amount of permanently dedicated space that most institutions neither have nor want to commit. Even when parts of an archive are on regular display, such as that of Louis Sullivan at the Art Institute of Chicago and Mies van der Rohe at the Museum of Modern Art, the vast wealth of the archive is held behind the scenes for the purposes of researchers. In the process of dividing a sum archive between showpieces and research pieces, a handful of museological dilemmas arise. For starters, there is the issue of relationships. Unlike painting, for example, where a final composition is typically seen as the logical endpoint of studies in a different media with no inherent value (some would say), the process of architectural representation, when it emerges from an archive and not for the predetermined purpose of display, is far more circular and iterative. A selection or a suite of selections must then be divorced from a process where representations mutually, as opposed to teleologically, support one another in a process of gestation.

Because of the inevitability that this will be done with the display of an archive, certain compromises are required from the outset. Does one look for what pieces fairly represent the collection, if that is even possible? Does one look for the most artistically impressive item in the archive? Does one focus on a particular project? These compromises would likely become increasingly complicated with a living architect who, with little doubt, would want to be involved in the (ostensibly third party) curatorial process and would likely see the process more as a representation of them as an architect than of a given project.

CONCLUSION

The removal of the ego from the process of collecting the archive of a living architect would seem to be the only way in which the process of the collection of architecture can maintain its curatorial integrity. The reasons for this are manifold, and I have attempted to evince both how and why in this reflection on the themes of authorship, fame, canonization, and museology. Architects may increasingly wish to see their life work perpetuate a lasting meaning, but they and the institutions they approach must also be aware that this is a delicate proposition, which bears conceptual burdens possibly

einem noch lebenden Architekten darstellen, der höchstwahrscheinlich immer wieder in den kuratorischen Auswahlprozess eingreifen und dabei vermutlich mehr an die eigene Selbstdarstellung als an das betreffende Projekt denken würde.

RESÜMEE

Wissenschaftlichen Ansprüchen würde ein Archiv mit Entwürfen und Plänen eines noch lebenden Architekten nur genügen, wenn dieser dem Sammlungsprozess die notwendige kuratorische Integrität zugestehen würde. Warum dies so wichtig ist, habe ich in diesem Essay darzulegen versucht, einem Text, der sich ausführlich mit den Themen Urheberschaft, Ruhm, Kanonisierung und Museologie befasst. Wie es scheint, gibt es immer mehr Architekten, die ihr Lebenswerk vor der Vergänglichkeit bewahren möchten. Die Institutionen, denen solche nicht ganz unbedenklichen Angebote unterbreitet werden, sollten sich daher darüber im Klaren sein, dass sie mit der Einwilligung ein beträchtliches kuratorisches Risiko eingehen. In Zukunft wird es deshalb vor allem darauf ankommen, eine archivalische Kultur zu entwickeln, die dem autografischen und dem allografischen Architekturverständnis gleich viel Raum gewährt und sich nicht dafür hergibt, vor allem dem Ruhm und der Kanonisierung der betreffenden Architekten zu dienen. Institutionen, die sich diesem Geist verpflichtet fühlen, müssten also dafür Sorge tragen, dass alle diese Aspekte angemessen zur Geltung kommen.

1 Robin Pogrebin, »For Architects, Personal Archives as Gold Mines«, in: *The New York Times*, 23.7.2007.

2 Ebd.

3 Ebd.

4 Sehr gründlich dokumentiert ist die Wertentwicklung der Architekturzeichnung bei Kendra Schank Smith, *Architect's Drawings*, Oxford und Burlington 2005.

5 Ebd., S. 19–45.

6 Mary Nan Rosenfeld, »The Royal Building Administration in France from Charles V to Louis XIV«, in: Spiro Kostof (Hrsg.), *The Architect*, New York 1977, S. 161–179.

7 Siehe Walter Benjamin, *Das Kunstwerk im Zeitalter seiner technischen Reproduzierbarkeit*, Frankfurt am Main 2007.

8 Roland Barthes, »Der Tod des Autors«, in: ders., *Das Rauschen der Sprache*, Frankfurt am Main 2006, S. 62.

9 Das Begriffspaar »autografisch / allografisch« habe ich einem Essay von Alfred Willis über die Geschichte des Architekturarchivs entnommen; siehe Alfred Willis, »The Place of Archives in the Universe of Architectural Documentation«, in: *The American Archivist. Special Issue on Architecture*, 59, 2, Frühjahr 1996, S. 197.

10 Ebd, S. 146 ff.

11 Mark Jarzombek, »The (Trans)formations of Fame«, in: *Perspecta 37. Famous*, 2005, S. 10–17.

12 Gülsüm Baydar, »The Cultural Burden of Architecture«, in: *Journal of Architectural Education*, 57, 4, Mai 2004, S. 19–27.

13 Hilarie M. Sheets, »Architect Goes Home, to Recall and to Work«, *The New York Times*, 24.1.2014.

outweighing custodial benefits. The key challenge will be to develop an institutional and archival culture that promotes both autographic and allographic understandings of architecture, one that exists outside of the promotion of fame and canonization as much as possible, furnishing an environment where interconnections between the archive's constituent units is not only promoted but encouraged.

1   Robin Pogrebin, "For Architects, Personal Archives as Gold Mines," *The New York Times*, July 23, 2007.

2   Ibid.

3   Ibid.

4   This topic, specifically as it relates to the evolution and valuation of architectural drawings, is well covered by Kendra Schank Smith, *Architect's Drawings* (Oxford and Burlington, 2005).

5   Ibid., pp. 19–45.

6   Mary Nan Rosenfeld, "The Royal Building Administration in France from Charles V to Louis XIV," in Spiro Kostof, ed., *The Architect* (New York, 1977), pp. 161–79.

7   See Walter Benajmin, *The Work of Art in the Age of Its Technological Reproducibility, and Other Writings on Media*, Michael W. Jennings et al., eds. (Cambridge, Massachusetts, 2008).

8   Roland Barthes, "The Death of the Author," in *Image, Music, Text* (New York, 1977), p. 147.

9   I use this conception of autographic and allographic from an essay discussing the history and development of architectural archives by Alfred Willis. See Alfred Willis, "The Place of Archives in the Universe of Architectural Documentation," *The American Archivist* 59.2, Special Issue on Architecture (Spring 1996), p. 197.

10   Ibid., pp. 146, 148.

11   Mark Jarzombek, "The (Trans)formations of Fame," *Perspecta* 37, Famous (2005), pp. 10–17.

12   Gülsüm Baydar, "The Cultural Burden of Architecture," *Journal of Architectural Education* 57.4 (May 2004), pp. 19–27.

13   Hilarie M. Sheets, "Architect Goes Home, to Recall and to Work," *The New York Times*, January 24, 2014.

BILD- UND FOTONACHWEIS | IMAGE CREDITS

Umschlagabbildung / Cover illustration, 6–9, 12, 15, 17, 18, 20/21, 25, 32/33, 36, 38, 39, 40, 41, 42, 43, 45, 48–51, 52, 57, 58, 59, 60, 62/63, 65, 68, 70, 73, 75, 80/81, 82, 84/85, 86, 88, 89, 90, 93, 94, 96/97: Architekturmuseum der TU München

Umschlagabbildung / Cover illustration: Foto / Photo: Myrzik und Jarisch

6–9, 12, 15, 17, 18, 20/21, 25, 32/33: Fotos / Photos: Markus Lanz

20/21: Film: Corinne Rose

57: © Bayerische Staatsbibliothek München / Bildarchiv, Foto / Photo: Heinrich Hoffmann

65: © 2014 VG Bild-Kunst, Bonn

70: Foto / Photo: Bayerische Akademie der Schönen Künste

75: Foto / Photo: Marcus Schlaf

76: SPIEGEL 30 / 1993

79: »Texte, die Gestalt annehmen«, Martin Thurau, *Süddeutsche Zeitung,* 27.12.2006

80/81: Foto / Photo: Achim Bunz

82: Foto / Photo: Laura Egger

83: Stiftung Pinakothek der Moderne, *Rotunde,* 1 / 2007, Foto / Photo: Markus Burke

84/85: Foto / Photo: Jens Weber

89: © Estate of Louis I. Kahn

90: © 2014 FLC / VG Bild-Kunst, Bonn

94: © Asymptote Architecture

96/97: Foto / Photo: Alexander Laurenzo, Die Neue Sammlung – The International Design Museum Munich

120/121: © 2014 VG Bild-Kunst, Bonn; Digital image © 2014 The Museum of Modern Art, New York / Scala, Florence, Foto / Photo: George H. Van Anda

122/123: © 2014 VG Bild-Kunst, Bonn; Digital image © 2014 The Museum of Modern Art, New York / Scala, Florence

127: © 2014 VG Bild-Kunst, Bonn; Best Products Company Architecture Fund, Digital image © 2014 The Museum of Modern Art, New York / Scala, Florence

133: © 2014 Burle Marx & Cia. Ltda.; © Oscar Niemeyer Foundation; Digital image © 2014 The Museum of Modern Art, New York / Scala, Florence

137: © 2014 VG Bild-Kunst, Bonn; Digital image © 2014 Mies van der Rohe / Gift of the Architect / MoMA / Scala

138–141: Fotos / Photos: Jonathan Muzikar, Photo courtesy of The Museum of Modern Art, New York

143: © 2014 VG Bild-Kunst, Bonn; Digital image © 2014 The Museum of Modern Art, New York / Scala, Florence

148, 151, 152: Archiv / Archive Jean-Louis Cohen

155: Fonds Prost. Académie d'architecture / Cité de l'architecture et du patrimoine / Archives d'architecture du XXe siècle

156: Fonds Lods. Académie d'architecture / Cité de l'architecture et du patrimoine /Archives d'architecture du XXe siècle

158/159: © 2014 FLC / VG Bild-Kunst, Bonn

161: © bpk / RMN – Grand Palais / Paris, Musée d'Orsay

162: Fonds Hennebique. CNAM / SIAF / Cité de l'architecture et du patrimoine / Archives d'architecture du XXe siècle

165: © 2014 VG Bild-Kunst, Bonn; © bpk / Centre Pompidou-CNAC-MNAM / Bibliothèque Kandinsky – Fonds Vera Cardot – Pierre Joly

168/169: Jakob + MacFarlane, Collection FRAC Centre, Orléans, Foto / Photo: François Lauginie

174/175: Foto / Photo: © Peter Cook

176–179, 181: © Victoria and Albert Museum London

189: © Cody Wilson

190: Foto / Photo: © Corinna Gardner

196/197: © Fondazione MAXXI, Foto / Photo: Sebastiano Luciano

198: Archivio Carlo Scarpa, Fondazione MAXXI, Collezione MAXXI Architettura

201: Archivio Pier Luigi Nervi, Fondazione MAXXI, Collezione MAXXI Architettura

208/209: © Sou Fujimoto Architects; © Fondazione MAXXI, Foto / Photo: Sebastiano Luciano

211–213: © Fondazione MAXXI, Foto / Photo: Cecilia Fiorenza

218/219: Gehry Partners, LLP, Foto / Photo: © Martin Crook

221: Archiv / Archive Peter Christensen

224: © 2014 VG Bild-Kunst, Bonn

233: Aldo Rossi fonds, Collection Centre Canadien d'Architecture / Candian Centre for Architecture, Montréal; © Eredi Aldo Rossi

DANK Der Kuratorin der Ausstellung *Show & Tell. Architekturgeschichte(n) aus der Sammlung,* Hilde Strobl, danke ich herzlich. Sie hat mit der Unterstützung von Klaus Altenbuchner, Markus Lanz, Hanna Böhm und Raphaela Rothenaicher die Sammlungsbestände durch diese Präsentation in ein neues Licht gerückt. Großer Dank auch an das Team des Hatje Cantz Verlags, besonders Birte Kreft und Julia Günther, für ihren starken Einsatz und die sorgsame Umsetzung. Weiter möchte ich Hannes Aechter für die anregende und produktive Zusammenarbeit bei Ausstellung und Buch danken.

Der wichtigste Dank geht an den Förderverein des Architekturmuseums der TU München, namentlich an dessen Präsidenten Uwe Kiessler, der die finanziellen Mittel für den Druck dieser Publikation bereitgestellt hat.

ACKNOWLEDGMENTS I would like to express my warmest thanks to Hilde Strobl, the curator of the exhibition *Show & Tell: Architectural (Hi)stories from the Collection.* With the help of Klaus Altenbuchner, Markus Lanz, Hanna Böhm, and Raphaela Rothenaicher she has shed new light on the holdings of the collection through this presentation. Many thanks also go to Hatje Cantz, in particular to Birte Kreft and Julia Günther for their commitment to the project and their careful attention to detail. I would also like to thank Hannes Aechter for the inspiring and productive collaboration on the exhibition and book.

Most importantly, I would like to thank the Förderverein des Architekturmuseums der TU München, and specifically its president Uwe Kiessler, for kindly funding the printing costs of this publication.

ANDRES LEPIK

DIESE PUBLIKATION ERSCHEINT ANLÄSSLICH DER AUSSTELLUNG |
THIS BOOK IS PUBLISHED IN CONJUNCTION WITH THE EXHIBITION

SHOW & TELL

ARCHITEKTURGESCHICHTE(N) | ARCHITECTURAL (HI)STORIES
AUS DER SAMMLUNG | FROM THE COLLECTION

ARCHITEKTURMUSEUM DER TU MÜNCHEN, PINAKOTHEK DER MODERNE
13. MÄRZ – 15. JUNI 2014 | MARCH 13 – JUNE 15, 2014

HERAUSGEBER | EDITOR
ANDRES LEPIK

LEKTORAT | COPYEDITING
**SANDRA-JO HUBER, BIRTE KREFT, LAURA SCHLEUSSNER,
HATJE CANTZ**

ÜBERSETZUNGEN | TRANSLATIONS
**NICOLA DENIS, CHRISTIAN HUBERT,
CHRISTIAN QUATMANN, LAURA SCHLEUSSNER**

GRAFISCHE GESTALTUNG | GRAPHIC DESIGN
HANNES AECHTER

SCHRIFT | TYPEFACE
FCC, BAU, SABON NEXT

PAPIER | PAPER
HELLO FAT MATT, 150 G/M²

HERSTELLUNG | PRODUCTION
JULIA GÜNTHER, HATJE CANTZ

REPRODUKTIONEN, DRUCK, BUCHBINDEREI |
REPRODUCTIONS, PRINTING, BINDING
DZA DRUCKEREI ZU ALTENBURG GMBH, ALTENBURG

DER DRUCK DIESES BUCHES WURDE ERMÖGLICHT DURCH DIE
FREUNDLICHE UNTERSTÜTZUNG DES | THE PRINTING OF THIS BOOK WAS
MADE POSSIBLE THROUGH THE KIND SUPPORT OF THE
**FÖRDERVEREIN DES ARCHITEKTURMUSEUMS
DER TU MÜNCHEN E.V.**

ERSCHIENEN IM | PUBLISHED BY
HATJE CANTZ VERLAG
ZEPPELINSTRASSE 32
73760 OSTFILDERN
DEUTSCHLAND | GERMANY
TEL. +49 711 4405-200
FAX +49 711 4405-220
WWW.HATJECANTZ.COM
EIN UNTERNEHMEN DER GANSKE VERLAGSGRUPPE | A GANSKE PUBLISHING GROUP COMPANY

HATJE CANTZ BOOKS ARE AVAILABLE INTERNATIONALLY AT SELECTED BOOKSTORES.
FOR MORE INFORMATION ABOUT OUR DISTRIBUTION PARTNERS,
PLEASE VISIT OUR WEBSITE AT WWW.HATJECANTZ.COM.

ISBN 978-3-7757-3801-9

PRINTED IN GERMANY

UMSCHLAGABBILDUNG | COVER ILLUSTRATION:
ADOLF ABEL, KIRCHENSTUDIE, MODELL | STUDY OF A CHURCH, MODEL, CA. 1955
FOTO | PHOTO: MYRZIK UND JARISCH